Science of the Supernatural

How can science explain ghost sightings, psychic readings, or the feeling of presence in an empty room?

This book explores eerie, unexplained experiences through the lens of neuroscience and psychology. With chapters on sleep paralysis, alien abductions, false memories, psychic readings, mystical experiences, and even zombies, it invites readers to examine how the brain generates strange sensations – and why we often interpret them as supernatural.

Designed to spark curiosity and sharpen critical thinking, this book blends scientific insight with storytelling. It is perfect for students, educators, and curious readers alike. Whether you're a skeptic, a believer, or somewhere in between, you'll come away with a deeper understanding of how our brains shape belief.

MELISSA MAFFEO is Associate Teaching Professor at Wake Forest University, specializing in the teaching of behavioral neuroscience. She cofounded the Neuroscience Teaching Conference and has received multiple awards for teaching innovation and excellence. Maffeo earned her PhD in neuroscience from Florida State University.

Science of the Supernatural

Critical Thinking for the Mind and Brain

MELISSA MAFFEO
Wake Forest University

CAMBRIDGE
UNIVERSITY PRESS

CAMBRIDGE
UNIVERSITY PRESS

Shaftesbury Road, Cambridge CB2 8EA, United Kingdom

One Liberty Plaza, 20th Floor, New York, NY 10006, USA

477 Williamstown Road, Port Melbourne, VIC 3207, Australia

314–321, 3rd Floor, Plot 3, Splendor Forum, Jasola District Centre, New Delhi – 110025, India

103 Penang Road, #05-06/07, Visioncrest Commercial, Singapore 238467

Cambridge University Press is part of Cambridge University Press & Assessment, a department of the University of Cambridge.

We share the University's mission to contribute to society through the pursuit of education, learning and research at the highest international levels of excellence.

www.cambridge.org

Information on this title: www.cambridge.org/9781009322331
DOI: 10.1017/9781009322348

When citing this work, please include a reference to the DOI 10.1017/9781009322348

First published 2026
Cover image: mikroman6 / Moment / Getty Images

A catalogue record for this publication is available from the British Library

A Cataloging-in-Publication data record for this book is available from the Library of Congress

ISBN 978-1-009-32233-1 Hardback
ISBN 978-1-009-32237-9 Paperback

My parents always put the X-Files on for me when I was feeling unwell.

This book is dedicated to them.

Contents

Figures

Acknowledgments

There are so many people without whose support this never would have happened.

Thank you to everyone at Cambridge University Press, and especially to Stephen Acerra. Stephen was there since the inception of this project, which, at the time, seemed like nothing more than a harebrained idea. He has encouraged me and helped me ever since.

Thank you to everyone who provided feedback on early drafts of this project. This includes Stephen Acerra, Terry Blumenthal, Eric Stottlemyer, Larah Wong, and my siblings, Nick Maffeo and Heather Maffeo. Your patience and eye for detail were extraordinary. Thank you to Annaelle Gackiere for copyediting and indexing support.

Thank you to all of my students, and especially to my biopsychology students. You let me rattle on about zombies and supernatural stuff far more than was appropriate. Thank you for being, and inspiring me to be, curiouser and curiouser.

Thank you to the Psychology Department at Wake Forest University for supporting this project and for being excited for my work. Y'all are the best.

Thank you to John Foster, who was the first person to believe I could do it.

Thank you to Larah Wong, who would show up with a shovel at any place and any time.

Thank you to my kids, Nicholas and Nora. It was Nora who coined the subtitle, "Rabie, baby." I love that my kids have inherited my morbid curiosity. Please do not ever lose it, because it will come in handy one day.

And thank you, Eric Stottlemyer. You talked me down from approximately 347 panic spirals and always believed in me, even when my amygdala was doing somersaults. You are the most patient person I know. I am so deeply grateful for you.

Introduction

Why Study the Science of the Supernatural?

The *Science of the Supernatural* might, at first, feel like an oxymoron. I don't think most people would immediately see the myriad connections between the paranormal and psychology. I didn't at first, either. I've always loved ghost stories, horror movies, and scary novels. I have a distinct memory of lying in my bed as a kid, trying unsuccessfully to go to sleep. I had just read Stephen King's short story "The Boogeyman." I remember staring at my closet door, sure that it was slowly creaking open. Certain that the boogeyman was on the other side, waiting to kill me.

As I got older (thankfully spared from the boogeyman), I fell in love with psychology and neuroscience. I thought the brain, which can change in response to the changing environment, was the coolest thing ever. Years later, I began teaching neuroscience to college students. After getting into the thick (dare I say doldrums?) of neuroscience research in graduate school and in my postdoctoral training years, teaching college students reignited my excitement for just how damn cool it all is. I love teaching about the senses and how easily our senses can be fooled. I love teaching about how memories are made, and how they can just as easily be fabricated. A colleague and I tell our students, "Trust yourself. But *don't trust yourself.*"

Anomalistic psychology is the branch of psychology that deals with empirically investigating extraordinary phenomena, including, but not limited to, phenomena that could be labeled "paranormal." Importantly, anomalistic psychology does not assume that paranormal forces exist (paranormal being defined as any phenomena that cannot be explained by conventional tools). This aligns with rigorous psychological research methods – one cannot conduct an unbiased experiment with the assumption that their hypothesis is correct.

It could skew the results. Anomalistic psychology should not be confused with *parapsychology*. Parapsychology is the investigation of paranormal activity. In parapsychology, an a priori belief in the paranormal is usually in place. The general goal of parapsychology is to produce evidence that paranormal activity exists, whereas anomalistic psychology takes a skeptical approach to these studies.

Why would psychologists spend all this effort studying the paranormal, even when they might not even think that paranormal activity exists? Well, according to one Gallup poll, about three in four Americans believe in some aspect of paranormal activity. That's 75 percent of the country. There doesn't seem to be a large difference across sex, age, race, education, and region of the country (Moore, 2005). What psychological, neurological, or paranormal forces could be at play to cause this mass belief? Maybe 75 percent of Americans are correct. We should definitely investigate this. Empirical evidence of the paranormal might be the most important scientific finding in history, and, at the time of this writing, this evidence does not exist. But if the 75 percent are wrong, and there is no such thing as paranormal or supernatural activity, then there is a widespread false belief that is endorsed by most of the population. This would be a psychological gold mine, and we should definitely investigate this.

When investigating paranormal claims, we need to take lots of psychological and neuroscientific phenomena into account. This includes cognitive biases, the fallibility of memory, hallucinations, hypnosis and altered states of consciousness, poor probabilistic reasoning and the psychology of coincidence, the power of suggestion and the placebo effect, activity in brain areas dedicated to the sense of self and agency, sleep disorders, and personality characteristics. More than likely, most paranormal claims can be explained by a combination of these factors.

The goal of this book isn't to debunk paranormal claims. No one has, of yet, been able to prove that the supernatural doesn't exist. Instead, the goal of this book is to teach about how humans perceive the world and the powerful factors that have profound influences over

FIGURE 0.1 Duck rabbit illusion.
An optical illusion showing a single image that can be perceived as either a duck facing left or a rabbit facing right.
Source: Wikimedia Commons

our perception. I hope that, by reading this book, you learn to appreciate the way our brains impact perception, and importantly, that our experiences aren't always accurate portrayals of the physical world. I think that this humbling knowledge can promote critical thinking, and I hope it helps people have an open and modest mind. Not everything is experienced the same way by every person.

You've probably seen illusions like the famous duck/rabbit illusion (Figure 0.1).

You can look at it quickly and you'll see a line drawing of an animal. Which animal did you see? Some people see a duck first. Others see a rabbit. When you know what to look for, most people can see both animals. The animal that you saw first doesn't open some window into who you really are or if you're more left-brained or right-brained (by the way, that whole left brain, right brain thing is a myth. Everyone uses both sides of their brain with only a few small differences). What it might tell you, though, is what you were unconsciously thinking of. Maybe you saw a rabbit dart across your yard this morning, and you've already forgotten about it. You might be more likely to see the rabbit. Or maybe you took your little brother to feed the ducks at the lake yesterday, and you might be more likely to see the duck first.

Another cool illusion is the blue-and-gold (its blue and gold, dammit!) dress that broke the Internet about a decade ago. A simple internet search for "The Dress" should pull it up. What colors do you see when you look at this dress? Some people look at this dress and see blue and gold. Some see white and gold, or blue and black. Why? Because the photo that went viral was a low-quality photograph with ambiguous visual cues. Our brains don't have enough visual information from the photograph alone to know the true color of the dress. With limited sensory information to go on, the brain makes up what it thinks you should see.

The brain works hard to interpret our world, and sometimes it takes some shortcuts. This is okay – thinking is hard work. But sometimes your brain makes perceptual mistakes. Sometimes, you have the perfect storm of mistakes, and this conjures a perception of something supernatural. This book is about exploring those perceptual errors.

If you're a lover of psychology, neuroscience, the paranormal, or all three, this book is for you. So read on. In the words of my esteemed colleague, "Trust yourself, but *don't trust yourself.*"

REFERENCES

Moore, D. W. (2005, June 16). Three in Four Americans Believe in Paranormal. Gallup.com. https://news.gallup.com/poll/16915/three-four-americans-believe-paranormal.aspx.

1 Why Are Scary Things Scary? The Neuroscience of Fear

Growing up, my brother, sister, and I would read *Scary Stories to Tell in the Dark* to each other. We stayed up late on Saturdays to watch *Are You Afraid of the Dark?* on Nickelodeon. And even though I devoured stories of the supernatural, the ones that scared me the most were the stories of real-life terrors – the man with the hook scratching on top of the car parked in the woods. The prank caller who was calling from inside the house. And the man who snuck into the back seat of a car driven by a young woman, the high beams of the car driving behind her the only thing stopping him from stabbing her to death. Looking back, I think it's interesting that the real-life terrors gave me more fear than the supernatural terrors (although that all might have changed when I read Stephen King's *It*). Fear was fun for my siblings and me, and since you've picked this book up, I'm guessing you, like me, fall into this camp of people who are fascinated by fear. Even now, as an adult neuroscientist, I'm still fascinated by things that go bump in the night. Why do people enjoy being afraid? What is "afraid," anyway? What is fear?

Fear is a feeling. Fear should, in theory, help keep us alive. In psychological and neuroscientific literature, fear is described as an adaptive mechanism to help learn to avoid potentially harmful threats. It is crucially important that we distinguish, though, between the *feeling* of fear and the physiological *response* to a threatening situation. When I stayed up at night under my covers with a flashlight reading Stephen King, I was inducing *feelings* of fear, which are different than my body's response to clear and present danger. To understand feelings of fear, we must first understand where conscious feelings come from. Luckily for us, we don't need to understand consciousness to study emotions, because emotions can, and do, derive from nonconscious processes.

It's important to operationalize and then describe what we're talking about when we use the word "fear." To do that, let's back up a moment and define what we mean by the word "emotion." Most psychologists agree that emotions have three main components: a subjective experience (a feeling), a physiological response, and a behavioral response. The feeling aspect of the emotion refers to the part that's the hardest to describe. It's how that emotion lives in you, it's when you feel happy or sad, or yes, fearful. It's how happiness colors your world and makes you want to greet each day with a smile, or how sadness makes you feel heavy and blue. The physiological response refers to what the body is doing. Has your heart started pounding? Has your breathing quickened? Perhaps your stomach and intestines have slowed the digestion of your breakfast to divert energy to your muscles. All of these are physiological responses to danger that prepare your body to fight – or flee. Finally, there's also a behavioral response – are you smiling or grimacing? Laughing or crying ... or running away in terror? Perceptions of emotions also require consciousness. From a psychological and neuroscientific perspective, the feeling and the conscious aspects of emotions are extraordinarily difficult to measure, especially when we want to measure them in laboratory animals. If I find a brain area that I believe corresponds to an emotion, how do I manipulate that brain area and ask a rat if it's feeling that emotion? Neuroscientists have found myriad creative ways to explore and understand the neurobiology of emotions in nonhuman brains, but we must interpret these results with caution. We must not anthropomorphize, assigning subjective mental states to animals whose mental states we cannot possibly understand, and then extend that assignment to the mental states of humans.

According to Merriam-Webster, fear is "an unpleasant often strong emotion caused by anticipation or awareness of danger" (Fear, n.d.). This definition describes the subjective emotional state that one can experience, but excludes the measurable behavior observed by virtually all animals in response to danger. It is a very human-centric definition. We cannot assume that nonhuman animals experience mental states the same way humans do simply because they have a well-defined behavioral response to danger. On the other hand, though, we can absolutely use nonhuman animals to learn more about brain areas that underlie behavioral or physiological responses to danger, and we can theorize how these relate to human feelings of fear. In this chapter, we'll dive into the so-called fear circuitry of the mammalian brain. I'll caution you to interpret "fear" in the sense of a neural and behavioral response to danger, and not as a subjective feeling. Later in this book, we'll explore the more human and conscious emotion of fear.

A LITTLE BIT OF NEUROANATOMY

Most people believe that the underlying biological substrate of fear is an almond-shaped cluster of neurons deep in the brain, roughly behind each ear, called the amygdala. This cluster of cells is an "evolutionarily conserved" region, meaning that it has been relatively unchanged in most animal species, probably for millions of years (Pabba, 2013; Swanson & Petrovich, 1998). Because it has been conserved for so many years, some neuroscientists refer to the amygdala and surrounding structures as the "reptilian brain." Neuroscientist Paul MacLean categorized brain structures as either reptilian, paleomammalian, or neomammalian, based on his understanding of the evolution of the brain. This was called the triune model of the brain (MacLean, 1985). In this model, the paleomammalian brain refers to structures that evolved early in mammalian evolution and have been fairly well-conserved over evolutionary time. The neomammalian structures are evolutionarily "newer," like the mammalian forebrain, which is important for planning and decision-making (more on this in a minute). Unfortunately for MacLean, these distinctions didn't turn out to be quite right, although many neuroscientists today still use the term "reptilian brain." I also want to point out here that modern reptiles are no less "evolved" than modern mammals –

all of our features have been selected for over generations in ways that suit the survival of our own species.

In order to understand how the amygdala plays a role in emotions, we should talk a little about the brain as a whole. In contrast to MacLean's divisions, neuroscientists today consider the major divisions of the brain to be the *forebrain, midbrain,* and *hindbrain*. Add in the spinal cord, and we have the *central nervous system*. The spinal cord contains neurons that send sensory information about touch and the position of the body to the central nervous system (*afferent* information arrives at the central nervous system), as well as neurons that send information from the brain to the muscles to control movement (*efferent* information exits the central nervous system).

The hindbrain, consisting of the medulla, pons, and cerebellum, is the most *caudal* (furthest back) part of the brain and emerges from the top of the spinal cord. The hindbrain is generally concerned with basic survival functions. For example, the medulla has regions devoted to controlling heart rate and respiration. The pons is crucial for communicating sensory and motor information between the brain and body. The cerebellum itself looks a bit like a head of cauliflower, and, despite its small size, has about 80 percent of the surface area of the cerebral cortex of the forebrain (Sereno et al., 2020). The neuron-dense cerebellum has an important job – it acts as a quality-control center for all the body's movements. The cerebellum takes in all our sensory information and uses it to talk to motor areas of the brain, fine-tuning the movements of our bodies to optimize balance and coordination.

The midbrain lies just *rostral* (forward) to the hindbrain. The midbrain contains subregions that process basic sensory information (i.e., nonconscious auditory and visual information) and provides important connections to other brain areas that regulate movement and motivated behavior. To give a couple of neat examples, the midbrain is home to both the ventral tegmental area and the substantia nigra. A portion of these neurons lives in the midbrain, and these neurons are so long (several inches, in a human brain) that they extend out of the midbrain and into the forebrain. One of the primary endpoints of the ventral tegmental area is a forebrain region called the nucleus accumbens. It is believed that the accumbens is a key brain reward area. Rewarding feelings, like outsmarting the zombie who is chasing you, are the result of these neurons releasing dopamine in the nucleus accumbens. Most drugs of abuse hijack this pathway. Next door to the ventral tegmental areas lies the substantia nigra. Substantia nigra neurons terminate in another set of forebrain structures, collectively called the basal ganglia. The basal ganglia are important for movement – so when you see a shadowy figure gliding toward you, your basal ganglia will definitely play a role in helping you run and hide.

Finally, the forebrain is what really controls our planned defensive behaviors, learning, memory, and, most intriguingly, our cognition. The *diencephalon* of the forebrain contains the thalamus and hypothalamus. The thalamus contains important nuclei that receive information from the senses and then projects that information to the so-called reptilian brain and cerebral cortex (this sensory-processing role of the thalamus will be a recurring theme in this book). The hypothalamus lies just *ventral* (underneath) to the thalamus. The hypothalamus controls internal states, like your bodily rhythms, hormone release, food and water balance, temperature, and so much more. Finally, the *telencephalon* of the forebrain contains the cerebral cortex and several clusters of neurons that lie underneath the cortex. The cerebral cortex is the wrinkly outer "bark" of the brain and is divided into four main lobes. Each lobe contains both primary sensory areas and association areas. Sensory areas process information from our various senses via the thalamus. Association areas, then, are areas that communicate with the rest of the cortex to connect our sensory experiences to form a seamless picture of our world. The association areas help us to understand our world based on sensory information coming in and based on our expectations, beliefs, and previous experiences. Readers can refer to Figures 1.1 and 1.2 for a visual representation of the divisions of the brain.

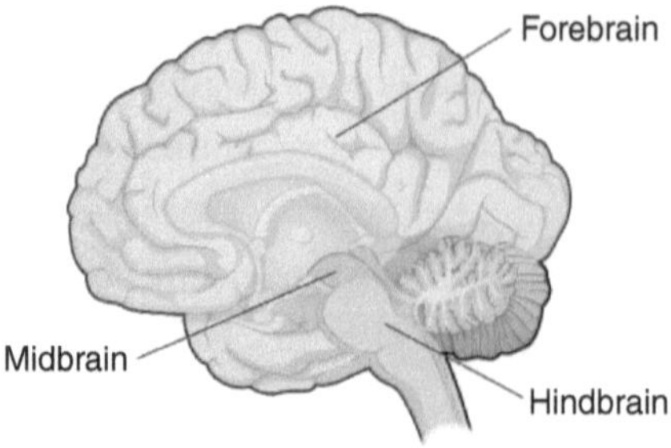

FIGURE 1.1 Divisions of the brain.
Labeled diagram of the brain showing major divisions, including forebrain, midbrain, and hindbrain.
Source: Simple Psychology

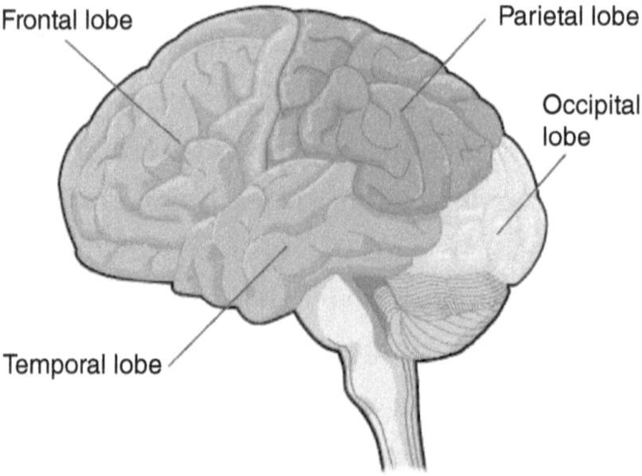

FIGURE 1.2 Lobes of the cortex.
Labeled diagram of the human brain indicating the frontal, parietal, temporal, and occipital lobes.
Source: Noba

Within the telencephalon, buried underneath the cortex, are brain areas that control various complex behaviors like movement, learning, and emotion. These include the basal ganglia and nucleus accumbens that were described earlier. There are other important areas, like the hippocampus (which is crucial for memory consolidation), and our friend, the amygdala. Most people agree that the amygdala plays an important role in emotion, but understanding just how the amygdala relates to emotion gets complicated. The amygdala is definitely important for detecting threat and generating defensive behaviors, and because humans have a pesky habit of anthropomorphizing, the amygdala has been colloquially dedicated as the "fear center" rather than the more objective and accurate "threat detection center."

Localizing structure and function has been a way to attempt to understand the brain that dates back hundreds of years. It's a simplistic approach, though. Brain structures don't exist in a vacuum, and activation or inhibition of a structure will have implications on the entire neural community. Thanks to the growing field of human neuroscience, we are better poised to understand how networks of cooperative brain areas interact to regulate our feelings and behaviors. Understanding cooperation in neural networks will help us take a minuscule step toward understanding nebulous ideas, like the neural basis of a thought. Or the neural representation of the boogeyman hiding in your closet.

KLUVER, BUCY, AND DOCILE MONKEYS

The story of how the amygdala came to be regarded for its role in emotion dates back to the 1930s in the research laboratory of psychologist Heinrich Kluver. Kluver was fascinated by the concept of mental imagery long before he inadvertently veered his research into emotionality (sadly, he never took the plunge into anomalistic psychology). Kluver's early work focused on eidetic (visual) memory in children, and this led him to begin studying the effects of the psychedelic compound mescaline. Kluver famously administered mescaline to himself on at least one occasion, to refute the idea that the hallucinations brought on by mescaline were similar in nature to the mental imagery of eidetic memory (Kluver, 1966; Nahm, 1997). All in the name of science, right? For a detailed review of the background and early works of Heinrich Kluver and Paul Bucy, refer to Nahm (1997).

Kluver's work administering mescaline to monkeys revealed a set of stereotyped behaviors that he ultimately spent his career studying, and which, serendipitously, led him to uncover some of the neurobiological mysteries of emotions. After mescaline treatment, Kluver's monkeys began to run their tongues around the outside of their lips, smack their lips, and investigate objects with their mouths. Kluver called this set of behaviors "oral syndrome" (Kluver, 1966), or hyperorality. Oddly, oral syndrome sometimes depended on whether there was someone watching the monkey or not – monkeys that didn't display hyperorality would suddenly begin this behavior when someone entered the space and watched them! This led Kluver to believe that oral syndrome was somehow related to the affective, or emotional, state of the monkey.

Kluver set out to determine the neuroanatomical substrate of oral syndrome. When a neuroscientist wants to understand the relationship between a brain area and a behavior, they might decide to conduct a lesion, or ablation, study. Here, they can destroy the brain area of interest and see how it affects behavior. This technique might seem extreme by today's standards. At the time, though, lesion studies were immensely helpful with understanding relationships between structure and function, and that structure–function relationships contained more subtleties than pioneering neuroanatomists believed.

Armed with his theory that oral syndrome was related to the animal's affective state, he sought to identify a neural substrate of oral syndrome. His first ablation studies, with the assistance of Karl Lashley (who would later conduct seminal research on the role of the cortex in rodent learning), targeted the occipital lobe. The occipital lobe is the most posterior region of the cerebral cortex and contains the primary visual cortex. Kluver was interested in the occipital lobe in its potential relationship to eidetic memory. Later, and in collaboration with Bucy, Kluver extended his ablation studies to include the temporal lobe. The temporal lobe is the bit of cortex behind the ears and contains the primary auditory cortex. Just underneath the temporal lobe lie the hippocampus and amygdala. While Kluver's occipital lobe studies were generally focused on mental imagery, his temporal lobe studies, inspired by patients with temporal lobe epilepsy, were focused on finding the locus of the hyperorality he observed in his mescaline-treated animals.

Kluver and Bucy's first temporal lobe ablation patient was a female monkey named Aurora. The first surgery they conducted on Aurora removed one temporal lobe – what we call a unilateral temporal lobectomy. After that surgery, Aurora, who previously was so aggressive that she could hardly be handled, became extraordinarily tame. The change in her behavior was so striking that, upon seeing Aurora for the first time since her surgery, Kluver called up Bucy and demanded, "What did you do to my monkey?" (Bucy, 1985, p. 351). Shortly thereafter, Kluver and Bucy ablated Aurora's contralateral temporal lobe to create a bilateral temporal lobectomy. This procedure was repeated on several other animals and led to similar findings, a behavioral condition that Kluver and Bucy referred to as "temporal lobe syndrome" (Bucy & Klüver, 1955). Temporal lobe syndrome would later come to be known as Kluver–Bucy syndrome.

Kluver–Bucy syndrome is characterized by very stereotyped behaviors (Kluver & Bucy, 1939). One of the most prominent behaviors is hyperorality, much like the behavior seen in the mescaline-treated animals. This, of course, did not support Kluver's original hypothesis that ablating the temporal lobe would stop hyperoral behaviors. On the contrary, temporal lobe ablation *increased* hyperoral behaviors. Animals with Kluver–Bucy syndrome excessively examine objects by licking, chewing, and mouthing them. Furthermore, animals didn't seem to recognize familiar objects, examining such objects with the same curiosity with which they would examine a novel object.

Another key symptom of Kluver–Bucy syndrome is a drastic change in affective behavior. Recall that Kluver and Bucy's first patient, Aurora, was so aggressive prior to her surgery that she could hardly be handled. Bucy had even referred to Aurora as "unmanageable" (Bucy, 1985, p. 351). After the surgery, though, she was docile and tame, a complete reversal of her aggressive nature. Kluver and Bucy also noticed that the subjects of their experiments, including Aurora, behaved in an unnatural, placid way. These animals did not show emotional responses to things that monkeys usually show emotion to, like snakes or strange and aggressive handlers (Kluver & Bucy, 1939). Although there are no published accounts of Kluver and Bucy's monkeys encountering ghosts, I don't think they would have reacted negatively to them, either.

Unbeknownst to Kluver and Bucy, the very syndrome that would later be named after them had been published fifty years prior by Sanger Brown and E. A. Schafer (Brown & Sharpey-Schafer, 1888). Brown and Schafer's patient, Monkey No. 6, who had undergone a complete temporal lobectomy, exhibited very similar behavioral traits as Aurora did fifty years later.

> A remarkable change is, however, manifested in the disposition of the monkey. Prior to the operations he was very wild and even fierce, assaulting any person who teased or tried to handle him. Now he voluntarily approaches all persons indifferently, allows himself to be handled, or even to be teased or slapped, without making any attempt at retaliation or endeavouring to escape.
>
> *(Brown & Sharpey-Schafer, 1888, pp. 301–311).*

Both independent groups of researchers reported that these behavioral disturbances were ameliorated after a period of weeks to months and monkeys returned to their presurgical state (Nahm, 1997). Neither group theorized about the specific anatomical locations underlying these unique behaviors. Indeed, both groups observed significant changes in affective behavior, but neither group attempted to localize affective states in the brain. Kluver and Bucy certainly did not presume to state that the amygdala played a role in the affective changes they observed.

WHERE IN THE BRAIN IS EMOTION?

Even though Kluver and Bucy didn't attempt to describe the neurobiology that underlies the change in emotional behavior they observed, they laid the foundation for pivotal findings in the field of affective neuroscience. James Papez was one of the key contributors to these findings. Papez extended theories of emotion that had been proposed by William James (who was well-regarded as the father of psychology) and later, by Walter Cannon (who actually coined the phrase "fight or flight"; Cannon, 1915). Kluver and Bucy later indicated (Kluver & Bucy, 1939) that their work lent support for Papez's ideas on the neural underpinnings of emotion (Papez, 1937). Let's back up for a moment, though, to pay homage to the ingenuity of James and Cannon and describe how this work paved the way for a more modern understanding of the role of the brain in emotional regulation.

The early theories of emotion from James and Cannon are important because they were the first to suggest that emotions are related to our *autonomic nervous system* – the collection of nerves in our bodies that can either allow our body to rest and digest or prepare for fight or flight. William James and Carl Lange suggested that the feeling aspect of emotion was a direct result of a perception of what is happening in your body, including your autonomic nervous system (James, 1918). For example, if you see a ghost, your heart rate will increase, your palms will become sweaty, and your body will increase its blood supply to muscles, all to prepare for action. This little thing called the fight or flight response is controlled by a branch of the autonomic nervous system called the *sympathetic nervous system* (conversely, the *parasympathetic nervous system* relaxes your body during times you have the freedom to rest and digest). The James–Lange theory suggests that animals perceive a specific bodily response and ascribe feelings to it. So, rather than saying, "I feel afraid because I saw a ghost and then my heart started racing," you would say, "I saw a ghost and my heart started racing, and therefore I felt afraid." If you've ever had a panic attack, you'll understand this. Panic attacks are a result of autonomic nervous system activation, even though they aren't always tied to an external stimulus. Nonetheless, people who suffer panic attacks experience true terror as a result of interpreting their body's signals.

Walter Cannon and his student, Phillip Bard, later modified the James–Lange theory. They appreciated the idea that the brain perceives bodily changes but believed perception of emotions must be more complex than that alone. Cannon and Bard believed that deep brain areas, below the cortex (i.e., subcortical brain areas) assess the situation, determine the appropriate physiological response, and send that information down through the brainstem to the autonomic nervous system. These same areas also send information about the situation to the cerebral cortex. Remember that the cortex plays a big role in complex cognition. So now, not only is your autonomic nervous system going crazy, the cortex allows you to have a conscious experience of the emotional event (Cannon, 1927). Your (very astute) train of thought might be something like, "I see a ghost, and this experience is activating my subcortical brain areas and my autonomic nervous system, and therefore I feel afraid." All right, back to Papez and his extensions of Kluver and Bucy's work.

James Papez liked the idea that there are subcortical structures that can influence autonomic nervous system arousal and conscious feelings. He also knew of the work of Kluver and Bucy and their strangely docile, temporal lobe-less monkeys. The Papez circuit, as it had begun to be called, originally described a circuit connecting the hippocampus, fornix, mammillary bodies, and anterior thalamic nucleus. In his landmark paper, Papez wrote, "It is proposed that the hypothalamus, the anterior thalamic nuclei, the gyrus cinguli, the hippocampus and their interconnections constitute a harmonious mechanism which may elaborate the functions of central emotion, as well as participate in emotional expression" (Papez, 1937, p. 743). Note that this early description of the circuitry of the emotive brain does *not* include the amygdala. The amygdala was later incorporated into this circuitry – termed the limbic system – through the work of the American psychiatrist Paul MacLean. MacLean, known for proposing the triune brain model discussed earlier in this chapter, expanded on Papez's ideas by including the septum, amygdala, and prefrontal cortex in 1949 (Maclean, 1952). However, it wasn't until 1956, when Lawrence Weiskrantz made specific lesions to the amygdalae in monkeys that the amygdala was identified as the likely structure that led to Kluver–Bucy syndrome, first described two

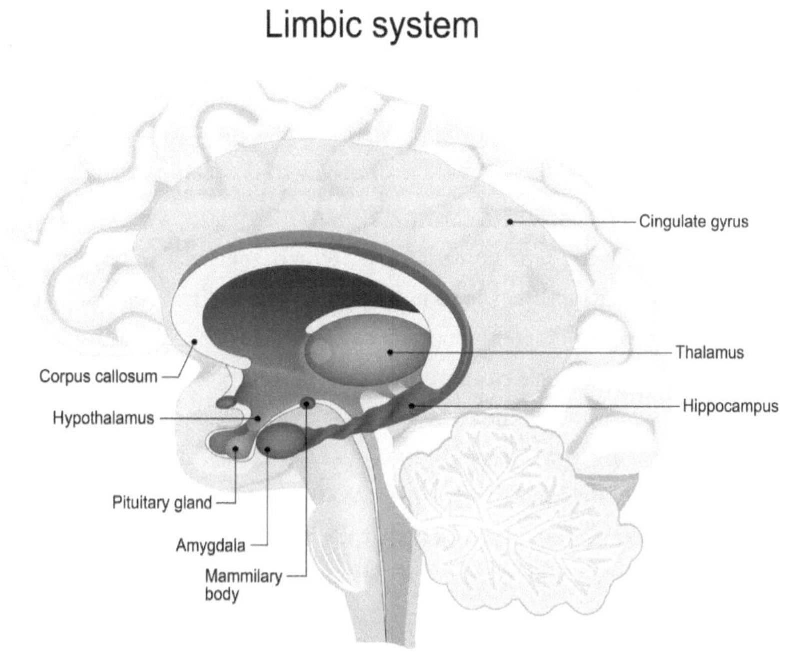

FIGURE 1.3 The limbic system.
Diagram of the brain highlighting the limbic system, including the amygdala, hippocampus, and hypothalamus.
Source: Getty Images

decades prior (Weiskrantz, 1956). Figure 1.3 depicts a modern conception of the mammalian limbic system.

THE AMYGDALA, THREAT DETECTION, AND FEAR

Following the work of Weiskrantz, research into the role of the amygdala and emotions exploded, although a clear role of the amygdala was yet to be determined. It wasn't until researchers began investigating the role of the amygdala in the context of emotional learning that our understanding of the amygdala began to solidify. This type of learning, called classical, or Pavlovian, conditioning is a type of learning where an organism learns to associate two or more stimuli. More specifically, the organism learns to associate a salient stimulus (salient is a fancy way to say important), like food, with a neutral stimulus, like a bell. We call the salient stimulus the unconditioned stimulus (US) because the organism doesn't really need to learn anything to respond to it. The neutral stimulus is termed the conditioned stimulus (CS), because, in order to have the same response that the US evokes, the organism has to do some learning.

In Pavlovian *fear* conditioning, which specifically requires the amygdala, an animal learns to associate a salient stimulus that would presumably signal danger (such as a foot shock) with a neutral stimulus (such as a tone). To give an example, imagine you're walking through the woods in the middle of the night, when suddenly, you realize a demonic spirit is chasing you. Somehow you escape unscathed. Later though, when walking through those same woods, you might feel that sympathetic nervous system activation that we talked about earlier – the fight or flight response. You might also demonstrate defensive or avoidance behaviors. Here, the demonic spirit (the unconditioned stimulus; US) evokes a very clear feeling of fear, and that feeling, appropriately, is related to sympathetic activation. The woods (the conditioned stimulus; CS) themselves, however, are nonthreatening, but your brain has associated the spirit with the woods. Your brain may even generalize this association to *all* woods, not just the woods where you saw the spirit. After this, the next time you stroll through the woods, your heart might start racing in anticipation of meeting that demonic spirit again. Please note that we're using the word "fear" in fear conditioning to refer (the conditioned response; CR) to the generation of species-specific behaviors in response to threat, not the conscious feeling of fear.

As decades of neuroscience research has taught us, circuitry to and from the amygdala is crucial for generating this Pavlovian fear response (for review, see LeDoux, 2000). In its simplest description, sensory regions of the brain (namely the thalamus) send information to the amygdala about the CS and US, and the amygdala regulates the appropriate output in the form of sympathetic activity, hormonal responses, and behavioral changes (like defensive or avoidance behaviors). The amygdala itself is made up of at least twelve specific subregions, but only a few of those appear to be crucial for fear learning. CSs, in the form of sensory information, like the soft crack of a tree branch right behind you, travel from thalamic nuclei and cortical areas into the lateral amygdala (LA), and the LA then sends that information to the central nucleus of the amygdala (CeA). When the CS is the environment of the animal (a contextual CS), the hippocampus is also recruited, and the hippocampus sends contextual information to the basal and accessory basal nuclei of the amygdala. The pathway of the US to the amygdala is a little more diffuse. Structures that code the US include the somatosensory cortex and the spinothalamic tract, important for processing touch and pain. The convergence of touch and pain information with input from the CS in the LA lends support for the idea that the LA is a key site for the formation of CS-US associations. When these associations are strengthened, the CS is thus able to elicit a stronger response from the CeA.

The LA appears to be important for the *acquisition* of conditioned fear, while the CeA appears to be important for the *expression* of conditioned responses, that is, the ability of the animal to demonstrate the learned association between the CS-US (such as by freezing, increasing its heart rate, etc.). This output can be thought of as the "action" component of the emotion. The CeA receives sensory projections from the LA, as well as other nuclei in the amygdala. The CeA, in turn, sends this information to various brainstem regions to trigger the expression of conditioned fear responses in the form of defensive behaviors, sympathetic, and endocrine responses. Thus, a previously meaningless stimulus, like the sound of a twig snapping in the woods, can elicit avoidance behaviors, like running away with your heart pounding. It can do this even in the absence of any observable danger.

The CeA also sends information to an area of the hindbrain called the caudal pontine reticular nucleus (PnC), a nucleus crucial for the acoustic startle response. When we're in scary situations, our anxiety is heightened and the CeA potentiates the activity of the PnC, increasing the startle response. No doubt you've experienced this before. If you've ever found yourself in a situation where you felt afraid or anxious, like walking alone in the woods at night, or in a movie theater watching a scary movie, you've probably jumped out of your skin at a sudden, loud noise. The fear-potentiated startle reflex is generally regarded as an important survival response (for an excellent review of this startle reflex, see Koch, 1999).

It's crucial to state here that this circuitry can result in conditioned fear responses even in the absence of conscious awareness, and this has huge evolutionary benefits. The faster an animal can learn to associate sights, smells, and other neutral stimuli with something dangerous, the faster its brain can react to the *potential* presence of danger, and the better likelihood for survival. Virtually all animals, and even some single-celled organisms, can react with conditioned defensive behaviors after CS-US pairings (LeDoux, 2012). It's also important to highlight that, since these associations can be made in the absence of conscious awareness, this circuitry cannot, at least fully, underlie the *emotion* of fear. Full understanding of the neurobiology of the emotion of fear would require an understanding of the neurobiology of consciousness, and though progress has been made, neuroscientists haven't yet unlocked that secret.

So, is the amygdala the so-called fear center of the brain? It is certainly crucial for threat detection and Pavlovian fear conditioning, and the neurobiology underlying these abilities has been selected for over millions of years of evolution. We have no way of asking a lab rat if it is feeling afraid. We can only measure its behavior, and the behavior of the rat tells a clear story that the rat can quickly learn CS-US associations and behave in a manner consistent with survival – defensive or avoidance behaviors. No, we cannot ask a rat if it is feeling afraid, but we *can* ask humans. Patients living with the rare genetic condition Urbach–Wiethe disease typically have damage to both amygdalae, and are thus the human equivalent of a rat with an amygdala lesion (Meletti et al., 2014). There have been a small number of publications examining the emotional differences in people with Urbach–Wiethe disease (Anderson & Phelps, 2002; Feinstein et al., 2011; Meletti et al., 2014; Siebert et al., 2003), and no one patient has been as extensively studied as Patient S.M.

S.M. is a middle-aged woman presenting with bilateral amygdala lesions. Most Urbach–Wiethe patients, including S.M., have difficulties interpreting facial expressions of fear (Adolphs et al., 1995; Meletti et al., 2014; Siebert et al., 2003). In addition, Patient S.M. doesn't seem to be able to experience the *feeling* of fear. Researchers have asked her to handle snakes and spiders, walk through haunted houses, and watch clips of scary movies. To all of these stimuli, S.M. has responded with positive emotions and a lack of fear ("This way, guys, follow me!" she said, as she took the lead through a haunted house as part of a study; Feinstein et al., 2011 p. 5).

The fact that S.M., a patient with no amygdala, has seemingly no experience with emotional fear certainly suggests that the amygdala is important for fear. In one bizarre study, though, researchers asked three patients with Urbach–Wiethe disease to inhale 35 percent CO_2. To their surprise, all three patients reported fear and panic, with panic in the Urbach–Wiethe patients even stronger than in control participants with intact amygdalae (Feinstein et al., 2013). These results suggest that whatever underlying circuitry caused these patients to experience fear and panic was independent of the amygdala. One possibility is that the amygdala might play a role in *decreasing* panic, which would explain why the amygdala-damaged patients reported more feelings of panic. Or there could be some sort of compensatory mechanism for detecting extreme danger that emerged in these patients due to the absence of more traditional threat-detection areas. These results could also suggest that the amygdala is not actually responsible for the subjective feelings of emotional fear (Feinstein et al., 2013). It's important to note, however, that not all studies on patients with amygdala damage report a difference in emotion identification compared to intact controls, too (Anderson & Phelps, 2002). This further muddies the water on our understandings of the role of the amygdala, threat detection, and fear.

Joseph Ledoux, one of the pioneering researchers who studied amygdala circuitry, makes a compelling argument against assigning emotional states to animals. "Problems especially arise," he argued, "when mental state words derived from human introspection are used to talk about behaviours that do not depend on mental states" (LeDoux, 2022, p. 4). It is abundantly clear that amygdala circuitry is crucial for threat detection and for generating species-specific defensive behaviors. Many behaviorists over the decades have referred to these behaviors as a demonstration of "fear," but those behaviorists weren't really referring to fear as an emotional state. Unfortunately, this distinction was never very clear, and as a result, the amygdala became known as the "fear center" of the brain. Ledoux's suggestion is to rename the amygdala fear circuitry to reflect defensive behaviors and not subjective feelings. "Conscious fear can cause us to act in certain ways, but it is not the cause of the expression of defensive behaviors and physiological responses elicited by conditioned or unconditioned threats. We should not have called it a fear system" (LeDoux, 2014, p. 2873).

So, is the amygdala related to the tingle in your spine as you walk home alone, with an unnerving sense of being watched by some*thing*? Does the amygdala become active when you're sitting at a séance and candlesticks slowly levitate from the table, and every fiber of your being is telling you get the hell out of there? What about when you wake up in the night and you sense a strange presence at the foot of your bed, and you are completely awash in terror?

And when we're awash in terror, what are we actually afraid of? Are those things truly happening, or is your brain making up ghost stories? Humans have a unique brain, and this uniqueness sets us apart from all other mammals. Our ability to use our forebrain, and especially our cerebral cortex, to think and plan and make decisions is quite remarkable. So remarkable and complicated, in fact, that our brains have figured out how to use mental shortcuts to make the hard work of thinking just a little easier. Our brains are constantly using our beliefs and past experiences as a filter for new information. And when our brains receive ambiguous information (which they really don't like), they fill in the gaps with information that our brains already believe to be true.

In the chapters that follow, we'll explore some of these mental shortcuts and whether they might explain some, if any, paranormal occurrences.

REFERENCES

Adolphs, R., Tranel, D., Damasio, H., & Damasio, A. (1995). Fear and the human amygdala. *The Journal of Neuroscience, 15*(9), 5879–5891. https://doi.org/10.1523/JNEUROSCI.15-09-05879.1995.

Anderson, A. K., & Phelps, E. A. (2002). Is the human amygdala critical for the subjective experience of emotion? Evidence of intact dispositional affect in patients with amygdala lesions. *Journal of Cognitive Neuroscience, 14*(5), 709–720. https://doi.org/10.1162/08989290260138618.

Brown, S., & Sharpey-Schafer, E. A. (1888). XI. An investigation into the functions of the occipital and temporal lobes of the monkey's brain. *Philosophical Transactions of the Royal Society of London (B), 179*, 303–327. https://doi.org/10.1098/rstb.1888.0011.

Bucy, P. C. (1985). Heinrich Klüver. In *Neurosurgical Giants: Feet of Clay and Iron* (pp. 349–353). New York: Elsevier Science Publishers.

Bucy, P. C., & Klüver, H. (1955). An anatomical investigation of the temporal lobe in the monkey (Macaca mulatta). *Journal of Comparative Neurology, 103*(2), 151–251. https://doi.org/10.1002/cne.901030202.

Cannon, W. B. (1915). *Bodily Changes in Pain, Hunger, Fear and Rage: An Account of Recent Researches into the Function of Emotional Excitement.* New York: Appleton-Century-Crofts.

Cannon, W. B. (1927). The James-Lange theory of emotions: A critical examination and an alternative theory. *The American Journal of Psychology, 39*(106), 106–124. https://doi.org/10.2307/1422695.

Fear. (n.d.). In *Merriam-Webster.com Dictionary*. www.merriam-webster.com/dictionary/fear?src=search-dict-box.

Feinstein, J. S., Adolphs, R., Damasio, A. R., & Tranel, D. (2011). The human amygdala and the induction and experience of fear. *Current Biology, 21*(1), 34–38. https://doi.org/10.1016/j.cub.2010.11.042.

Feinstein, J. S., Buzza, C., Hurlemann, R., Follmer, R. L., Dahdaleh, N. S., Coryell, W. H., Welsh, M. J., Tranel, D., & Wemmie, J. A. (2013). Fear and panic in humans with bilateral amygdala damage. *Nature Neuroscience, 16*(3), 270–272. https://doi.org/10.1038/nn.3323.

James, W. (1918). *The Principles of Psychology*. New York: H. Holt.

Kluver, H. (1966). *Mescal and Mechanisms of Hallucinations*. Chicago: University of Chicago Press.

Kluver, H., & Bucy, P. C. (1939). *Preliminary analysis of functions of the temporal lobes in monkeys. 1939 [classical article]*. https://doi.org/10.1176/jnp.9.4.606.

Koch, M. (1999). The neurobiology of startle. *Progress in Neurobiology, 59*(2), 107–128. https://doi.org/10.1016/s0301-0082(98)00098-7.

LeDoux, J. E. (2000). Emotion circuits in the brain. *Annual Review of Neuroscience, 23*, 155–184. https://doi.org/10.1146/annurev.neuro.23.1.155.

LeDoux, J. E. (2012). Evolution of human emotion: A view through fear. *Progress in Brain Research, 195*, 431–442. https://doi.org/10.1016/B978-0-444-53860-4.00021-0.

LeDoux, J. E. (2014). Coming to terms with fear. *Proceedings of the National Academy of Sciences, 111*(8), 2871–2878. https://doi.org/10.1073/pnas.1400335111.

LeDoux, J. E. (2022). As soon as there was life, there was danger: The deep history of survival behaviours and the shallower history of consciousness. *Philosophical Transactions of the Royal Society of London. Series B, Biological Sciences, 377*(1844), 20210292. https://doi.org/10.1098/rstb.2021.0292.

MacLean, P. D. (1952). Some psychiatric implications of physiological studies on frontotemporal portion of limbic system (visceral brain). *Electroencephalography and Clinical Neurophysiology, 4*(4), 407–418. https://doi.org/10.1016/0013-4694(52)90073-4.

MacLean, P. D. (1985). Brain evolution relating to family, play, and the separation call. *Archives of General Psychiatry, 42*(4), 405–417. https://doi.org/10.1001/archpsyc.1985.01790270095011.

Meletti, S., Cantalupo, G., Santoro, F., Benuzzi, F., Marliani, A. F., Tassinari, C. A., & Rubboli, G. (2014). Temporal lobe epilepsy and emotion recognition without amygdala: A case study of Urbach-Wiethe disease and review of the literature. *Epileptic Disorders: International Epilepsy Journal with Videotape, 16*(4), 518–527. https://doi.org/10.1684/epd.2014.0696.

Nahm, F. K. (1997). Heinrich Klüver and the temporal lobe syndrome. *Journal of the History of the Neurosciences, 6*(2), 193–208. https://doi.org/10.1080/09647049709525702.

Pabba, M. (2013). Evolutionary development of the amygdaloid complex. *Frontiers in Neuroanatomy, 7*, 27. https://doi.org/10.3389/fnana.2013.00027.

Papez, J. (1937). A proposed mechanism of emotion. *Archives of Neurology & Psychiatry, 38*(4), 725–743. https://doi.org/10.1001/archneurpsyc.1937.02260220069003.

Sereno, M. I., Diedrichsen, J., Tachrount, M., Testa-Silva, G., d'Arceuil, H., & De Zeeuw, C. (2020). The human cerebellum has almost 80% of the surface area of the neocortex. *Proceedings of the National Academy of Sciences, 117*(32), 19538–19543. https://doi.org/10.1073/pnas.2002896117.

Siebert, M., Markowitsch, H. J., & Bartel, P. (2003). Amygdala, affect and cognition: Evidence from 10 patients with Urbach–Wiethe disease. *Brain, 126*(12), 2627–2637. https://doi.org/10.1093/brain/awg271.

Swanson, L. W., & Petrovich, G. D. (1998). What is the amygdala? *Trends in Neurosciences, 21*(8), 323–331. https://doi.org/10.1016/s0166-2236(98)01265-x.

Weiskrantz, L. (1956). Behavioral changes associated with ablation of the amygdaloid complex in monkeys. *Journal of Comparative and Physiological Psychology, 49*(4), 381–391. https://doi.org/10.1037/h0088009.

2 Bravery in the Shadows

Altruism, Empathy, and the Neurobiology of Heroism

Imagine walking through a cornfield at night. The waning moon casts only a dim light. The cornstalks are tall and grow so dense that you can't even see the adjacent rows. The dried husks on the ground *crunch* under your feet. You hold your breath and step as lightly as you can, keen to hear any new sounds. So far there are none. You proceed down this path slowly and cautiously, sure that you're headed in the right direction, out of this nightmare. Suddenly and without warning, a figure steps into the path in front of you. Fog circles its legs. The figure is tall and thick and wears a white hockey mask. Worse still, the figure is holding a chainsaw. It slowly advances toward you, revving the chainsaw with unmistakable cruelty. You let out a blood-curdling scream, jump backward, feel your heart beating madly in your chest. The figure continues to walk toward you, and instead of turning on your heel, you ... laugh. You laugh and yell, with an exhilarated exhale, "Oh, that was good. You got me." You walk straight past the figure (giving it a large berth), down the cornfield path, out onto the pavement – to greet your friends. Your night exploring this haunted attraction has only just begun, and you excitedly anticipate the next good scare.

The fear you felt when you saw the figure advance toward you was, of course, a result of amygdala activation, alerting you to a threat. Based on what we know about the amygdala as a threat-detector, your brain should be telling you to stay *away* from scary things like chainsaw-wielding maniacs, even when you know they're fake. Because even when we know they're fake, we still feel fear. And yet, we can override that avoidance response, and some of us even derive pleasure from fear. What's more, people love being afraid so much that they flock to haunted attractions year after year, bringing in roughly $300 million annually (Haunted House Facts, n.d.). It's obviously a lucrative industry. *But why, though?* From a neurobiological perspective, we should be avoiding these places! Amygdala activation *is* amygdala activation, and that should trigger defensive or avoidance behaviors, and negative emotions. And yet, we're able to learn that (1) these threats aren't real (actual) threats, and (2) these threats are actually *fun*.

In this chapter, we'll explore the so-called paradox of horror. Why is fear sometimes pleasurable? Why would we seek out aversive stimuli that our brains are supposed to tell us to run from? And what does it say about a person if they enjoy being terrified? We can go even further down this road and ask ourselves how people can show courage, even in the face of fear. When every fiber of our being tells us to get out of there, we sometimes stand our ground and use our higher order brain areas to help us behave in complex ways. *How?*

THE PARADOX OF HORROR

Millions of people every year are attracted to things that scare them. This behavior is paradoxical and can't be explained by the basic amygdala circuitry and fear conditioning. Chainsaw-wielding maniacs signal a threat, the amygdala goes on red alert and triggers avoidance or defensive behaviors. Based on this premise alone, a killer on TV should still trigger negative emotions by way of the amygdala and thus, defensive or – more appropriately – avoidance behaviors. But despite the negative emotions, avoidance behaviors don't follow fear. This is the paradox of horror. We might not be able to explain the paradox on the sole basis of amygdala circuitry, but we can tap into some social evolutionary psychology to better understand it.

Horror movies are like simulations of other worlds and experiences with which we can explore potential outcomes. This is a *fascinating* idea. By watching horror, we're transported into fictional worlds filled with murderers, aliens, or zombies, and we can explore possible outcomes and futures, thus gathering information to use if we ourselves are ever posed with such a threat (Clasen et al., 2020;

Scalise Sugiyama, 2001). Now, of course, many of these monsters don't exist in our world (probably). That doesn't really matter for this theory because the plots in horror movies can be analogous to real-life situations. Take zombie movies, for example. In some movies, like *28 Days Later*, there's an outbreak of a highly contagious virus. In others, like the HBO series *The Last of Us*, zombieism is caused by a fast-growing variant of the real fungus, *Ophiocordiceps unilateralis*. When we watch movies like this, we see characters locking down to avoid infection. We see alliances forming between survivors. Inevitably, we see the breakdown of society, betrayal, death, and, eventually, adaptation. All of these can help prepare us for the very real threat of a global pandemic (Clasen, 2017).

In fact, movies about the outbreak of an infectious disease became notably more popular during the early days of the COVID-19 pandemic. The 2011 movie *Contagion* soared into iTune's top ten most streamed movies in late January of 2020, when just a couple of months prior, it wasn't even in the top 100 (Mack, 2020). By March 14th (for reference, this was the day President Donald Trump extended the US travel ban to include the United Kingdom) searches for *Contagion* peaked (Scrivner, 2021). It is a curious thing that so many people chose to watch movies depicting the global disaster through which they were currently living. Such people (and I include myself among them) are said to have the trait of *morbid curiosity*. Morbid curiosity can be thought of as an interest in information that could be a threat to survival and should normally inspire avoidance (such as information about deadly viruses, true crime, and violent acts; Scrivner, 2021). So, when a brand-new virus takes over the planet in just a few short months, killing thousands and shutting the entire world down, one can quench their morbid curiosity by devouring fictional stories of just that scenario. And it makes sense – these movies can give us a framework to think about the ongoing pandemic. Maybe they remind us how bad the pandemic could really be, or maybe they help us play through possible scenarios of what we would do if our best friend came into contact with the Rage virus from

28 Days Later. Horror movies can bring some peace through realistic escapism.

Morbid curiosity can even be a good thing. When people have fear and anxiety surrounding things like viral outbreaks, it can trigger avoidance, which then spirals into increased fear (Dillard et al., 2018). Presumably, people who consume a lot of horror fiction are more familiar with the feelings of fear and anxiety and, because of that, can employ emotion regulation strategies that help mitigate fear. So when a real-world crisis occurs, folks with morbid curiosity can employ the emotion regulation strategies they've been training for with their steady diet of horror and are therefore more equipped to deal with the anxiety (Kerr et al., 2019). As we know, the evolutionary purpose of fear is to trigger defensive or avoidance behaviors, which can be lifesaving. On the surface, being an avid lover of horror seems paradoxical because horror triggers fear, which should then trigger avoidance. But if the *goal* is avoidance (say, avoiding being killed by an evil poltergeist or a deadly virus), then practicing being afraid so you can better avoid deadly threats is an adaptive behavior (Kerr et al., 2019; Tamir & Ford, 2009). Research supports this. One group of researchers found that people actually prefer the feeling of fear over other emotions if the goal is to be able to avoid a stimulus (Tamir & Ford, 2009). Another group found – and I love this – that people who have a lot of morbid curiosity were actually more emotionally resilient during the early months of the pandemic. The same group also found that fans of the "prepper" genre of horror films (movies about alien invasion or the end of the world) were more emotionally resilient and showed greater emotional preparedness for the lockdown phase of the pandemic (Scrivner et al., 2021).

The idea that we consume horror movies to model other realities and to practice for possible future events can be thought of as analogous to play behavior in juvenile animals. When animals play, especially rough-and-tumble play, they're practicing for dangerous situations that could be encountered later in life. This engages cognitive and motor skills that would be required for those real-world dangerous situations, like fighting. Because rough-and-tumble play increases skills that are important for survival, it makes sense that animals that practice it more have a better chance at survival and find more pleasure in these behaviors (Scalise Sugiyama, 2001; Scrivner et al., 2021). So go ahead and hit play on that new slasher flick – it's good for you!

THE NEURAL BASIS OF EMPATHY

You know that feeling when, as you're watching a horror movie, the victim doesn't yet know that the killer is right behind them, and suddenly, you feel like the killer is right behind *you*? What you're feeling is empathy for the person who you know is about to be dismembered. You're not the one who's about to be dismembered – a fictional character on the TV is. So why do you have that shiver running down your spine?

A group of neurons in the frontal lobe, called *mirror neurons*, might be responsible. Mirror neurons have received a lot of attention, because they seem to be related to the neural basis of empathy. They were originally discovered in the macaque premotor cortex, a brain area important for the execution of planned movements. Mirror neurons have since been found in other cortical areas of the macaque, like the primary motor cortex and the parietal lobe. Mirror neurons are unique compared to other neurons because they become active, not when engaging in a behavior, but when one animal *observes* another animal perform a goal-oriented task (like reaching and grasping an object). Activity stops when the task is completed and begins firing again when the animal initiates the task itself (Gallese et al., 1996). Thus, if one macaque watches another macaque forage fruit from a tree, for example, mirror neurons in the first macaque's brain are probably active. From an evolutionary perspective, this has great prosocial benefits. Animals in groups can learn from each other, and this can benefit the group as a whole. Although macaques don't imitate behavior, humans do, and it's possible that mirror neurons can underlie social learning. Moreover, some have suggested that mirror neurons may play a role in complex social cognition, and individuals with differences in this area (e.g., Autism Spectrum Disorders) may have reduced mirror neuron functioning (Dapretto et al., 2006).

Are mirror neurons a component of the neural basis of empathy? Possibly, but much more work needs to be done. One reason that this is difficult to study is that it is difficult to manipulate empathy – it's not something we can turn on and off and observe differences in brain areas. One potential way, though, to study empathy and the brain is to look into the brains of people who have a demonstrable lack of empathy – psychopaths.

Psychopaths are individuals who have the psychiatric disorder of psychopathy. Generally, psychopathology is characterized by blunted emotional responses, impulsivity, and a lack of empathy (Cleckley, 1951). Importantly, not all psychopaths are violent or sharp-tempered. However, when we think about people high on the psychopathy spectrum, our minds tend to move toward famous serial killers like Ted Bundy and Jeffrey Dahmer. Our morbid curiosity begs us to ask why killers kill. Some killers, though certainly not all, exhibit high levels of antisocial behavior and psychopathy. If empathy is the emotion that allows us to be prosocial, then it follows that antisocial psychopaths are low on empathy. And *that's* something we can study.

One neural culprit for reduced empathy in psychopaths might be the amygdala, which appears to be changed in the brains of psychopaths. Studies have demonstrated a reduced volume in the amygdala, as well as in the prefrontal and orbitofrontal cortices in incarcerated inmates (Ermer et al., 2012; Yang et al., 2010). As we know, the amygdala is important for Pavlovian fear conditioning and the initiation of fear. The amygdala is also important for some aspects of social learning, especially social learning that requires a bit of empathy. Psychopaths are blunted in aspects of *affective theory of mind* – the ability of a person to entertain another's point of view – and are less able to take the emotional viewpoint of others (Shamay-Tsoory et al., 2010). Research has shown that early life damage to the amygdala (which in turn would disrupt amygdala-orbitofrontal connections) disrupts theory of mind (Shaw et al., 2004). So, connectivity between the amygdala and orbitofrontal cortex may indeed be important for the development of empathy.

Another groundbreaking study recorded activity directly from neurons in a forebrain region called the anterior cingulate cortex (ACC) while rodents were experiencing an anthropomorphic version of empathy. Basically, rats watched other rats experience a painful stimulus, like a footshock paired with a neutral tone. When rats had previously experienced the pain of the footshock, they demonstrated vicarious (empathetic?) fear-like responses when they observed distress in others (Atsak et al., 2011). Researchers found that the ACC had increased activity both when the animal experienced pain from the footshock *and* when the animal watched another animal receive a footshock. ACC neurons did not fire when the animal heard the tone alone, suggesting that it is not fear the neurons are responding to, but the actual (empathetic or lived) experience of pain (Carrillo et al., 2019).

The ACC is among the structures that were originally reported to be involved in complex affective states (MacLean, 1985; Papez, 1937). It extends under the cortex from the rostral (front) toward the caudal (back) parts of the brain and has myriad connections through the limbic system and orbitofrontal cortex (Margulies et al., 2007). Readers can refer back to Figure 1.3, which depicts circuitry thought to be involved in emotion. Neuroimaging studies have shown that humans have heightened activity in the ACC both when they experience pain and when they witness pain in others (Lamm et al., 2011). Vicarious activity in the ACC is increased in more empathetic individuals (Singer et al., 2004) and is reduced in psychopaths (Meffert et al., 2013). One meta-analysis evaluated the results of eight neuroimaging studies of participants viewing pained facial expressions in others. Regions activated include the ACC, the anterior central gyrus, the fusiform gyrus (important for facial recognition), and the insula (which may be related to feelings of disgust; Xiong et al., 2019).

Next time you're curled up on the couch cozily watching *The Texas Chainsaw Massacre*, you can think about how your brain is responding. You're imagining what you might do if you're held hostage by Leatherface – how you could save your friends and escape. Even though you're terrified, this is good practice for hostage situations that hopefully never come to fruition. Your amygdala is telling you to *run run run*. Your orbitofrontal cortex is probably giving you some subjective and affective state of fear. And your anterior cingulate cortex is giving you empathy for poor Pam as she gets impaled on a meat hook. This all, of course, presumes you're not a psychopath.

COURAGE IN THE FACE OF FEAR

On January 2, 2007, Wesley Autry's life changed forever. Autry and his two young daughters stood on the platform of the 137 Street City College station in Manhattan. Suddenly, a man standing nearby collapsed into a convulsive seizure. Autry and two bystanders ran to help the man, whose name was Cameron Hollopeter. Autry held a pen in Hollopeter's mouth to protect Hollopeter from his own convulsions. The convulsions slowed and finally stopped, and everyone breathed a sigh of relief. Hollopeter stood up, unsteady, and stumbled across the platform. He suddenly fell onto the tracks. Autry saw the headlight of the oncoming train and knew he couldn't hesitate. He jumped down onto the tracks, seconds ahead of the train. The driver sounded the horn and braked the train, but to no avail. Autry would never have been able to hoist Hollopeter off the tracks in time, so he did the next best thing. He pushed Hollopeter down into a drainage ditch between the tracks and threw his own body on top of the stranger's, pressing both their bodies into the ditch below as the train whizzed over them with less than an inch to spare. They were so close that the train covered the top of Autry's hat with grease. The two men lay in a ditch of water, Autry pinning Hollopeter's flailing arms, afraid of electrocution. Autry yelled up to the aghast onlookers, "We're OK down here, but I've got two daughters up there. Let them know their father's OK." The onlookers applauded (Buckley, 2007).

Both men left the platform miraculously unscathed. Hollopeter was admitted to St. Luke's-Roosevelt Hospital Center with "only bumps and bruises." Autry refused medical attention simply because he didn't need any, he said. Autry visited Hollopeter in the hospital before he began his night shift. Autry was later awarded New York City's Bronze Medallion by Mayor Michael Bloomberg, the highest award for exceptional citizenship and outstanding achievement. "I don't feel like I did anything spectacular, I just saw someone who needed help. I did what I felt was right," Autry later told the *New York Times* (Buckley, 2007).

Autry put his own life in jeopardy to save the life of a stranger. Autry's own daughters were there and narrowly missed seeing their father die a very grisly death. Of course, Autry didn't stop to think about these things before jumping out onto the train tracks to cover Hollopeter's body with his own. He just felt that what he had done was "right." Our brains are wired to promote our own survival. How can neuroscience explain Autry's downright reckless behavior?

Recall that sensory information enters the brain through sensory pathways into the thalamus. The thalamus then acts like a relay station to send sensory information to the appropriate brain area. And because we're talking about fear (or, more accurately, threat-detection), we know that the amygdala must become activated so that it can regulate downstream emotional and hormonal responses. For the amygdala to properly regulate responses, it needs to be activated rapidly and without conscious awareness. For this to take place, there must be a path from the sensory systems to the amygdala that remains entirely subcortical, that is, it will not cause any cortical activation (Öhman et al., 2007). Of course, areas in the cortex will eventually become activated by fear, otherwise we wouldn't have any conscious awareness of the thing that we're afraid of! They just lag a little behind the subcortical activation. The path from the thalamus directly to the amygdala (bypassing the cortex and, thus, conscious awareness) is sometimes called the *low road*, whereas the path from the thalamus to the cortex and then to the amygdala (which is slower but has the benefit of conscious awareness) is referred to as the *high road*. Figure 2.1 illustrates these two paths from sensory organ to amygdala.

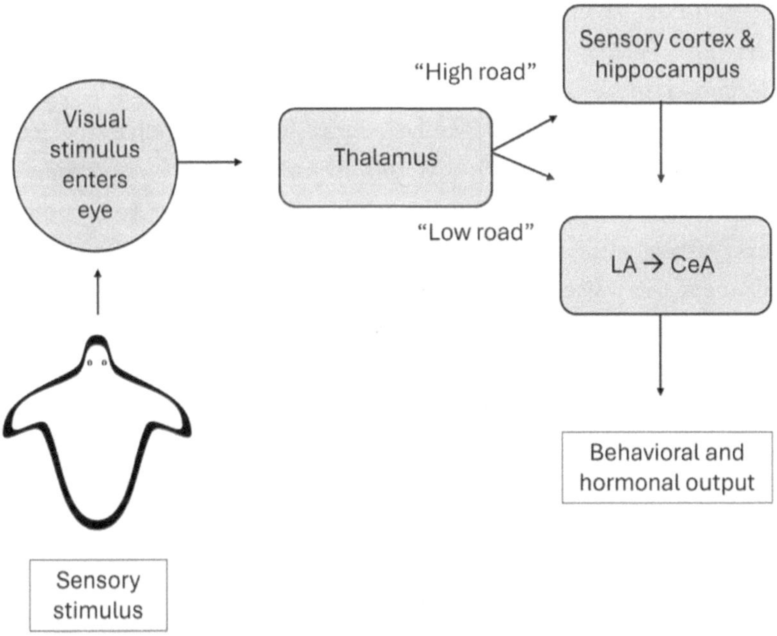

FIGURE 2.1 Low and high roads in the amygdala.
Diagram illustrating the low road (thalamus to amygdala) and high road (thalamus to cortex/hippocampus to amygdala) pathways for fear processing.

There are a few things to unpack before we tackle the question of why Autry put his own life in danger to help a stranger.

Remember that the amygdala triggers defensive or avoidance behaviors. For this to happen, the amygdala must receive sensory information from either the thalamus or the cortex. In mammals, much of this sensory input comes from vision circuitry. In response to a potential threat, rodents engage in one of two types of survival behaviors: saliency-reducing behaviors that help the rodent avoid detection by the predator (such as freezing or hiding), or saliency-enhancing behaviors to avoid capture (fleeing or aggressive behaviors; Salay et al., 2018). Cells in the thalamus regulate the animal's decision to engage in saliency-reducing or saliency-enhancing behaviors in response to a visual threat. Specifically, the *ventral midline thalamus (vMT)* is crucial for making this decision.

In the lab of Andrew Huberman at Stanford University, researchers have been interested in understanding how the vMT regulates responses to visual threats. To study this, the Huberman lab used a technique called viral-mediated gene transfer to manipulate the activity of vMT neurons. Basically, this technique allows researchers to inject a (noninfectious) virus into the brains of mice. The genome of this virus is altered to also include the genetic code for a protein that changes the way the cell functions, either inactivating or overacting those cells. Here, researchers divided mice into three groups: a control group of mice with a normally active vMT; a group of mice that had an inactivated vMT; and a group of mice that had an overactive vMT. All mice were exposed to a video that showed an overhead looming shadow, which reliably produces fear-like responses in rodents.

When the neurons in the vMT were inactivated, mice engaged in typical saliency-reducing behaviors, like freezing and hiding, and exhibited drastically fewer defensive behaviors, like tail-rattling (an aggressive behavior). Conversely, when the vMT was overactivated, mice exhibited *more* tail-rattling, even though freezing and hiding remained the same. These findings show that the vMT is important for regulating adaptive behaviors, and in particular saliency-enhancing behaviors, in response to a visual threat. But to understand how the vMT regulates behavioral output, we need to look at which brain regions are affected by vMT activity.

The vMT has two output paths. One path sends information from the vMT to the basolateral amygdala (BLA), while the other sends it to the medial prefrontal cortex (mPFC). These two pathways comprise the nonconscious low-road and conscious high-road fear circuitry, respectively. When Lindsey Salay, working in Huberman's lab, selectively activated the neurons projecting from vMT to BLA (low road) while projecting an overhead looming shadow, mice showed an increase in freezing behavior, but did not increase aggressive tail-rattling behaviors. Selective vMT to mPFC (high road) activation had the opposite effect: mice showed an increase in tail-rattling aggressive behaviors. Activating the vMT, and specifically the vMT to mPFC pathway, which corresponds to high road conscious fear, results in a shift from freezing to aggressive behaviors in mice (Salay et al., 2018). Perhaps this circuitry is a portion of the neural underpinnings of courage in the face of fear.

We've alluded to the concept of neural projections, but I'd like to pause for a moment to explicitly describe the structure of a neuron and just what neural projections are. This should help readers understand how brain areas communicate with each other.

To understand what a neuronal projection is, we need to understand how the shape of the neuron relates to its function. Neurons have a unique shape compared to other animal cells, illustrated in Figure 2.2a. As you probably know, neurons have the very important role of sending and receiving information in the nervous system. Some neurons can receive information about the senses (from the eyes, skin, etc.) and are called sensory neurons. Other neurons can send motor information from the brain to the muscles. These are called motor neurons. Still other neurons can talk directly to each

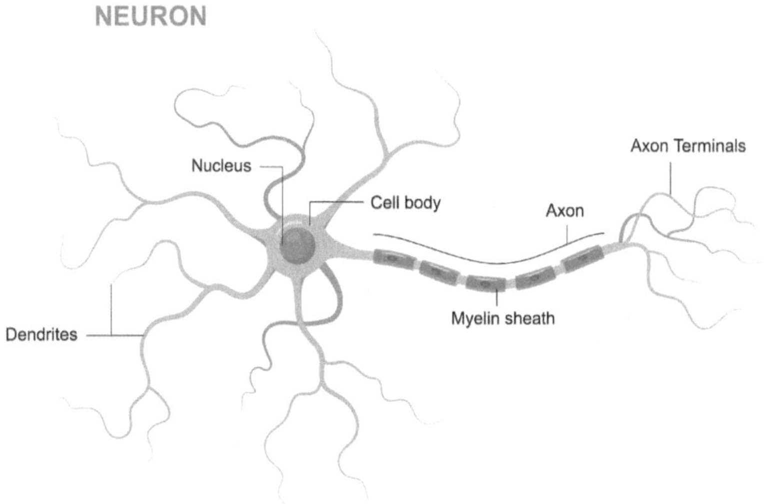

FIGURE 2.2A Diagram of a neuron.
Illustration of a neuron labeled with dendrites, soma, axon, and axon terminals.
Source: Getty Images

other, neuron-to-neuron. These are called interneurons. When a neuron becomes excited, it fires a nerve impulse, or *action potential*, which travels the length of the neuron.

Neurons receive information primarily through *dendrites*. Dendrites are branchlike arborizations that extend from the *soma*, or cell body. Each dendrite has many small protrusions, sort of like little mushrooms, growing from them. These are called *dendritic spines* and serve to increase the potential number of connections a neuron can make. When the action potential is generated in response to excitatory inputs, it travels, sort of like a wave, down the axon. The *axon* can be thought of as the conduction zone of the neuron, propagating the action potential down the axon. The axon is wrapped in a fatty covering, called the *myelin sheath*, which insulates the axon and speeds up the action potential. In most mammalian neurons, there are gaps in the myelin sheath called nodes of Ranvier. The action potential is regenerated at each of these nodes; thus, the action potential appears to "jump" from node to node. Once the action potential reaches the end of the neuron, the *axon terminal*, it triggers the release of chemical messengers, called *neurotransmitters*, from the *presynaptic neuron*. The neurotransmitters cross the microscopic distance of the synaptic cleft and bind to protein receptors on the surface of the *postsynaptic neuron*. Figure 2.2b shows a chemical synapse with the presynaptic cell sending neurotransmitters into the synapse, to be detected by neurotransmitter receptors on the postsynaptic cell. The interaction between neurotransmitter and receptor now becomes the input received by the next neuron, which may then fire an action potential.

When we talk about projections from one brain area to another, like from the vMT to the BLA, we mean that there are groups of cell bodies of neurons all clustered together whose axons extend to another part of the brain. A cluster of cell bodies in the central nervous system is called a *nucleus* (not to be confused with the organelle in the cell body that contains DNA). Axons from each of these cell bodies bundle together to form a *tract* (think of a bundle of electrical cords) which travel to another brain area, and the axon terminals are in that other brain area. We can therefore say that the

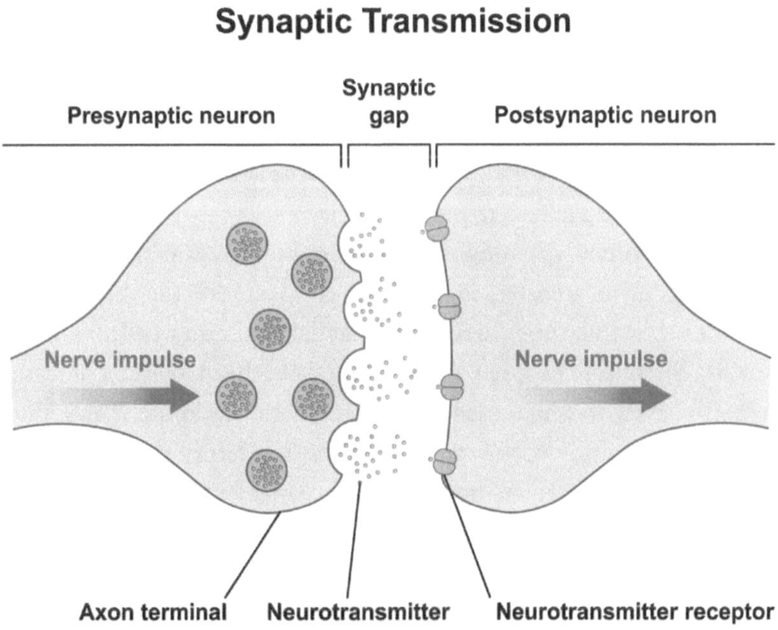

FIGURE 2.2B Diagram of a synapse.
Close-up diagram of a synapse showing the release of neurotransmitters from a presynaptic neuron to a postsynaptic receptor.
Source: Getty Images

vMT is a nucleus along the midline of the thalamus that sends divergent projections to the BLA and the mPFC. This circuitry seems to underlie attack and avoidance behaviors in mice in response to visually looming threats. But, the vMT doesn't receive direct visual input, so where does it get its information from? Lindsey Salay, working in the lab of Andrew Huberman, asked this very question.

Vision is the primary sense that many mammals use to detect threats in their environment. Vision is first processed in the retina, by light-sensitive cells called rods and cones. Rods and cones are the initial light detectors in the eye, and they send information to the brain by way of bipolar and ganglion cells, both of which also live in the retina. Visual information leaves the retina via the optic nerve, which is a bundle of ganglion cell axons. The optic nerve finally terminates in several nuclei of the thalamus. One specific retinorecipient nucleus in the thalamus is called the ventral lateral geniculate nucleus (vLGN; say that three times fast). The vLGN sends projections to the superior colliculus of the midbrain, the periaqueductal gray of the midbrain, and, importantly for this story, a portion of the vMT called the nucleus reuniens.

In a follow-up study, the Huberman lab again utilized viral-mediated gene transfer to increase or decrease the behavior of neurons, but this time, they only targeted inhibitory neurons in the vLGN. Mice were exposed to a simulated overhead looming predator. When activity was increased in inhibitory neurons in the vLGN, mice reduced their time spent freezing. When inhibitory neurons in this nucleus were shut down, however, mice displayed significantly more freezing behavior. Slowing the activity of inhibitory neurons in the vLGN not only increased time spent freezing, but mice also engaged in other behaviors that would similarly avoid detection, like staying in burrows instead of foraging for food.

Lead author on this study, Lindsay Salay, next investigated two pathways originating in the vLGN. The first of these pathways terminates in the nucleus reuniens, which is part of the vMT. The other pathway originates in the vLGN and terminates in the superior colliculus (SC) of the midbrain, which helps to process visual information. Activating only the vLGN to reuniens resulted in a robust *increase* in freezing behavior in mice. This finding contradicted the earlier finding that activating certain cells in the vLGN alone decreased freezing. vLGN activation, of course, would affect both the reuniens and the SC, leading researchers to theorize that the SC might play a pivotal role in modulating visual threat behavior. To investigate this, researchers stimulated the pathway from the vLGN to SC. Activating the pathway from vLGN to SC (but not the inhibitory pathway alone) decreased freezing behaviors, providing evidence that divergent pathways from the vLGN work together to produce adaptive behavioral responses to visual threat (Salay & Huberman, 2021). This is visualized in Figure 2.3.

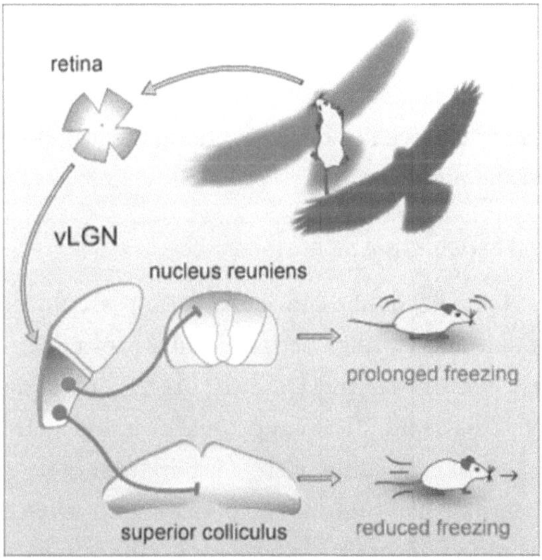

FIGURE 2.3 Divergent outputs of vLGN.
Schematic showing different visual output pathways from the lateral geniculate nucleus involved in defensive behaviors.
Source: Figure reproduced from Salay & Huberman (2021), "Divergent outputs of the ventral lateral geniculate nucleus mediate visually evoked defensive behaviors," Cell Reports, 37(7), 110009.

Yes, I know that this is very complex – let's review. Visual information comes into the eyes and makes its way to the thalamus. Within the thalamus, visual information makes an early stop in the vLGN. The vLGN has many outputs, including the vMT and SC. The vLGN to vMT pathway appears to increase behaviors that would reduce the saliency of the animal and thus reduce predation, like freezing. The vMT itself has divergent pathways that regulate response to visual threat: the pathway from the vMT to the BLA increases freezing behavior, whereas vMT to the mPFC increases aggressive behaviors.

The vLGN → vMT → BLA pathway might, then, be a likely piece of the so-called low road to the amygdala, bypassing the cortex and thus conscious awareness of the behavior. This research also shows that there are distinct neural pathways that regulate behaviors in response to visual threat. This is important because the choice between freezing, hiding, and fighting could mean life or death. Could turning on or off these pathways be a courage switch in the brain? Could altered activity in these pathways, say, cause a man to jump onto subway tracks to save a stranger's life, just seconds before the train pulled into the platform?

THE NEUROSCIENCE OF ALTRUISM

Autry's actions were no doubt brave. And they would have been contrary to any survival instinct he had. Had Autry never acted, he would never have been in danger. Despite that, he suppressed everything in his body that said, "It's dangerous to jump in front of an oncoming train," so that he could, well, jump in front of an oncoming train. Altruistic actions like these are actions that are taken to benefit another without a clear benefit to the donor. Oftentimes, altruistic behaviors aren't taught or rewarded, and even young children display natural altruism. Toddlers as young as fourteen months will help others obtain an out-of-reach object or open a cabinet door, without any reward or encouragement, or expectation of retribution (Warneken & Tomasello, 2009). Altruism is difficult to explain in the context of evolutionary psychology. Why would an animal go far out of its own way, even putting itself at risk, to benefit another? Some suggest that altruistic actions improve the inclusive fitness of the species, and that altruism increases the ability of a species, and not one individual member, to survive.

One model of altruism used in psychology labs is a game called "The Dictator Game." Briefly, the game involves two people, the Dictator and the Recipient. The Dictator is given a sum of money and can choose how to allocate it between themselves and the recipient. The recipient has no say in the Dictator's choice allocation. This game has, interestingly, been adapted to a rodent model, which gives us a closer look at the potential neural correlates of altruism.

In the rodent Dictator Game, the Dictator rat has access to two nose-poke holes with a compartment between them where food can be dispensed. Poking a nose into one hole results in food for the

Dictator rat (the selfish choice), while poking a nose into the other hole results in food being dispensed for the Recipient rat (the altruistic choice). Remarkably, when playing the Dictator Game over several days, rats overwhelmingly choose to give food to the Recipient rather than keep the food for itself. Male Dictators choose to donate food to the Recipient more than female Dictators; and animals who make more altruistic choices also spend more time sniffing and investigating the Recipient. Overall levels of altruism increase when the Dictator is familiar with the Recipient, reinforcing the idea that familiarity increases prosocial behaviors. And, speaking of prosociality, altruism appears to relate to empathy. In the model of emotional contagion described earlier (where one animal observes another receive a painful stimulus, like a footshock), researchers found that vicarious freezing behaviors were more prevalent in altruistic rats, and fear conditioning via observation correlated with the social dominance hierarchy such that dominant rats show more emotional contagion (Scheggia et al., 2022).

The basolateral amygdala (BLA) may mediate altruistic behaviors. In the same Dictator Game, if the BLA is silenced, altruistic behavior is abolished. While the game itself increases BLA activity, prosocial decisions significantly increase activity in the BLA as compared to selfish decisions. The BLA entertains reciprocal projections to important decision-making areas, namely limbic areas of the prefrontal cortex (PFC). When researchers silenced the projections from BLA to the PFC, altruistic choices were reduced, but not abolished, and were altogether eliminated when the PFC to BLA projections were silenced (Scheggia et al., 2022).

CONCLUSIONS

In *A Song of Ice and Fire*, by George R. R. Martin, young Bran Stark asked his father Ned whether a man can still be brave if he is afraid. Ned replied, "That is the only time a man can be brave." Bran and

Ned could have had no idea what amount of fear and bravery they would need to call upon to play the game of thrones.

Being afraid requires activation of the amygdala, and I'm willing to bet that young Bran had quite a bit of low- and high road activation as he processed the terrifying reality of why that man abandoned his post at The Wall. And as the series progressed, Bran and the other Stark children learned how to have courage in the face of fear. Even though there were so many times when Bran wanted to turn and flee, as his low road would have him, he stood his ground and did what was right. Reciprocal connections between the amygdala and frontal areas, like the orbitofrontal and prefrontal cortex, help promote empathy and social decision-making. The anterior cingulate cortex, as well, is a major neural substrate to empathy and Theory of Mind, the ability to take another's perspective. I'm not sure that altruism was a trait that took center stage in *Game of Thrones*, but if anyone in the Realm was altruistic, it would have been Ned Stark. Ned would have made the altruistic choice in the Dictator Game, especially if he saw it as for the good of the Realm.

REFERENCES

Atsak, P., Orre, M., Bakker, P., Cerliani, L., Roozendaal, B., Gazzola, V., Moita, M., & Keysers, C. (2011). Experience modulates vicarious freezing in rats: A model for empathy. *PLOS ONE*, *6*(7), e21855. https://doi.org/10.1371/journal.pone.0021855.

Buckley, C. (2007, January 3). Man Is Rescued by Stranger on Subway Tracks. *The New York Times*. www.nytimes.com/2007/01/03/nyregion/03life.html.

Carrillo, M., Han, Y., Migliorati, F., Liu, M., Gazzola, V., & Keysers, C. (2019). Emotional mirror neurons in the rat's anterior cingulate cortex. *Current Biology*, *29*(8), 1301–1312.e6. https://doi.org/10.1016/j.cub.2019.03.024.

Clasen, M. (2017). *Why Horror Seduces*. Oxford: Oxford University Press.

Clasen, M., Kjeldgaard-Christiansen, J., & Johnson, J. A. (2020). Horror, personality, and threat simulation: A survey on the psychology of scary media. *Evolutionary Behavioral Sciences*, *14*(3), 213–230. https://doi.org/10.1037/ebs0000152.

Cleckley, H. M. (1951). The mask of sanity. *Postgraduate Medicine*, *9*(3), 193–197. https://doi.org/10.1080/00325481.1951.11694097.

Dapretto, M., Davies, M. S., Pfeifer, J. H., Scott, A. A., Sigman, M., Bookheimer, S. Y., & Iacoboni, M. (2006). Understanding emotions in others: Mirror neuron dysfunction in children with autism spectrum disorders. *Nature Neuroscience, 9*(1), 28–30. https://doi.org/10.1038/nn1611.

Dillard, J. P., Yang, C., & Li, R. (2018). Self-regulation of emotional responses to Zika: Spiral of fear. *PLOS ONE, 13*(7), e0199828. https://doi.org/10.1371/journal.pone.0199828.

Ermer, E., Cope, L. M., Nyalakanti, P. K., Calhoun, V. D., & Kiehl, K. A. (2012). Aberrant paralimbic gray matter in criminal psychopathy. *Journal of Abnormal Psychology, 121*(3), 649–658. https://doi.org/10.1037/a0026371.

Gallese, V., Fadiga, L., Fogassi, L., & Rizzolatti, G. (1996). Action recognition in the premotor cortex. *Brain: A Journal of Neurology, 119*(2), 593–609. https://doi.org/10.1093/brain/119.2.593.

Haunted House Facts. (n.d.). *America Haunts.* Retrieved June 17, 2023, from www.americahaunts.com/ah/facts/.

Kerr, M., Siegle, G. J., & Orsini, J. (2019). Voluntary arousing negative experiences (VANE): Why we like to be scared. *Emotion, 19*(4), 682–698. https://doi.org/10.1037/emo0000470.

Lamm, C., Decety, J., & Singer, T. (2011). Meta-analytic evidence for common and distinct neural networks associated with directly experienced pain and empathy for pain. *NeuroImage, 54*(3), 2492–2502. https://doi.org/10.1016/j.neuroimage.2010.10.014.

Mack, D. (2020, March 3). Everyone Is Watching "Contagion," A 9-Year-Old Movie About A Flu Outbreak. *BuzzFeed.* www.buzzfeednews.com/article/davidmack/contagion-movie-coronavirus.

MacLean, P. D. (1985). Brain evolution relating to family, play, and the separation call. *Archives of General Psychiatry, 42*(4), 405–417. https://doi.org/10.1001/archpsyc.1985.01790270095011.

Margulies, D. S., Kelly, A. M. C., Uddin, L. Q., Biswal, B. B., Castellanos, F. X., & Milham, M. P. (2007). Mapping the functional connectivity of anterior cingulate cortex. *NeuroImage, 37*(2), 579–588. https://doi.org/10.1016/j.neuroimage.2007.05.019.

Meffert, H., Gazzola, V., den Boer, J. A., Bartels, A. A. J., & Keysers, C. (2013). Reduced spontaneous but relatively normal deliberate vicarious representations in psychopathy. *Brain: A Journal of Neurology, 136*(8), 2550–2562. https://doi.org/10.1093/brain/awt190.

Öhman, A., Carlsson, K., Lundqvist, D., & Ingvar, M. (2007). On the unconscious subcortical origin of human fear. *Physiology & Behavior, 92*(1), 180–185. https://doi.org/10.1016/j.physbeh.2007.05.057.

Papez, J. (1937). A proposed mechanism of emotion. *Archives of Neurology & Psychiatry, 38*(4), 725–743. https://doi.org/10.1001/archneurpsyc.1937.02260220069003.

Salay, L. D., & Huberman, A. D. (2021). Divergent outputs of the ventral lateral geniculate nucleus mediate visually evoked defensive behaviors. *Cell Reports, 37*(1), 109792. https://doi.org/10.1016/j.celrep.2021.109792.

Salay, L. D., Ishiko, N., & Huberman, A. D. (2018). A midline thalamic circuit determines reactions to visual threat. *Nature, 557*(7704), 183–189. https://doi.org/10.1038/s41586-018-0078-2.

Scalise Sugiyama, M. (2001). Food, foragers, and folklore: The role of narrative in human subsistence. *Evolution and Human Behavior, 22*(4), 221–240. https://doi.org/10.1016/S1090-5138(01)00063-0.

Scheggia, D., La Greca, F., Maltese, F., Chiacchierini, G., Italia, M., Molent, C., Bernardi, F., Coccia, G., Carrano, N., Zianni, E., Gardoni, F., Di Luca, M., & Papaleo, F. (2022). Reciprocal cortico-amygdala connections regulate prosocial and selfish choices in mice. *Nature Neuroscience, 25*(11), 1505–1518. https://doi.org/10.1038/s41593-022-01179-2.

Scrivner, C. (2021). An infectious curiosity: Morbid curiosity and media preferences during a pandemic. *Evolutionary Studies in Imaginative Culture, 5*(1), 1–12. https://doi.org/10.26613/esic.5.1.206.

Scrivner, C., Johnson, J. A., Kjeldgaard-Christiansen, J., & Clasen, M. (2021). Pandemic practice: Horror fans and morbidly curious individuals are more psychologically resilient during the COVID-19 pandemic. *Personality and Individual Differences, 168,* 110397. https://doi.org/10.1016/j.paid.2020.110397.

Shamay-Tsoory, S. G., Harari, H., Aharon-Peretz, J., & Levkovitz, Y. (2010). The role of the orbitofrontal cortex in affective theory of mind deficits in criminal offenders with psychopathic tendencies. *Cortex, 46*(5), 668–677. https://doi.org/10.1016/j.cortex.2009.04.008.

Shaw, P., Lawrence, E. J., Radbourne, C., Bramham, J., Polkey, C. E., & David, A. S. (2004). The impact of early and late damage to the human amygdala on 'theory of mind' reasoning. *Brain, 127*(7), 1535–1548. https://doi.org/10.1093/brain/awh168.

Singer, T., Seymour, B., O'Doherty, J., Kaube, H., Dolan, R. J., & Frith, C. D. (2004). Empathy for pain involves the affective but not sensory components of pain. *Science, 303*(5661), 1157–1162. https://doi.org/10.1126/science.1093535.

Tamir, M., & Ford, B. Q. (2009). Choosing to be afraid: Preferences for fear as a function of goal pursuit. *Emotion, 9*(4), 488–497. https://doi.org/10.1037/a0015882.

Warneken, F., & Tomasello, M. (2009). The roots of human altruism. *British Journal of Psychology, 100*(3), 455–471. https://doi.org/10.1348/000712608X379061.

Xiong, R.-C., Fu, X., Wu, L.-Z., Zhang, C.-H., Wu, H.-X., Shi, Y., & Wu, W. (2019). Brain pathways of pain empathy activated by pained facial expressions: A meta-analysis of fMRI using the activation likelihood estimation method. *Neural Regeneration Research, 14*(1), 172–178. https://doi.org/10.4103/1673-5374.243722.

Yang, Y., Raine, A., Colletti, P., Toga, A. W., & Narr, K. L. (2010). Morphological alterations in the prefrontal cortex and the amygdala in unsuccessful psychopaths. *Journal of Abnormal Psychology, 119*(3), 546–554. https://doi.org/10.1037/a0019611.

3 The EMF Is Going Crazy

Ghosts, Gadgets, and the Temporal Lobe

If you've ever watched a show on paranormal investigations, you've probably seen someone on the show walk into a room, their eyes trained on a handheld electronic device, and mutter something like, "The EMF's going crazy in here." The investigator (think *Supernatural*'s Dean Winchester) is measuring the electromagnetic frequency (EMF) of the area, which is reportedly disturbed when there is supernatural activity. Paranormal investigators regularly use EMF field recordings as a tool to help assess activity in an area. But is this an accurate measurement?

As psychologists, we want to test the hypothesis that electromagnetic fluctuations are related to paranormal activity. The fact that there is no reliable or valid measure of paranormal activity makes testing this hypothesis quite difficult. Moreover, the Earth's magnetic field is rife with fluctuations, and these can occur from many very natural sources. How can we sort out fluctuations due to paranormal activity from the fluctuations due to natural changes in the Earth's magnetosphere? When paranormal investigators determine that there are ghosts nearby because their EMF detector is "going crazy," they might be making what psychologists refer to as *Type I error* – they're assuming there is a real finding when there might not actually be, a false positive. Conversely, *Type II error* means that you're not picking up on a finding that might truly be there, a false negative. Imagine this scenario. You're walking through the creepy woods and you hear a twig snap behind you. You could pretend nothing had happened, or you could run like mad. If you make a Type I error, you'd run away, even if the twig snap was from a squirrel. You might feel silly, but you'd be alive. If you made a Type II error, though, you'd stay where you are, but the evil spirit could be right behind you, and if that were the case, you'd be toast.

WHAT CAME FIRST, THE EMF OR THE GHOST?

So, how can we test whether EMF fluctuations are related to paranormal activity, doing our best to avoid Type I and Type II error? Anomalistic psychologist Richard Wiseman visited some of the most haunted places in the United Kingdom to answer this very question.

Hampton Court Palace, just outside London, was originally constructed in the early 1500s and was famously home to King Henry VIII, his wives, and many courtiers. Many ghosts are said to be in residence at Hampton Court Palace, but none so famous as Catherine Howard, King Henry's fifth wife. Catherine was accused of adultery and sentenced to death by beheading. As the story goes, Catherine broke free from her guards and ran down the corridor yelling and begging for Henry's mercy. The guards recaptured her and her sentence was carried out. It is said that her ghost can be seen wandering that same corridor, the so-called Haunted Gallery. When it is very quiet, you can hear her distant cries for mercy. In Edinburgh, Scotland, the South Bridge vaults (see Figure 3.1) are home to another set of ghosts. Originally built as a space for merchants, the vaults beneath the bridge were soon abandoned due to poor ventilation and horrific sanitation. With the vaults now abandoned, the city's poorest sought shelter within them. Over time, the vaults became a haven for grave-robbed corpses, illegal distilleries, criminal hideouts, prostitution and gambling rings, and poverty-stricken families with nowhere else to go. Box 3.1 gives an especially horrific account of grave robbers and body snatchers in Edinburgh. Eventually, the vaults were filled with rubble and forgotten about. In 1985, a chance excavation exposed the forgotten vaults, the rubble was cleared, and the vaults were back in the public eye. The former dwellers had left behind clues about their lives that allowed historians to piece together what life was like in the subterranean vaults in eighteenth-century Edinburgh. It wasn't good. Nowadays, visitors to the vaults frequently report inexplicable lights and sounds, a strange sense of presence, and if they are very lucky, a toy ball might be rolled to them from the ghost of a little boy who roams the vaults in hopes of a game of catch.

BOX 3.1 **Murder for medicine**

It's nineteenth-century Edinburgh. The city was the leading center of anatomical study in Europe, yet there was a dire shortage of cadavers for medical training. Under Scottish law, bodies for dissection could only be provided by executed prisoners or victims of suicide. This led to a drastic shortage of corpses and an increase in grave robbing. A fresh corpse could earn a body snatcher enough money to feed their family for a month. When a lodger in William Hare's house died suddenly, Hare turned to his friend William Burke, who suggested that they sell the body to a local physician named Robert Knox. Knox paid handsomely for this corpse. Not long after, another lodger in Hare's house fell ill. According to some accounts, Hare feared the illness would scare off future tenants, so he and Burke murdered the woman and sold the corpse to Knox. This began a chilling string of murders – sixteen in all. Each victim was sent to Knox for medical dissection. Eventually, suspicions arose, and Hare turned King's Evidence against Burke in exchange for immunity. Burke was tried, found guilty, and hanged. His body was given to the medical school for dissection and his skeleton remains on display in the Edinburgh's Anatomical Museum to this day. It is not clear what happened to Hare. Some say he fled to London, others say he returned to his home in Ireland. As for Knox, he was never tried for his involvement in the murders. The Royal College of Surgeons pressured him to resign from his position and he moved to London. His reputation was irreparably damaged, and he was never again hired to teach at a university. Instead, he worked as an anatomist at a free hospital and published several highly controversial, and deeply racist, books.

If the Haunted Gallery and South Bridge vaults are truly haunted, then perhaps the EMF is measurably wonky in those areas. So, Wiseman did what any good psychologist would do – he used the scientific method to design and carry out the best experiment he could in the most haunted places available. In one study, Wiseman visited Hampton Court Palace and recruited participants that were about to enter. He was interested in EMF fluctuations and people's perceptions of, well, weird happenings in the palace. Participants wandered the palace and noted any odd sensations as well as the location within the palace where these sensations occurred. The participants then filled out a survey designed to measure paranormal belief. Wiseman discovered a difference in the experiences of believers and nonbelievers. Believers in the paranormal reported more strange experiences in the palace than nonbelievers did. They reported things like heightened emotions, a sensed presence, odd sounds, changes in temperature, dizziness, smells, sights, and tastes. Believers were also more likely to attribute these sensations to the presence of ghosts instead of natural phenomena, like drafts. When Wiseman's group compared these experiences with EMF data, they discovered that strange experiences were much more likely to have occurred in areas of the palace that were associated with greater EMF fluctuations (Wiseman et al., 2002). Self-report data certainly has its flaws. It is entirely possible that believers in the paranormal are more likely to notice things like odd sounds and changes in temperature and therefore report them more. But, if these data are to be believed, they suggest that there might be a relationship between EMF fluctuations and paranormal experiences.

When experiments test to see how likely certain things are to occur together (e.g., does the number of reported ghostly perceptions increase as the variance in EMF recordings increases), they're measuring a *correlation*. A correlation is a measured relationship between two or more variables. These can be informative but should always be interpreted with caution – a correlation can tell us whether there is a relationship between two variables, but it cannot tell us whether a change in one variable causes a change in another. Let's use an example of a spurious and non-supernatural correlation. Cheese consumption in the United States has been steadily increasing from the years 2000 to 2009. So has the number of people who have died by being tangled in their bedsheets. Can the amount of cheese eaten by your neighbor impact whether your bedsheets become murderous? Of course not. This is a wonderful example of two variables changing together, though a change in one is *probably* not related to a change in the other.

Wiseman found that there *was* in fact a correlation between variations in EMF activity and people's reports of unusual experiences at Hampton Court Palace. This is interesting but doesn't tell us anything causal. And if there is a causal relationship between EMF variations and unusual experiences, is it related to paranormal activity or to something else? Wiseman wondered whether the visitors to Hampton Court Palace had any prior knowledge of the alleged hauntings by Catherine Howard. If they expected, or even hoped, to get a glimpse of Catherine, and then coincidently felt an inexplicable draft or drop in temperature (hardly unlikely in a sixteenth century castle), how likely would they be to misattribute that to supernatural causes? Probably very likely, especially if they already have a high belief in the paranormal. Quite a bit of research supports the idea that when people expect to see ghosts, they are more likely to see ghosts. We'll explore the relationship between expectation and experience throughout the book.

All right, let's go back to Hampton Court Palace. After analyzing the data from the Hampton Court Palace experiment, Wiseman did two things: First, he cautioned his readers to take these interesting findings with a grain of salt – this is a correlation based on a small sample size. Then, he went back to Hampton Court Palace to collect more data.

In order to assess the role of expectation and natural contextual cues, like EMF changes, Wiseman repeated his research, but with some modifications. This time, he asked visitors to Hampton Court Palace whether they had previously heard rumors of hauntings in the palace. Then, like before, he asked them to walk through reportedly haunted and non-haunted parts of the palace, documenting anything unusual that they might experience. Finally, Wiseman and his team took EMF recordings in those same locations of the palace. Participants reported a variety of anomalous experiences, and when asked whether these experiences were due to a ghost, 14 percent of them answered "definitely yes" or "probably yes." Interestingly, prior knowledge of hauntings in the palace did not significantly affect ghostly experiences. Additionally, these experiences predominantly occurred in areas of the palace that were rumored to be haunted where there was also a wider range of EMF variance than non-haunted parts of the castle. This provides further evidence of a possible relationship between EMF fluctuations and paranormal experiences, and tells us that expectation might not be the whole story.

As I mentioned a few moments ago, the vaults underneath the South Bridge in Edinburgh, Scotland, are also home to a number of alleged ghosts. In another study, researchers ranked each vault according to the number of anomalous experiences that had occurred in the vault. Thus, each vault was assigned a rank that was referred to as the "Haunted Order." Participants were randomly assigned to a vault and asked to sit alone in it for ten minutes, recording any strange or unusual feelings. Like the results from the Hampton Court Palace experiments, participants experienced more unusual sensations in areas that had a higher Haunted Order. This was true even for participants that reported no prior knowledge of the hauntings. There was a small, but nonsignificant, correlation between the paranormal experiences in the vault and EMF fluctuations (Wiseman et al., 2003). The question remains: Are there natural environmental disturbances that some people interpret as paranormal activity, or is there truly paranormal activity in these areas?

FIGURE 3.1 The South Bridge vaults, Edinburgh, Scotland.
Photograph of the dark, stone-walled interior of the South Bridge vaults, historically used as underground chambers.
Source: Flickr

EMF AND THE BRAIN

Measurement techniques in science should have both *validity* and *reliability*. Having validity means that the instrument is truly measuring what it is intended to measure. In this case, an EMF detector should measure Earth's electromagnetic field (and not, say, radio waves). Reliability, on the other hand, refers to consistency. An instrument could be reliable but not valid if, for example, it consistently measures EMF levels 200Hz too low. It's wrong, but it's wrong the same way every time.

EMF are invisible areas of energy that are created by both natural sources, like the Earth's magnetic field, and man-made sources, like power lines. Devices that detect this energy can be purchased fairly inexpensively at most home improvement stores and are regularly used to detect electric and magnetic currents in an environment. Rest assured, though, there is no data to suggest that everyday levels of EMF exposure are dangerous. As we know, EMF detectors are also used by paranormal investigators. These detectors are probably valid at detecting EMF, and, depending on the model, are probably fairly reliable too. But understanding the data is difficult without an understanding of natural electromagnetic activity. For example, for correct interpretation of the data, one would need to know how electromagnetic energy decays over time and space, and how the data are triangulated among various sources of current. It is unlikely that any "blip" in EMF corresponds to a specific location in time and space. This could be a potential Type I error, but let's look a little closer.

Another problem, then, in assessing the relationship between EMF and paranormal activity is that the research on the subject is sparse, and the existing research is fraught with methodological variations that render each study noncomparable to other studies. Thus, even though Wiseman found a relationship between EMF and unusual experiences, the actual measured EMF variation was very small. Moreover, very few field studies of EMF and paranormal activity find a correlation between EMF variability and unusual experiences (Braithwaite, 2008). Besides EMF, there are other environmental and contextual factors that could alter a person's perception of the environment in ways that may correlate with experiences of paranormal activity. These include room temperature, low levels of light, sounds just below our hearing threshold, or draftiness of the room (Braithwaite, 2011). Again, this is all correlational, and correlations, as we know, do not tell us about causation. These findings also do not rule out the idea that actual ghosts might be causing these contextual disturbances. But, of course, this is a non-falsifiable hypothesis. To test it, we need to get more creative.

In one very famous and ingenious study, anomalistic psychologist Chris French actually built a haunted room in his laboratory (French et al., 2009)! This experiment was called "The Haunt Project." The room was designed to manipulate certain contextual cues that have been linked to hauntings. In this experiment, researchers manipulated EMF complexity and infrasound, or sound that is so low-pitched that it is not detectable by humans. Participants were invited into the lab and asked to fill out two surveys. The first, called the Australian Sheep-Goat Scale (ASGS) measures overall belief in the paranormal. The second, called the Temporal Lobe Signs (TLS), reportedly measures flexibility, or lability, of the temporal lobe of the cerebral cortex (more on this in a minute). Afterward, participants spent fifty minutes in the dimly lit, artificially haunted room and were asked to report any unusual sensations they experienced while in the room. The context of the room varied such that some participants experienced complex EMF *and* infrasound, complex EMF *or* infrasound, or nothing.

Remarkably, participants reported all sorts of unusual sensations. 79.7% of participants reported that they felt dizzy or odd; 49.4% felt like they were spinning around; 22.8% felt detached from their bodies; 22.8% felt a presence; 8.9% even experienced terror. However, the reports of unusual experiences did *not* correlate at all to experimental conditions. Whether the participant experienced EMF, infrasound, a combination of the two, or neither, had no bearing on whether they reported unusual or anomalous experiences. What, then, could have caused these anomalous experiences? According to French, the most parsimonious explanation is that the participants were primed. In psychology, priming is the idea that ideas can be planted or suggested in the mind. Research ethics dictate that participants must be informed about the tasks they will be asked to do in the experiment, and they must provide their consent to participate. Here, participants filled out surveys related to paranormal activity and then were told that they might experience unusual sensations during the experiment. Thus, participants were likely primed to expect strange sensations. Expectation led to reality for those who were believers in the paranormal.

Other studies have shown that mere suggestion can cause people to think they're experiencing something supernatural. Lange and Houran reported on the power of suggestion after they asked participants to walk through a non-haunted, but disused, cinema, telling some people that it has a history of paranormal activity. You guessed it – the people that were told that the cinema had a history of paranormal activity were much more likely to experience the paranormal for themselves (Lange & Houran, 1997). Wiseman's group (Wiseman et al., 2003) has reported on this when they suggested that tabletop top objects – and even the table! – were levitating in a fake séance. Unsurprisingly, in both studies, participants that were expecting paranormal activity were more likely to experience paranormal activity. We'll get to that in Chapter 6.

TEMPORAL LOBE, MYSTICISM, AND THE SELF

What would have caused people to experience unusual sensations – sensations that have the power to evoke terror – in a setting that was almost certainly not haunted? In The Haunt Project, Chris French found that participants that reported the unusual sensations scored high in overall belief in the paranormal. They also scored high on the Temporal Lobe Signs (TLS) scale. The TLS scale is a subset of the Personal Philosophy Inventory, a scale developed by Michael Persinger that reportedly measures the lability, or overall activity, of the temporal lobe. Persinger's long-standing argument has been that people that score high on the TLS, and therefore have greater temporal lobe lability, are more susceptible to environmental factors like EMF, and thus are more likely to report supernatural experiences (Persinger, 1984). This idea isn't that far out of left field. There are people with temporal lobe epilepsy whose seizures bring on hyper-religious or spiritual experiences (see Aaen-Stockdale, 2012; Dewhurst & Beard, 1970). Joan of Arc, who famously had visions of God, very likely had temporal lobe epilepsy. (Nicastro & Picard, 2016).

Luckily, the relationship between a labile temporal lobe and unusual experiences *is* a testable relationship, and Michael Persinger spent his life work devoted to investigating it. He believed that God "exists" in the right temporal lobe region, and direct stimulation to that area could induce a sensed presence (similar to what a person with temporal lobe epilepsy might experience). In the early 2000s, Persinger famously fitted a helmet with solenoid coils that could deliver magnetic current to the temporal lobe of the brain. Hundreds of participants wore this so-called God Helmet (originally and briefly called the Koren Helmet, after its designer), and with magnetic current delivered to the right temporal lobe, reported religious experiences. In Persinger's opinion, this proved that humans' perceptions of God are generated in the right temporal region.

In one case study, Persinger brought a subject into his lab who had experienced regular "haunts" in his life. This man had moved into a new home with his family in the early 1990s and quickly experienced strange sensations, like sudden depression and anxiety, feelings of being watched, cold and drafty spots in the house, strange sounds, and unexplained electrical bursts in light bulbs. In this case study, the participant was invited to the lab and was fitted with the God Helmet that would deliver transcranial stimulation to the left or right temporal regions. Remarkably, this stimulation brought on a variety of unusual sensations, including feelings of the body being controlled and twisted, feelings of extreme happiness ("I want to burst into laughter") or sadness ("feeling weepy," "depression, malaise"), and finally, an actual apparition ("I see an apparition – that's it," "See a pair of eyes approaching looking at me ... it's taking definite form"; Persinger et al., 2010). Did this person's home contain naturally occurring fluctuations in EMF that acted on the temporal lobe to cause anomalous sensations? Or could it be that supernatural forces themselves induced this man's anomalous experiences, and these experiences were mimicked by stimulating the temporal lobe with the God Helmet?

Persinger's work suggests that complex stimulation to the temporal lobes, and specifically, the temporal-parietal region, could induce a sense of a presence. One of the hallmarks of good science, however, is replicability, and in this respect, Persinger's work falls short. There has been a paucity of studies that attempted to recreate the bizarre effects of the God Helmet, and those attempts were mostly unsuccessful. One well-known replication attempt found no effect of transcranial magnetic stimulation on the experience of a presence, even in people who were predicted to have high levels of suggestibility (Granqvist et al., 2005). It was thus concluded that the effects of stimulation that Persinger so prolifically published were probably due to suggestion and not brain stimulation. Persinger replied to these findings in a Letter to the Editor, retorting that there were major methodological variations in the replication attempt that would explain the null findings. That, and perhaps those participants just weren't temporal lobe-y enough (Persinger & Koren, 2005).

There probably is *something* in stimulating the temporal lobe, though. One weird report from a group of neurologists described applying stimulation to the junction between the temporal and parietal lobes (the temporoparietal junction; TPJ; see Figure 3.2) in a nonpsychiatric patient who was being evaluated for surgical treatment for epilepsy (Arzy, Seeck et al., 2006). In this report, the patient had a small amount of stimulation to the TPJ and reported the sensation of *a human-like presence standing behind her*. As the current was increased over the TPJ, the intensity of the sensation increased, such that the patient now observed this presence as man. The man

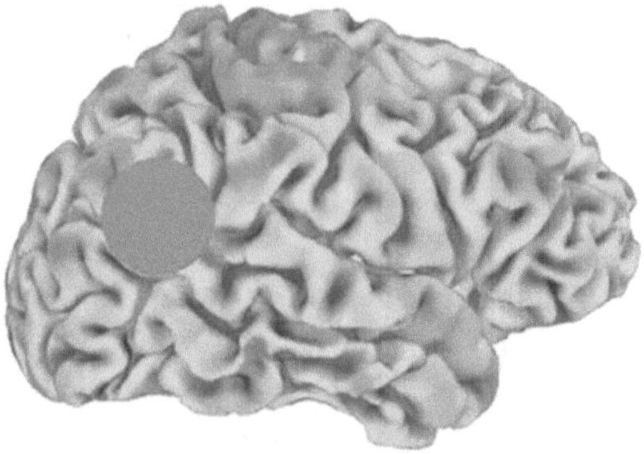

FIGURE 3.2 The temporoparietal junction.
Brain diagram highlighting the temporoparietal junction, a region involved in multisensory integration and self-perception.

was described as grasping her in an unpleasant way. Finally, the man stood on her right side and attempted to interfere with a card-naming task that she was asked to complete ("He wants to take the card"; Arzy et al., 2006, p. 287). Other subsequent work has shown that direct stimulation to the TPJ can induce self-other illusions, like a feeling of presence (Blanke et al., 2014) or even an out-of-body experience (Arzy, Thut et al., 2006; Blanke et al., 2002; Blanke & Arzy, 2005).

A good deal of work has gone into understanding the role the brain plays in feelings of self, agency, and embodiment. The TPJ, along with nearby regions, are crucial for these feelings. Let me give an example. When I think to myself, "Gosh, I hope I see a ghost on my next trip to Hampton Court Palace," I know that that thought was generated by me and not an external source. When I walk into a haunted house with a team of paranormal investigators, I know that it was my own volition that got me there and that an external force isn't controlling my body. With an overactive TPJ, a person might experience an illusory own-body perception – essentially a perception of yourself outside your body or a belief that it is another presence in your extra-bodily space. Basically, the TPJ helps integrate bodily senses like touch with the spatial location of our bodies. When that integration becomes disturbed, we may misperceive our bodies (Arzy, Thut et al., 2006; Blanke et al., 2002, 2014). This is probably what happened in the case study I described a moment ago. Stimulation to the patient's TPJ confused the sense and location of the self. Sometimes, the self might be perceived as a sensed presence. Other times, the self might be experienced as being outside one's own body (an out-of-body experience, or OBE).

TPJ activation is the probable basis for out-of-body experiences (OBEs). In OBEs, a person feels that their self is suddenly and unpredictably outside its normal location inside the body. In one person's words, "I was in bed and about to fall asleep when I had the distinct impression that 'I' was at the ceiling level looking down at my body in the bed. I was very startled and frightened; immediately [afterward] I felt that, I was consciously back in bed again" (as cited in Blanke & Arzy, 2005).

Most scientists believe that OBEs are due to disintegration of feedback from muscles, visual, tactile, and vestibular senses. These senses typically converge in the brain to give us a sense of our whole self as a resident of our own bodies. The TPJ is crucial for neural integration of these various senses, thus producing our sense of embodiment. When there is a lack of integration, our sense of self, or the location of the self, may be altered. In such cases, one might experience an OBE. It's not entirely clear why this may be the case, but it's possible that temporal lobe stimulation can induce feelings of "others" because our neural sense of self, agency, and embodiment are, well, confused.

One patient, who was being examined for temporal lobe epilepsy, experienced repeated OBEs when electrical stimulation was applied to the TPJ. Interestingly, this patient only experienced OBEs when they were looking straight ahead. When the patient looked at their limbs, they experienced other illusions, as if their limbs were shortening or lengthening (Blanke et al., 2002). Other research, too, has provided evidence that the TPJ, along with the extrastriate body, responds to body position with reference to the self. The extrastriate body is part of the occipital lobe that is heavily involved in visual processing, particularly of the human body. In one study, authors manipulated mental own-body imagery by having participants imagine either embodied or disembodied images. Cortical activation was measured by EEG. The extrastriate body was more activated when the participant used embodied imagery, whereas the TPJ was more active when the participant entertained *disembodied* imagery (Arzy, Thut et al., 2006). When the TPJ is temporarily inhibited by transcranial magnetic stimulation, healthy participants were impaired at disembodied mental imagery. But, inhibiting the TPJ did not impair imagining external objects in other places (Blanke et al., 2005).

And speaking of illusions of shortening and lengthening limbs ... these are primary symptoms in Alice in Wonderland syndrome. Alice in Wonderland syndrome is a unique syndrome generally affecting young children following viral infections and fever.

The primary symptom of Alice in Wonderland syndrome is the illusion that specific parts of the body are shrinking or growing, just like the protagonist in Lewis Carroll's *Alice's Adventures in Wonderland*. Case studies of children with Alice in Wonderland syndrome show abnormal activity in the extrastriate cortex and the temporal-occipital junction, providing further evidence that these structures help maintain the representation of the self within our body (Brumm et al., 2010; Shah et al., 2020).

Thus, taken together, this small body of research suggests that the TPJ and the extrastriate cortex are important areas for interpreting our sense of self and knowing that the self resides inside our body. When regions like the TPJ become overactive, bodily perceptions are altered. Moreover, the TPJ seems to be particularly important in *dis*embodiment, the feeling that the self is no longer inside one's own body.

In the reports on the induction of an illusory shadowy figure by TPJ stimulation, the authors propose that the stimulation disturbed bodily sensations coming into the brain and induced an own-body illusion of another body in extrabodily space. Like we talked about, hallucinations like these can occur in temporal lobe epilepsy patients. They also occur in some psychiatric disorders, namely schizophrenia.

Schizophrenia is a psychiatric disorder characterized by disturbances in thought, perception, and behavior. It usually has its onset anywhere from the late teenage years to mid-thirties, with the most common onset of symptoms in the twenties. Recently, schizophrenia has been named a spectrum disorder, meaning that the symptoms can range from mild to severe and vary significantly from person to person. Symptoms are classified as either positive, negative, or cognitive in nature. Positive symptoms (things that are there that shouldn't be) are usually delusions or hallucinations, or false beliefs or perceptions, respectively. Negative symptoms (things that are absent that should be present) take the form of anhedonia, social withdrawal, and flat affect. Cognitive symptoms are symptoms that impair thinking, like memory loss, planning future actions, and following a logical train of thought. Interestingly, there appears to be dysregulation in the temporoparietal regions in schizophrenic individuals. This may be why some of these hallucinations and delusions occur – their sense of self is compromised, and they therefore attribute their own thoughts and actions to external sources.

The relationship between TPJ activity and schizophrenia isn't totally clear, but there are a few pieces of evidence that suggest that there might be TPJ hyperactivity in schizophrenic patients. First, the amount of hippocampal activation prior to the onset of schizophrenia is related to the time of onset and severity of clinical symptoms (Schobel et al., 2009). The hippocampus also undergoes developmental changes that coincide with the usual onset of schizophrenia. Finally, hippocampal connectivity is correlated with TPJ activity, meaning that hippocampal overactivation should result in TPJ overactivation. In fact, temporoparietal areas are targets of the hippocampus (Wible, 2012). Furthermore, in nonpsychiatric patients, injury to the TPJ can cause changes in perceptions of self and agency. While there isn't a proven overactivation in the TPJ in schizophrenics, it is a reasonable hypothesis that this might induce hallucinations and delusions that are hallmarks of this disorder.

WHICH CAME FIRST, THE EMF OR THE GHOST?

The EMF Has Indeed Gone Crazy

Can EMF be used as a measurement for paranormal activity? Well, the jury's still out on that, but it doesn't look good. Most handheld EMF detectors probably do reliably measure EMF, but based on signal strength and decay, varied potential sources for EMF, and methods of signal triangulation, paranormal investigators are most likely committing Type I error when they interpret a "blip" as evidence for ghosts. That said, though, there is a small amount of research that shows that reportedly haunted places may be linked with complex EMF. Perhaps sensitive individuals can unconsciously detect those disturbances and interpret them as unusual sensations? Couple that with a preexisting belief in the paranormal and perhaps a cool draft, and we may have ourselves a ghost!

In The Haunt Project, Chris French designed an artificially haunted room. In this room, he varied EMF and infrasound, with the hypothesis that if EMF or infrasound can induce unusual sensations, they would see that in this experiment. The Haunt Project did induce a number of unusual experiences, but those experiences did not relate to EMF or infrasound at all. The unusual experiences strongly correlated with belief in the paranormal, and interestingly, with scores on the TLS scale, which measures temporal lobe lability.

There might be something to this temporal lobe thing, though. The history of research is complicated and fraught with methodological issues, but thanks to newer and more specified techniques, research has been successful in inducing feelings of a presence when current is applied to the temporal lobe. This might be because this region of the temporal lobe is important for integration of bodily senses with the sense of self, knowing that your body is your body and that your self is located within this body, and also that movements, behavior, and thoughts generated by this body belong to the self.

Does this explain why some people see the ghost of Catherine Howard wandering the Haunted Gallery at Hampton Court Palace? Not quite. More work needs to be done on the relationship between naturally occurring changes in EMF and unusual experiences. But it does offer some insight into the neural basis of the self, which is a fascinating and not well-understood subject.

REFERENCES

Aaen-Stockdale, C. (2012). *Neuroscience for the Soul.* BPS. www.bps.org.uk/psychologist/neuroscience-soul.

Arzy, S., Seeck, M., Ortigue, S., Spinelli, L., & Blanke, O. (2006). Induction of an illusory shadow person. *Nature, 443*(7109), 287–287. https://doi.org/10.1038/443287a.

Arzy, S., Thut, G., Mohr, C., Michel, C. M., & Blanke, O. (2006). Neural basis of embodiment: Distinct contributions of temporoparietal junction and extrastriate body area. *The Journal of Neuroscience, 26*(31), 8074–8081. https://doi.org/10.1523/JNEUROSCI.0745-06.2006.

Blanke, O., & Arzy, S. (2005). The out-of-body experience: Disturbed self-processing at the temporo-parietal junction. *The Neuroscientist, 11*(1), 16–24. https://doi.org/10.1177/1073858404270885.

Blanke, O., Mohr, C., Michel, C. M., Pascual-Leone, A., Brugger, P., Seeck, M., Landis, T., & Thut, G. (2005). Linking out-of-body experience and self processing to mental own-body imagery at the temporoparietal junction. *The Journal of Neuroscience, 25*(3), 550–557. https://doi.org/10.1523/JNEUROSCI.2612-04.2005.

Blanke, O., Ortigue, S., Landis, T., & Seeck, M. (2002). Stimulating illusory own-body perceptions. *Nature, 419*(6904), 269–270. https://doi.org/10.1038/419269a.

Blanke, O., Pozeg, P., Hara, M., Heydrich, L., Serino, A., Yamamoto, A., Higuchi, T., Salomon, R., Seeck, M., Landis, T., Arzy, S., Herbelin, B., Bleuler, H., & Rognini, G. (2014). Neurological and robot-controlled induction of an apparition. *Current Biology, 24*(22), 2681–2686. https://doi.org/10.1016/j.cub.2014.09.049.

Braithwaite, J. (2011). *Magnetic Fields, Anomalous Experiences: A Sceptical Critique of the Current Evidence.* www.academia.edu/1009539/Magnetic_Fields_Anomalous_Experiences_A_Sceptical_Critique_of_the_Current_Evidence.

Braithwaite, J. (2008). Putting magnetism in its place: A critical examination of the weak-intensity magnetic field account for anomalous haunt-type experiences. *Journal of the Society for Psychical Research, 72*(890), 34–50.

Brumm, K., Walenski, M., Haist, F., Robbins, S. L., Granet, D. B., & Love, T. (2010). Functional magnetic resonance imaging of a child with Alice in Wonderland syndrome during an episode of micropsia. *Journal of AAPOS, 14*(4), 317–322. https://doi.org/10.1016/j.jaapos.2010.03.007.

Dewhurst, K., & Beard, A. W. (1970). Sudden religious conversions in temporal lobe epilepsy. *The British Journal of Psychiatry, 117*(540), 497–507. https://doi.org/10.1192/bjp.117.540.497.

French, C. C., Haque, U., Bunton-Stasyshyn, R., & Davis, R. (2009). The "Haunt" project: An attempt to build a "haunted" room by manipulating complex electromagnetic fields and infrasound. *Cortex, 45*(5), 619–629. https://doi.org/10.1016/j.cortex.2007.10.011.

Granqvist, P., Fredrikson, M., Unge, P., Hagenfeldt, A., Valind, S., Larhammar, D., & Larsson, M. (2005). Sensed presence and mystical experiences are predicted by suggestibility, not by the application of transcranial weak complex magnetic fields. *Neuroscience Letters, 379*(1), 1–6. https://doi.org/10.1016/j.neulet.2004.10.057.

Lange, R., & Houran, J. (1997). Context-induced paranormal experiences: Support for Houran and Lange's model of haunting phenomena. *Perceptual and Motor Skills, 84*(3), 1455–1458. https://doi.org/10.2466/pms.1997.84.3c.1455.

Nicastro, N., & Picard, F. (2016). Joan of Arc: Sanctity, witchcraft or epilepsy? *Epilepsy & Behavior, 57*, 247–250. https://doi.org/10.1016/j.yebeh.2015.12.043.

Persinger, M. A. (1984). Propensity to report paranormal experiences is correlated with temporal lobe signs. *Perceptual and Motor Skills, 59*(2), 583–586. https://doi.org/10.2466/pms.1984.59.2.583.

Persinger, M. A., & Koren, S. A.. (2005). A response to Granqvist et al. "Sensed presence and mystical experiences are predicted by suggestibility, not by the application of transcranial weak magnetic fields." *NeuroscienceLetters, 380*(3), 346–347.

Persinger, M. A., Saroka, K., Koren, S. A., & St-Pierre, L. S. (2010). The electromagnetic induction of mystical and altered states within the laboratory. *Journal of Consciousness Exploration & Research, 1*(7), 808–830. https://jcer.com/index.php/jcj/article/view/100.

Schobel, S. A., Lewandowski, N. M., Corcoran, C. M., Moore, H., Brown, T., Malaspina, D., & Small, S. A. (2009). Differential targeting of the CA1 subfield of the hippocampal formation by schizophrenia and related psychotic disorders. *Archives of General Psychiatry, 66*(9), 938–946. https://doi.org/10.1001/archgenpsychiatry.2009.115.

Shah, A., Magaña, S. M., & Youssef, P. E. (2020). Do you see what I see? A case of Alice in Wonderland syndrome with EEG correlate. *Child Neurology Open, 7*, 2329048X20932714. https://doi.org/10.1177/2329048X20932714.

Wible, C. G. (2012). Hippocampal temporal-parietal junction interaction in the production of psychotic symptoms: A framework for understanding the schizophrenic syndrome. *Frontiers in Human Neuroscience, 6*, 180. https://doi.org/10.3389/fnhum.2012.00180.

Wiseman, R., Greening, E., & Smith, M. (2003). Belief in the paranormal and suggestion in the seance room. *British Journal of Psychology, 94*(3), 285–297. https://doi.org/10.1348/000712603767876235.

Wiseman, R., Watt, C., Greening, E., Stevens, P., & O'Kefffe, C. (2002). An investigation into the alleged haunting of Hampton Court Palace: Psychological variables and magnetic fields. *Journal of Parapsychology, 66*(4), 387–408.

Wiseman, R., Watt, C., Greening, E., Stevens, P., & O'Kefffe, C. (2003). An investigation into alleged "hauntings." *British Journal of Psychology, 94*(2), 195–211. https://doi.org/10.1348/000712603321661886.

4 They Only Come Out at Night

The Brain's Role in Nighttime Hallucinations

In Brazil, an old hag lurks on the rooftops of homes. She is tall and gaunt and has long yellow fingernails. She peers through windows and watches families as they eat their dinners. She waits while they put their bedclothes on. Finally, when they go to sleep, she silently creeps into the bedroom. She glides toward the bed, and in one deft leap, pounces on their chest. All her weight presses down onto the neck and chest of her victim. The victim wakes but cannot breathe. They try to scream, try to throw her off – anything – but her magic keeps them motionless. With eyes wide and mouth open in a silent scream, they look pleadingly into the face of the hag. The hag grins and puts more weight on the victim's chest. And then, as suddenly as she appeared, the hag leaves, the pressure on the chest is relieved, and the victim is safe in their bed.

The hag is the Pisadeira of Brazilian folklore. It is said that she watches families from a rooftop and, if a person sleeps on their backs with a full stomach, she enters the bedroom and sits on the chest of the victim. The victim cannot breathe, move, or scream. Versions of the ghastly Pisadeira appear in folklore around the world – tales of evil beings sitting on the chests of sleeping victims, rendering them motionless and helpless. In northern Canada, Inuit people describe *uqumangirniq*, a sleep state where the sleeper is unable to move and a frightening force tries to separate their body from soul. In Japan, a *kanashibari* may be summoned to attack an enemy while they sleep. In Cambodia, a *khmaoch sângkât*, or "the ghost that pushes you down," attacks when the victim is asleep by putting its hands on their neck and chest. Around 400 BC, Hippocrates named the feeling of waking up with a demon pressing on your chest "ephialtes," which translates "to pounce upon someone." In American cultures, people describe nighttime visitors, chest pressure, sometimes accompanied by feelings of immobility, a threatening presence, or levitation. These experiences are sometimes interpreted as extraterrestrial visits, or even abductions (de Sá & Mota-Rolim, 2016). Figure 4.1 is an image of a famous painting by Henry Fuseli called *The Nightmare*. It depicts a demonic spirit perched upon the chest of a sleeping woman.

There actually is a very *natural* thing that can account for these seemingly supernatural events – sleep paralysis. Over the course of a night of sleep, we cycle through various stages. One of these stages, REM, or rapid eye-movement, is characterized by – you guessed it! – rapid eye movement. It's an odd state because, even though the body is in deep sleep, the brain is highly active, with brain waves more like an awake brain than a brain in deep sleep. REM sleep is also the sleep stage where we do our most vivid dreaming. Weirdly, though, the

FIGURE 4.1 *The Nightmare*, by Henry Fuseli.
Painting of a sleeping woman with a demonic incubus on her chest and a ghostly horse head emerging from the shadows behind her.
Source: Detroit Institute of Art

body, except for eyes and genitals, is completely paralyzed during REM sleep. Our brain's way of keeping us safe during REM sleep is to release inhibitory neurotransmitters onto our motor neurons, paralyzing us from the neck down, preventing us from getting out of bed and acting out our dreams. But, for at least 20 percent of the population (Cheyne et al., 1999a; Cheyne et al., 1999b; French & Stone, 2014), this doesn't always work. Some people are prone to sleep paralysis – waking during REM sleep. Often people are in the middle of a dream, and when they wake, they try to move their bodies but find that they cannot. This can be very scary, and sufferers report strange things – including a sensed presence, flashing lights, and feelings of floating. In the pages that follow, we'll explore sleep, sleep paralysis, disorders of sleep, and whether the things that go bump in the night might be science, or supernatural.

WHAT IS SLEEP?

Humans spend about a third of their lives asleep. For most people, this equates to about *twenty-seven years*. With the amount of time we dedicate to sleep, it must be important, right?

Why we sleep so much, though, has stumped scientists and philosophers for hundreds of years. Aristotle observed that all animals require sleep (and different animals have different sleep needs). According to his writing, sleeping and waking lie together in the same part of the soul, and the two states exist in opposition to each other. If the waking state is the ability to sense the world, then sleep is the incapacitation of the senses. Sleep offers access to areas of the self that can't be accessed during wakefulness, as sleep is the "borderland between living and not living" (Wohl, 2020). Aristotle did not believe that dreams came from the gods, as the Ancient Greeks did. Instead, Aristotle believed that dreams come from within and are simply an after-image of wakefulness (Wohl, 2020). This idea later received support from Sigmund Freud, who believed that dreams could be interpretated and yield great insight to the inner workings of the mind (Gregoric & Fink, 2022; Wohl, 2020).

Even today, scientists don't fully understand the purpose of sleep. What we *do* know, however, is that the brain is highly active during sleep despite our bodies showing reduced activity. Our bodies generate cyclical rhythms that regulate all sorts of things – temperature, hormone release, sleep, wakefulness, and more. Some of these rhythms are twenty-four-hour rhythms, called *circadian rhythm* (from Latin *circa*, meaning "about" and *dies*, meaning "a day"). *Ultradian rhythms*, like the stages of sleep, occur more frequently than once per day and are nested within the broader circadian rhythm. During a 24-hour window, various cues tell your body when to feel awake, when to feel sleepy, and when to go to sleep. One very important cue that regulates circadian rhythms is sunlight. A unique subset of retinal cells called *retinal ganglion cells* sends light information from the retina to the *suprachiasmatic nucleus* in the hypothalamus. The suprachiasmatic nucleus controls the release of melatonin from the pineal gland, which helps us feel sleepy at bedtime.

There are two main types of sleep: non-rapid eye movement sleep (NREM) and rapid eye movement (REM) sleep. For most healthy adults, nightly cycles of NREM and REM sleep follow a predictable pattern. Each sleep cycle lasts about 90–110 minutes, comprising four NREM stages and one bout of REM per cycle. By measuring cortical brain activity with an *electroencephalogram* (EEG), we can learn about what happens in the brain during each sleep stage, and how sleep cycles change throughout a night of sleep. The awake, relaxed brain exhibits high frequency *beta activity*. When we first fall asleep, we enter Stage 1 of NREM sleep, which is our lightest and briefest sleep stage. Sleep Stage 1 is characterized by low-voltage *theta activity* and makes up only about 5 percent of our total night's sleep. Muscle tone is present, and breathing is regular. As we descend further into sleep, Stage 2 maintains theta activity, although EEG readings indicate the slowing down of the brain by the emergence of high amplitude *delta waves* called *K-complexes* and short bursts of activity called *sleep spindles* (more on the functional role of these in a minute). Our deepest sleep is Stage 3 sleep. Stage 3 sleep is also called *slow-wave sleep* because of the characteristic high amplitude, low-frequency delta waves that are predominant during this stage. Stage 3 is the hardest stage to wake from, and is also when sleepwalking, night terrors, and bedwetting typically occur. Finally, roughly sixty minutes after falling asleep, we experience our first bout of REM for the night. During REM sleep, EEG patterns resemble a waking brain – very low-amplitude and high-frequency. And, as we've established, our bodies are mostly paralyzed during REM sleep. Your eyelids may be closed, but eyes are moving rapidly (hence the name), your genitals are likely engorged, and yet, the rest of your body is effectively paralyzed (McNamara, 2023). You can see the difference in EEG patterns across sleep states in Figure 4.2.

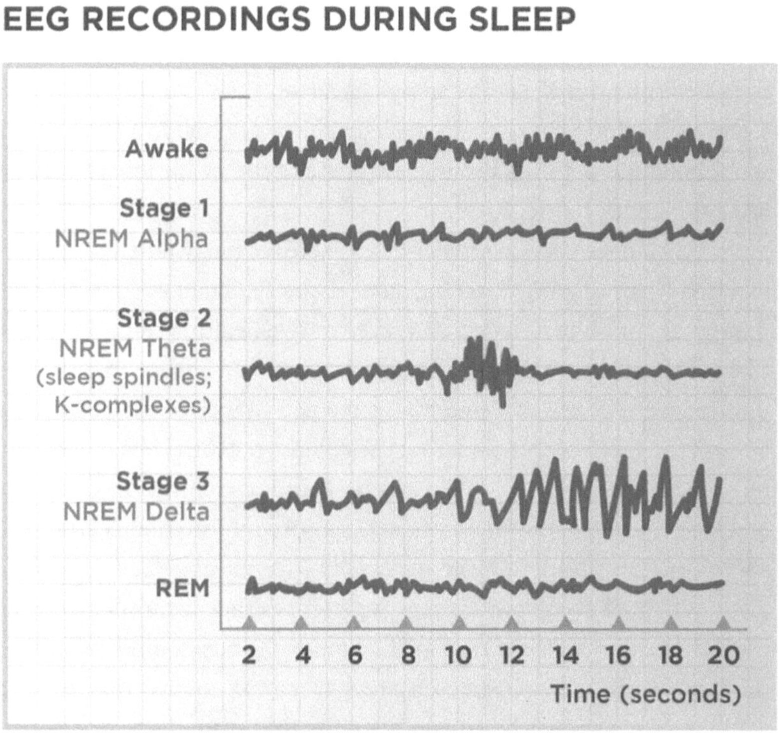

FIGURE 4.2 Electroencephalogram of the stages of sleep.
EEG waveforms showing characteristic brain activity during different stages of sleep, including REM and non-REM sleep.
Source: Lumen Learning

During one sleep cycle, a healthy adult human will pass from NREM Stages 1 and 2 to the deep state of Stage 3. Even though the sleeper remains asleep, brain activity quickens, and the sleeper moves from Stage 3 back through Stage 2 and even Stage 1 before they enter their first bout of REM, roughly an hour after they have fallen asleep. Sometimes, either before or after REM, we experience brief awakenings, though most people don't remember having woken up. Sleep stages change a bit as sleep progresses through the night, with REM bouts becoming longer and NREM stages becoming shorter.

WHY DO WE NEED TO SLEEP?

"If we didn't need eight hours of sleep and we could survive on six," Professor Matthew Walker, of UC Berkeley, mused on a Hidden Brain podcast, "Mother Nature would have done away with 25 percent of our sleep time millions of years ago because when you think about it, sleep is an idiotic thing to do. If sleep does not provide a remarkable set of benefits, then it's the biggest mistake the evolutionary process has ever made" (NPR, 2017).

Why do we need so much sleep? There are many possible benefits of sleep – improving learning and memory, energy conservation, improving immune function and regenerative health, promoting niche adaptation in the wild, and allowing our brain to engage in processes that reduce the risk of dementia as we age (Winer et al., 2020). It is beyond the scope of this book to review all the potential benefits of, and reasons for, sleep. Here, we'll focus on learning and memory, because understanding how our brains encode sensory information is crucial to answering the question, "Is it science, or supernatural?"

When we sleep, our sensory experiences that accumulate during the day become consolidated into memories. Thus, a memory can be thought of as a neural representation of an experience that we had when we were awake. The set of neurons that store these representations are called neuronal ensembles, or engrams. When we live through a sensory experience, a set of neurons becomes activated. When these neurons are active together, they form stronger connections between themselves. When those connections are strong enough, activation in one or some of those neurons will then trigger activation in the entire ensemble. The more this happens, in theory, the stronger the ensemble and, therefore, the stronger the memory. These types of connections are endearingly referred to as Hebbian synapses, after neurophysiologist, Donald Hebb, who first described cell assemblies that connect in this way (Hebb, 1949). In Chapter 5, we'll spend more time with Dr. Hebb and how his work helped elucidate the neuroscience of memory formation.

The formation of memories from sensory experiences is referred to as *consolidation*. There is a lot of research that tells us that our various sleep stages each play a unique role in the consolidation of memories. During Stage 2 sleep, low-voltage theta waves predominate, although we see the emergence of higher voltage delta waves called K-complexes and bursts of low amplitude neuronal activity called sleep spindles. Both K-complexes and sleep spindles are important for neuronal plasticity and for the consolidation of memories (Patel et al., 2023).

As we descend from Stage 2 sleep to Stage 3 sleep, we start to transition into slow-wave sleep. In slow wave sleep, there is an increase in high amplitude delta activity. Additionally, more of the hippocampus, a brain area crucial to memory consolidation, becomes active. Within the hippocampus, cells of the dentate gyrus send axonal projections to CA3, make a synapse, and in turn project to CA1 (see Figure 4.3). One theory posits that, during wakefulness, a sensory experience (which will later become a memory) causes connections to form between the pyramidal neurons in layers CA3 and CA1. During Stage 3 sleep, fast oscillatory activity called sharp-wave ripples reverberate between CA3 and CA1, thus reactivating neuronal ensembles that contain representations of events (Girardeau & Lopes-Dos-Santos, 2021). Sharp-wave ripples are believed to be essential for memory consolidation.

But how do we *know* that sharp-wave ripples lead to memory consolidation? We observe them, and then we block them! In one study, van de Ven and colleagues identified a group of neurons important for navigating spatial environments in the mouse hippocampus. They measured activity in these neurons, both while the mouse

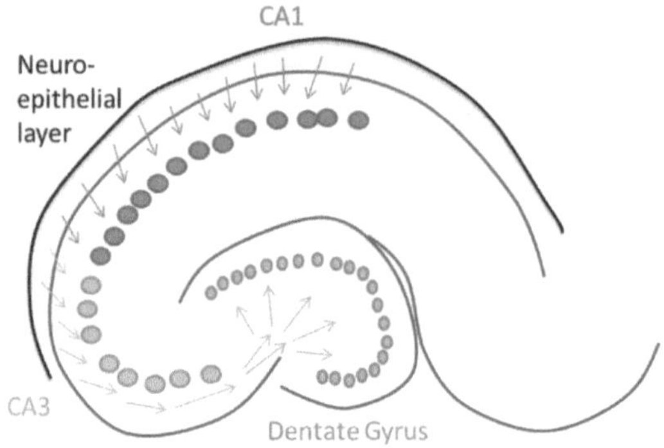

FIGURE 4.3 Schematic of the hippocampus.
Anatomical diagram of the hippocampus in the medial temporal lobe, labeled with major subregions such as CA1 and dentate gyrus.
Source: Wikimedia Commons

explored a new environment compared to a familiar environment, and again while the mouse was in a resting state (akin to sleep). The goal was to identify groups of neurons in the hippocampus that were active both while exploring a new environment and while in a rest state. The correlational neural activity between exploring an environment (i.e., spatial learning) and rest is called "coincident activation." They found that coincident activation between exploration and the rest state was greater when the animal explored a novel, compared to familiar, environment. In other words, groups of neurons that were activated when having a new experience were more likely to also be active when the mouse was resting. The reactivation of assembly patterns was strongest during times of sharp-wave ripples. Sharp-wave ripple activity was subsequently inhibited using optogenetics (refer to the description of optogenetics in Box 4.1). When sharp-wave ripples were inhibited during rest, reactivation of the neural assembly was reduced when the animal explored the same environment. Conversely, when the sharp-wave ripples were left intact during rest, reactivation was heightened when the animal was reexposed to that environment. This suggests that sharp-wave ripples are important to stabilize the neuronal assembly that contains the representation of the sensory experience (van de Ven et al., 2016).

BOX 4.1 Optogenetics

When reading about optogenetics in the media, you might have noticed a catchy phrase like, "scientists can control neurons in the brain with the flick of a switch!" That's a little simplified, but it's also eerily accurate. Optogenetics was first used by neuroscientist Karl Deisseroth at Stanford University in 2004. By 2010, optogenetics had taken off and was named "Method of the year," by Nature Methods. Optogenetics is a biological technique that utilizes the genes that code for light-sensitive ion channels in algae. These ion channels are similar to the light-sensitive rods and cones in our retina – when a photon of light hits them, it causes the ion channel to allow ions to pass into the cell, which ultimately can change the activity of the cell. Scientists can take the gene for these ion channels and insert the genes into a virus, like the herpes simplex virus (HSV). HSV is a great candidate because of its large genome and preference for neurons for reproduction. Importantly, the virus has been modified so that it is noninfectious. By injecting this virus into target areas in an animal's brain, the virus then incorporates itself, along with the light-sensitive ion channel, into the neurons it comes into contact with. Later on, scientists can surgically implant a fiber-optic cable to deliver light to the brain of the animal, specifically over the cells that express light-sensitive channels. Then, when they turn on the light, it will activate all of the cells that express that ion channel. This technology has become so sophisticated that scientists can even target subpopulations of cells to express light-sensitive ion channels. This allows for highly specific manipulation of certain cell groups, which allow us to map neuronal circuits, explore functional connectivity, and further tie structure, function, and behavior together in an awake and moving animal model. The fear circuits of the amygdala have been extensively studied using optogenetics.

WHAT IS DREAMING?

While dreams can occur in all sleep stages, REM sleep is most associated with dreaming. During REM, we experience a vivid and often bizarre series of highly visual imagery. Comedian Mitch Hedberg famously complained, "I hate dreaming, because dreaming takes energy. Sleeping is supposed to be a relaxing affair. I lay down in the bed, it feels great. Next thing you know, I have to build a go-cart with my ex-landlord!"

Neuroscientists and psychologists haven't landed on a one-size-fits-all definition of dreaming, in part because dreaming is so hard to study. Neuroscientist Patrick McNamara defines dreams as cognitions that occur during sleep that are sensitive to social factors and will not be constrained by some forms of external perceptions. Dreams are thoughts that are generated entirely by the sleeping brain (McNamara, 2023). J. Allan Hobson and colleagues (Hobson et al., 2000) further describe common features of REM dreaming:

(1) Dreams contain hallucinatory perceptions that are primarily visual and motor
(2) Dream imagery can change rapidly and is often bizarre in nature
(3) Dreams are delusional. When we are dreaming, we believe that we are awake
(4) When we are dreaming, we engage in little, if any, self-reflection
(5) In dreams, people, time, and places are not fixed and can change rapidly
(6) Dreams show increased and intense emotions, especially fear and anxiety
(7) In our dreams, we follow our instincts. Our instincts drive the storyline of our dreams
(8) We generally do not have volition in our dreams

We do our most vivid dreaming during REM sleep, which is electrographically and behaviorally distinct from NREM sleep. NREM sleep, and Stage 3 sleep in particular, is characterized by large amplitude, low frequency delta waves. During REM, however, our brain activity resembles that of the waking brain, with beta and theta waves dominating the polysomnograph. REM is also a time of heightened parasympathetic activity, which allows our bodies to "rest and digest," which comes with the side effect of engaged sexual organs. Paradoxically, though, our bodies are paralyzed from the neck down, preventing any sort of movement. As we succumb to REM, our brains disengage from the external world, we lose volition over our thoughts, and we are carried through the strange and surreal landscape of our dreams.

Our complex descent from NREM into REM sleep is regulated by many brain areas and molecular signals. Some of the earliest studies on sleep employed a technique called transection. In transection studies, sections of forebrain and midbrain were removed, usually in a feline model, and the resulting changes to REM sleep were noted. When the forebrain and midbrain were removed, cats still displayed normal amounts of REM sleep. These results indicate that the forebrain and midbrain are not required for the generation REM sleep, and rather, there must be a region in the hindbrain that generates REM sleep. This region was later identified as the pons (Jouvet, 1962). Further research indicated that the dorsolateral pons is important for the muscle atonia that accompanies REM sleep. Cats with lesions to the dorsolateral pons do not experience muscle atonia – and seem to act out their dreams (Hendricks et al., 1982; Henley & Morrison, 1974)! (The reader should plug 'cat REM w/o paralysis' into the search box at YouYube for a video of a sleeping cat acting out its dream of chasing a fly.)

REM-specific brain activity originates in the pons. During REM sleep, projections from the pons to the lateral geniculate nucleus (LGN; a vision center of the thalamus) are highly active. The astute reader will recall our exploration of divergent outputs from the LGN in Chapter 2. These outputs help to regulate responses to an overhead looming predator. After REM-specific activity is sent from pons to LGN, the LGN, in turn, redirects these signals to the occipital lobe. Pons-geniculate-occipital activity, called PGO waves, is thought to be, at least in part, what underlines the visual imagery in dreams. During REM sleep, external sensory input is blocked so that the dreamer is at the mercy of internally created sensorimotor cortical activation, resulting in strange narratives and imagery that exists only within one's mind (Hobson et al., 2000; Hobson & McCarley, 1977; Tsunematsu, 2023).

Consider the odd case of a generally healthy seventy-three-year-old woman who was admitted to the hospital in August of 1997. She reported sudden vision loss and weakness in the left side of her body. Upon examination, it was discovered that she had suffered a stroke deep in the occipital lobes, with evidence of the stroke present in both hemispheres of her brain. After two days, the vision problems subsided, but new, strange, symptoms emerged. Three days after she suffered the stroke, the patient had a short but highly vivid dream. In this dream, someone gave her a very large piece of cotton with pictures of tiny, odd men printed on it. Later in the dream, she couldn't find the men on the cotton and she became upset. But after that dream, that night, the patient never dreamed again (Bischof & Bassetti, 2004).

Charcot–Wilbrand syndrome (CWS) is a rare syndrome exhibiting dream loss following focal brain damage. And since it is so rare, there has been a paucity of data related to the sleep architecture of CWS sufferers. In the case of the seventy-three-year-old woman, though, complete polysomnographs were obtained, and it became clear that her sleep architecture was more or less normal, with little to no alteration in REM sleep amount or depth. In other words, this patient had perfectly intact REM sleep, and yet lacked dreams. This tells us that REM activity is not inextricably tied to dreaming and that dreaming is necessitated by another, more elusive, neural mechanism.

In addition to PGO waves reverberating through the hindbrain to forebrain, neurons in the pons release inhibitory neurotransmitters, like GABA and glycine, onto motor neurons. When these motor neurons become inhibited, they stop communicating with our muscles, thus preventing any movement (Brooks & Peever, 2012). So, if you're running through the woods to escape a sinister killer in your dream, your motor cortex might be generating the command for your legs to move. The inhibition of motor neurons ensures that you're running only in your dream and not in real life. It can be problematic – and downright dangerous – when motor neurons are not inhibited during dream states. This happens in a parasomnia called *REM Behavior Disorder* (RBD). Patients with RBD often act out their dreams. In his one-man comedy show *Sleepwalk with Me*, comedian Mike Birbiglia describes his struggles with RBD, ranging from dreaming about climbing a podium to accept an award for Olympic-level dust bustering (and in real life, climbing up and then falling from the bookshelf in his living room), to actually crashing through a – well, I won't spoil it. Go watch the movie.

DREAMING THE FUTURE

Some believe that dreams can be a glimpse into the future. Indeed, many people believe that they have dreamed something, only to have it come true the very next day. These sorts of dreams are called prophetic, predictive, or precognitive dreams. I'll stick to the term "precognitive" to describe dreams that precede conscious awareness, or cognition, of an event. Precognition that occurs during wakefulness will be addressed in later chapters, don't worry!

Researching dreams can be very difficult. At the time of this writing, the most accurate studies on dreaming are done by waking the sleeper and asking them to recount their dreams right then and there. Unfortunately, these types of measurements are still highly subjective. First, there are no (known) neurophysiological correlates of dreaming, so if a person is asleep, we can't tell for certain whether they are dreaming. Second, people vary greatly in their ability to recall dreams. For those of us who can remember our dreams, those memories still deteriorate rapidly upon waking and even more throughout the day. Interestingly, there appear to be several neurological and personality differences in both our ability to remember our dreams and the significance we place on our dreams.

High dream recallers tend to have higher cerebral blood flow to the temporoparietal junction (TPJ) and medial prefrontal cortex, as compared to low dream recallers (Eichenlaub et al., 2014). High dream recallers also have more functional connectivity, or a high amount of correlated blood flow, between nodes of the Default Mode Network (Vallat et al., 2020, 2022). The Default Mode Network is a functional neural network that is associated with autobiographical thought, mind wandering, and inferential reasoning. The TPJ and prefrontal cortex are core nodes along this network, along with the posterior cingulate cortex and precuneus. High dream recallers also have personality traits that differ from low dream recallers – they score higher on creativity (Vallat et al., 2022), openness to new experience, and thin boundary structure (Schredl et al., 2003a; Schredl et al., 2003b).

There are also differences in personality traits among those who, more generally, believe in the paranormal compared with those who don't. The trait of openness to new experience is usually associated with curiosity, a desire for variety and a dislike for the mundane. There seems to be a positive relationship between different facets of openness to new experience and belief in the paranormal (French & Stone, 2014). Other traits, too, are associated with a higher belief in paranormal, like fantasy-proneness, absorption, and hypnotic-suggestibility (reviewed in French & Stone, 2014). An interesting overlap here is the trait of openness to new experience, which is high in believers of the paranormal, believers of precognitive dreaming, and also in high dream recallers. It's interesting that openness tends to be high among these groups of people. Perhaps high dream recall is related to the belief that dreams may be predictive?

Precognitive dreaming is inherently impossible to study empirically, as both the dream itself and its potential predictive nature are both highly subjective. Research has, though, looked at the relationship between belief in precognitive dreams and probabilistic reasoning – how well a person can determine whether an event was due to random chance. In one study, 46 percent of participants had a dream that they believed to be predictive in nature. The more precognitive dreams a person reported, the more likely they were to attribute a paranormal explanation as a source of the dreams (e.g., "It's always/usually something paranormal that can't be explained naturally"). Moreover, the same participants that attributed precognitive dreams to paranormal sources performed worse on a task that assessed the probability of an event occurring by chance. This finding was also related to the education level of the participant – those with university-level education had higher probabilistic reasoning and lower belief in the paranormal (Blagrove et al., 2006). Other studies, too, have correlated belief in the paranormal with errors in probabilistic reasoning, thus providing further evidence that believers are more likely to attribute chance occurrences to paranormal activity (Musch & Ehrenberg, 2002).

Perhaps one reason people believe their dreams are precognitive is that, when they're awake, they experience a strange sensation of having done something before. Most people have experienced déjà vu at one time or another. Sometimes, déjà vu can be quite strong. People might feel that they must have dreamed their experience before it happened. Déjà vu is commonly experienced during temporal lobe epilepsy, due to the overactivation of memory formation networks around regions buried in the temporal lobe. Déjà vu can even be induced by focal stimulation of the perirhinal areas, which are also in the temporal lobe. These areas are important for encoding some types of long-term memories (Barbeau et al., 2005). Episodic memories, the memories of our life experiences, are formed through circuits involving the hippocampus, perirhinal areas, and other surrounding areas. The hippocampus, in turn, communicates with the cortex both to store the memory as a long-term memory, and to compare that memory to other experiences we may have had previously. When we have the distinct feeling that we're reliving something that has already happened, we're probably experiencing a nontypical synchronization of the hippocampal-cortical circuits (Gillinder et al., 2022). What follows, then, is a disconnect where we simultaneously live and relive the sensory experience. It's a weird sensation. When we try to remember how or when we experienced that moment before, we might erroneously attribute it to a moment experienced in a dream.

SLEEP PARALYSIS

Recall the nighttime visits from the Pisadeira at the opening of this chapter. Versions of the Pisadeira appear in folklore from around the world. Many cultures describe malevolent nighttime visitors stealing the breath of their victims and causing tightness in their chests. Do these evil spirits truly exist? Perhaps – but perhaps these occurrences can also be explained by instances of sleep paralysis.

During REM sleep, our bodies are paralyzed, and yet our brains are highly active. Heightened and specific brain activity creates the rich landscape of dreams. When one experiences an episode of sleep paralysis, they wake just before (hypnogogic) or just after (hypnopompic) the REM state with dreams spilling over into wakefulness. Awakenings during REM sleep are usually coupled with very strange sensory experiences. These sensory experiences can involve threatening intruders; physical assaults involving pressure on the chest, choking, or suffocation; or out-of-body experiences (Cheyne, 2003; Cheyne et al., 1999b). A person experiencing this would justifiably feel extreme terror and confusion, and thus grasp for meaning.

It's hard to know precisely what percentage of the population experiences sleep paralysis. Cultures around the world have stories and folklore about malevolent nighttime visitors; presumably, sleep paralysis affects humans globally (Cheyne et al., 1999b; de Sá & Mota-Rolim, 2016). Some studies estimate that 25–40 percent of people have had at least one episode of sleep paralysis (Cheyne et al., 1999a; Cheyne et al., 1999b). Most sufferers of sleep paralysis report a sensed presence and fear, although a smaller proportion report visual hallucinations (Cheyne et al., 1999a). Those who wake up the next morning with a memory of their sleep paralysis episode, and perhaps a vague recollection of a sensed nighttime visitor, also search for meaning. Chalking the experience up to a dream or nightmare feels unsatisfying, because the experience seemed more real than that. A nighttime visitor or presence is a far more satisfying explanation.

We don't know why our brains search for meaning and interpretation in dreams when there isn't meaning to be had – not external meaning, that is. Psychologically, humans like patterns and we like explanations for coincidences. When there isn't an easily accessible explanation, we search for one because we don't like ambiguity. Why?

One possibility lies in the actions of the neurotransmitter serotonin. When our brains are waking up from sleep, the dorsal raphe nucleus of the hindbrain, which is the brain's principal source of serotonin, becomes active. As the raphe nucleus shuts off REM centers in the hindbrain, it also releases serotonin in several places throughout the brain, thus stimulating its receptors. One type of serotonin receptor, the $5HT_{2A}$ receptor, is a known target of psychedelic drugs like LSD and psilocybin. Activation of these receptors by psychedelics increases attributions of personal relevance to everyday stimuli and may be one reason psychedelics can bring about mystical experiences (Preller et al., 2017). Activation of $5HT_{2A}$ receptors in the cortex may cause hallucinations geared toward interpreting anomalous experiences, and those in the limbic system may induce deep emotions, such as fear (Jalal, 2018). Perhaps $5HT_{2A}$ receptors are activated by serotonin as the brain moves from REM sleep to a waking state. If an episode of sleep paralysis occurs, the serotonergic system might prompt us to search for meaning and interpretation of anomalous sensations, real or imagined. Thus, visual hallucinations and a sensed presence give a person the terrifying perceived reality of something visiting them in the night.

This idea is an extension of the *activation-synthesis model of dreaming* (Hobson & McCarley, 1977). According to this model, REM is induced by turning off brain areas devoted to keeping the brain awake. Once in REM sleep, the pons inhibits both motor output and sensory input, while the cortex is provided with rhythmic, internally generated activity via the pons and thalamus (the PGO waves described earlier). The cortex then creates meaning and patterns from this internal activity. Thus, dreams. When this is taken a step further, and the dreamer is partially awake, but REM patterns prevail, the initial feelings of fear and a sensed presence push the cortex to create further meaning and increasingly elaborate interpretations of the experience (Cheyne et al., 1999b). During a threatening event that occurs during wakefulness, sensory projections to the thalamus activate the amygdala, which can generate defensive or avoidance behaviors. The cortex, then, corroborates (or refutes) the interpretation that danger is present (LeDoux, 2000). During episodes of sleep paralysis, however, the activity in the cortex is internally generated and the cortex is therefore unable to make any judgments about external stimuli.

Sometimes, an episode of sleep paralysis can trigger an out-of-body experience, or OBE. As you know, most scientists believe that OBEs are due to disintegration of feedback from muscles, visual, tactile, and vestibular senses. These senses typically converge in the brain to give us a sense of our whole self as a resident of our own bodies. When there is a lack of integration, our sense of self, or the location of the self, may be altered. In such cases, one might experience an OBE (Arzy, Seeck et al., 2006).

Some believe that OBEs can be intentional and self-guided, such as in shamanistic rituals involving astral projection. Sometimes, though, an OBE can occur during the night in an otherwise healthy person. When wakefulness intrudes into a REM state, the brain is confused. Muscles are paralyzed. Proprioceptive feedback does not align with lived experience. This confuses the integration of sensory stimuli from our inner ears, our joints and muscles, and our eyes. Rationally, this could induce feelings of terror, including sympathetic activation manifesting as intense pressure on the chest. Our cortex, still dreaming and responding to internally generated stimuli, searches for an interpretation of this nonsense. Serotonin receptors are stimulated, causing us to perhaps apply meaning where there is none and create hallucinations, like that of an old hag. In some people, the lack of integration in the temporal lobe is so extreme that the brain misinterprets the *location* of the self and places the self outside the body. Finally, people are more at risk for this when they sleep in the supine position, as our TPJ responds differently to disembodied mental imagery in different bodily positions (Arzy, Thut et al., 2006). The Pisadeira, as well, visits those who sleep on their backs, and prefers those with full bellies (de Sá & Mota-Rolim, 2016).

NEAR-DEATH EXPERIENCES

Near-death experiences (NDEs) can occur when a person has escaped a brush with death. The Internet is rife with accounts of those who have come close to death but were brought back. These accounts tend to have a lot of similarities, including OBEs, passing through a tunnel, moving toward a bright light, entering a beautiful place, or encountering a loved one (see French & Stone, 2014 for a review). There are many natural explanations for NDEs, although no one explanation tracks for every NDE. Some are discussed here, and for further reading, I highly suggest Chris French's 2005 detailed review of NDEs (French, 2005).

One plausible explanation for NDEs is that there is a lack of oxygen in the brain, resulting in specific hallucinations, like moving toward a bright light. For obvious ethical reasons, we cannot restrict oxygen and ask a person about how they're feeling. But we *can* study the brains of people who have experienced an acute lack of oxygen and compare those sensations to those of NEDs. G-LOC syndrome can happen in fighter pilots who experience a sudden, large increase in g-force. This results in a loss of consciousness due to low blood supply (and thus oxygen) to the brain. Symptoms of G-LOC syndrome parallel those of NDEs, including moving through a tunnel, moving toward a light, feelings of floating, and a strong desire to understand the experience (Whinery, 1997). These similarities suggest that, at least in some cases, hypoxia in the brain might induce some of the sensory features of NDEs. Rats undergoing experimental asphyxia display a "brainstorm" of activity in the cortex prior to death (Li et al., 2015). This could perhaps explain some of the subjective feelings in an NDE. Certainly, lack of oxygen does not explain every NDE, as there are reports of NDEs in individuals who don't appear to be suffering from any lack of oxygen.

Another potential explanation of NDEs is that there is a surge of naturally occurring brain chemicals that are released in the moments prior to death. There is a popular theory that when we die or are about to die, our brains release large quantities of the psychedelic *N,N*-Dimethyltryptamine, or DMT. DMT can be found in several plant species that are native to Central and South America. Effects of acute DMT highly resemble those of NDEs (Timmermann et al., 2018). The idea that our brains can produce and release enough DMT to produce intense psychedelic trips is an attractive idea from the novelty alone, and also from a spiritual perspective. A pioneer of this idea, Rick Strassman, wrote in his book that DMT is produced in the brain and released during times of extreme stress (like birth and death) and facilitates the movement of the soul in and out of the body. According to Strassman, this is an integral aspect of not only birth and death, but also of highly spiritual experiences, like extreme meditative states and sexual transcendence (Strassman, 2001). New Age and metaphysical literature place a great deal of emphasis on the pineal gland as the "third eye" and Strassman himself refers to it as the "spirit gland." Historically, too, the pineal gland has been regarded as the "seat of the soul" by Renè Descartes, which adds even more attraction to Stassman's ideas.

As attractive as Strassman's ideas are, there is little evidence to support them. DMT has been found in the mammalian brain and even in the pineal gland, but in quantities far too small to induce any psychological effects. The principal job of the pineal gland is to produce melatonin during sleep, which helps us regulate our sleep-wake cycles. The pineal gland produces about 20–35 μg of melatonin per day (males secrete a bit more melatonin than females). Conversely, the pineal gland would have to very quickly – over the course of twenty-five minutes, because DMT is very rapidly metabolized – produce about 25 mg of DMT to achieve the concentrations needed to induce a subjective experience. From a neuroendocrine gland weighing approximately 100 mg itself, this seems like a great feat. Not to mention, there is little evidence that the synthetic material is even present in the pineal gland in order to produce this massive amount of DMT (Nichols, 2018).

Although DMT is not released in large quantities at the time of death and likely not the culprit for NDEs, this does not preclude the idea that there is a neurochemical responsible for NDEs. One candidate for such a chemical could be an opioid peptide. Endorphins, which are a class of opioid peptide, are chemically similar to morphine, naturally produced in our brains, and are also released when we experience pain and stress. The caveat to this hypothesis, however, is that a large release of endorphins would feel like taking opiate drugs, like morphine or heroin, and the subjective effects of taking opiates does not parallel those of NDEs. Another type of opioid, though, might be a better candidate. Dynorphin is an opioid peptide that is produced in the brain and also released during times of stress. Exogenous substances that are chemically similar to dynorphin, like the psychedelic salvinorin A, produce dissociative amnesia and out-of-body experiences that more closely parallel the subjective effects of NDEs (Nichols, 2018; Roth et al., 2002).

Clearly, more research needs to be done before we have a clear understanding of what neural and psychological processes happen to cause NDEs. The Neurophysiological Evolutionary Psychological Theory Understanding Near Death Experiences (NEPTUNE) model attempts to combine our current understanding of NDE's into a single parsimonious model. Here, oxygen depletion (for example) sets off a chain reaction in the brain that includes rapid neurophysiological changes such as serotonin and glutamate release, activation of regions like the TPJ and extrastriate cortex, and a massive release of endogenous opioids. These neurophysiological events have the evolutionary benefit of inducing a calm state of mind and vivid hallucinations, thus allowing individuals to better cope with life-threatening situations (Martial et al., 2025).

CONCLUSION: WHAT REALLY GOES BUMP IN THE NIGHT?

So you've fallen asleep, only to wake up in the middle of the night. The lights outside the window cast eerie shadows on the wall. You sense something in the corner and try to sit up, but you can't. There's an inexplicable pressure on your chest. Your eyes are wide and you sense that the thing in the corner is coming closer. You know that its intentions are sinister. You still can't move and the pressure in your chest is getting worse. You feel pure terror.

Suddenly the pressure is gone and you can sit up. You reach madly for the light switch and flip it on, bathing the room in light. The *thing* is gone. Your heart is still racing but you know now that you're safe.

The next morning, you remember the old hag that visited you in the night. You remember the pressure in your chest and that you could not move your body. You picture the hag in your mind, trying to remember every detail. But … did you really see anything, or are you imagining it?

While science can't rule out the idea of ghouls and hags visiting us in the night, we can offer other (testable) explanations. Some people wake up during REM sleep. During episodes of sleep paralysis, people may feel terror, a sensed presence, and a lack of ability to integrate bodily senses. Because our brains are largely still asleep, our dreams spill over into wakefulness and we cannot tell the difference between reality and dreams. We search for meaning, to make sense of it all. And, if we are prone to accepting paranormal explanations for events, we are more likely to attribute this to the paranormal, rather than an experience generated by our sleeping brain.

We also know that we have brain regions that are important for our sense of self and self-agency. When the activity in these regions becomes disrupted, it is possible to experience the self outside the body, or to experience a sensed presence nearby.

Later, when we reconstruct our memories from the previous night, we're likely to adulterate those memories with things that make sense to us. Our memories are notoriously fallible, which is a hard pill to swallow. Everything that we remember is simply an interpretation of an experience we've had, and ambiguous experiences, like sleep paralysis, leave a lot of room for interpretation. It makes you wonder how many of our truths are just well-polished guesses.

REFERENCES

Arzy, S., Seeck, M., Ortigue, S., Spinelli, L., & Blanke, O. (2006). Induction of an illusory shadow person. *Nature, 443*(7109), 287–287. https://doi.org/10.1038/443287a.

Arzy, S., Thut, G., Mohr, C., Michel, C. M., & Blanke, O. (2006). Neural basis of embodiment: Distinct contributions of temporoparietal junction and extrastriate body area. *The Journal of Neuroscience, 26*(31), 8074–8081. https://doi.org/10.1523/JNEUROSCI.0745-06.2006.

Barbeau, E., Wendling, F., Régis, J., Duncan, R., Poncet, M., Chauvel, P., & Bartolomei, F. (2005). Recollection of vivid memories after perirhinal region stimulations: Synchronization in the theta range of spatially distributed brain areas. *Neuropsychologia, 43*(9), 1329–1337. https://doi.org/10.1016/j.neuropsychologia.2004.11.025.

Bischof, M., & Bassetti, C. L. (2004). Total dream loss: A distinct neuropsychological dysfunction after bilateral PCA stroke. *Annals of Neurology, 56*(4), 583–586. https://doi.org/10.1002/ana.20246.

Blagrove, M., French, C. C., & Jones, G. (2006). Probabilistic reasoning, affirmative bias and belief in precognitive dreams. *Applied Cognitive Psychology, 20*(1), 65–83. https://doi.org/10.1002/acp.1165.

Brooks, P. L., & Peever, J. H. (2012). Identification of the transmitter and receptor mechanisms responsible for REM sleep paralysis. *Journal of Neuroscience, 32*(29), 9785–9795. https://doi.org/10.1523/JNEUROSCI.0482-12.2012.

Cheyne, J. A. (2003). Sleep paralysis and the structure of waking-nightmare hallucinations. *Dreaming, 13*(3), 163–179. https://doi.org/10.1023/A:1025373412722.

Cheyne, J. A., Newby-Clark, I. R., & Rueffer, S. D. (1999a). Relations among hypnagogic and hypnopompic experiences associated with sleep paralysis. *Journal of Sleep Research, 8*(4), 313–317. https://doi.org/10.1046/j.1365-2869.1999.00165.x.

Cheyne, J. A., Rueffer, S. D., & Newby-Clark, I. R. (1999b). Hypnagogic and hypnopompic hallucinations during sleep paralysis: Neurological and cultural construction of the night-mare. *Consciousness and Cognition, 8*(3), 319–337. https://doi.org/10.1006/ccog.1999.0404.

de Sá, J. F. R., & Mota-Rolim, S. A. (2016). Sleep paralysis in Brazilian folklore and other cultures: A brief review. *Frontiers in Psychology, 7*. https://doi.org/10.3389/fpsyg.2016.01294.

Eichenlaub, J.-B., Nicolas, A., Daltrozzo, J., Redouté, J., Costes, N., & Ruby, P. (2014). Resting brain activity varies with dream recall frequency between subjects. *Neuropsychopharmacology, 39*(7), 1594–1602. https://doi.org/10.1038/npp.2014.6.

French, C. C. (2005). Near-death experiences in cardiac arrest survivors. In S. Laureys (Ed.), *Progress in Brain Research* (Vol. 150, pp. 351–367). Amsterdam: Elsevier. https://doi.org/10.1016/S0079-6123(05)50025-6.

French, C. C., & Stone, A. (2014). *Anomalistic Psychology: Exploring Paranormal Belief and Experience.* London: Red Globe Press.

Gillinder, L., Liegeois-Chauvel, C., & Chauvel, P. (2022). What déjà vu and the "dreamy state" tell us about episodic memory networks. *Clinical Neurophysiology, 136*, 173–181. https://doi.org/10.1016/j.clinph.2022.01.126.

Girardeau, G., & Lopes-Dos-Santos, V. (2021). Brain neural patterns and the memory function of sleep. *Science, 374*(6567), 560–564. https://doi.org/10.1126/science.abi8370.

Gregoric, P., & Fink, J. L. (2022). Sleeping and dreaming in Aristotle and the Aristotelian tradition. In C. T. Thörnqvist & J. Toivanen (Eds.), *Forms of Representation in the Aristotelian Tradition* (Vol. 2, pp. 1–27). Leiden: Brill. https://doi.org/10.1163/9789004506091_002.

Hebb, D. O. (1949). *The Organization of Behavior: A Psychological Theory.* New York: Wiley.

Hendricks, J. C., Morrison, A. R., & Mann, G. L. (1982). Different behaviors during paradoxical sleep without atonia depend on pontine lesion site. *Brain Research, 239*(1), 81–105. https://doi.org/10.1016/0006-8993(82)90835-6.

Henley, K., & Morrison, A. R. (1974). A re-evaluation of the effects of lesions of the pontine tegmentum and locus coeruleus on phenomena of paradoxical sleep in the cat. *Acta Neurobiologiae Experimentalis, 34*(2), 215–232.

Hobson, J. A., & McCarley, R. W. (1977). The brain as a dream state generator: An activation-synthesis hypothesis of the dream process. *The American Journal of Psychiatry, 134*(12), 1335–1348. https://doi.org/10.1176/ajp.134.12.1335.

Hobson, J. A., Pace-Schott, E. F., & Stickgold, R. (2000). Dreaming and the brain: Toward a cognitive neuroscience of conscious states. *Behavioral and Brain Sciences, 23*(6), 793–842. https://doi.org/10.1017/S0140525X00003976.

Jalal, B. (2018). The neuropharmacology of sleep paralysis hallucinations: Serotonin 2A activation and a novel therapeutic drug. *Psychopharmacology, 235*(11), 3083–3091. https://doi.org/10.1007/s00213-018-5042-1.

Jouvet, M. (1962). Research on the neural structures and responsible mechanisms in different phases of physiological sleep. *Archives Italiennes De Biologie, 100*, 125–206.

LeDoux, J. E. (2000). Emotion circuits in the brain. *Annual Review of Neuroscience, 23*, 155–184. https://doi.org/10.1146/annurev.neuro.23.1.155.

Li, D., Mabrouk, O. S., Liu, T., Tian, F., Xu, G., Rengifo, S., Choi, S. J., Mathur, A., Crooks, C. P., Kennedy, R. T., Wang, M. M., Ghanbari, H., & Borjigin, J. (2015). Asphyxia-activated corticocardiac signaling accelerates onset of cardiac arrest. *Proceedings of the National Academy of Sciences, 112*(16), E2073–E2082. https://doi.org/10.1073/pnas.1423936112.

Martial, C., Fritz, P., Gosseries, O., Bonhomme, V., Kondziella, D., Nelson, K., & Lejeune, N. (2025). A neuroscientific model of near-death experiences. *Nature Reviews Neurology, 21*(6), 297–311. https://doi.org/10.1038/s41582-025-01072-z.

McNamara, P. (2023). *The Neuroscience of Sleep and Dreams* (2nd ed.). Cambridge: Cambridge University Press.

Musch, J., & Ehrenberg, K. (2002). Probability misjudgment, cognitive ability, and belief in the paranormal. *British Journal of Psychology, 93*(2), 169–177. https://doi.org/10.1348/000712602162517.

Nichols, D. E. (2018). N,N-dimethyltryptamine and the pineal gland: Separating fact from myth. *Journal of Psychopharmacology, 32*(1), 30–36. https://doi.org/10.1177/0269881117736919.

NPR. (2017). *The "Swiss Army Knife" Of Health: A Good Night's Sleep* (No. November 13, 2017) [Broadcast]. www.npr.org/transcripts/563831137.

Patel, A. K., Reddy, V., Shumway, K. R., & Araujo, J. F. (2023). *Physiology, Sleep Stages*. Treasure Island: StatPearls. www.ncbi.nlm.nih.gov/books/NBK526132/.

Preller, K. H., Herdener, M., Pokorny, T., Planzer, A., Kraehenmann, R., Stämpfli, P., Liechti, M. E., Seifritz, E., & Vollenweider, F. X. (2017). The fabric of meaning and subjective effects in LSD-induced states depend on serotonin 2A receptor activation. *Current Biology, 27*(3), 451–457. https://doi.org/10.1016/j.cub.2016.12.030.

Roth, B. L., Baner, K., Westkaemper, R., Siebert, D., Rice, K. C., Steinberg, S., Ernsberger, P., & Rothman, R. B. (2002). Salvinorin A: A potent naturally occurring nonnitrogenous κ opioid selective agonist. *Proceedings of the National Academy of Sciences, 99*(18), 11934–11939. https://doi.org/10.1073/pnas.182234399.

Schredl, M., Ciric, P., Götz, S., & Wittmann, L. (2003a). Dream recall frequency, attitude towards dreams and openness to experience. *Dreaming, 13*(3), 145–153. https://doi.org/10.1023/A:1025369311813.

Schredl, M., Wittmann, L., Ciric, P., & Götz, S. (2003b). Factors of home dream recall: A structural equation model. *Journal of Sleep Research, 12*(2), 133–141. https://doi.org/10.1046/j.1365-2869.2003.00344.x.

Strassman, R. (2001). *DMT: The Spirit Molecule: A Doctor's Revolutionary Research into the Biology of Near-death and Mystical Experiences*. Rochester: Park Street Press.

Timmermann, C., Roseman, L., Williams, L., Erritzoe, D., Martial, C., Cassol, H., Laureys, S., Nutt, D., & Carhart-Harris, R. (2018). DMT models the near-death experience. *Frontiers in Psychology, 9*, 1424. doi:10.3389/fpsyg.2018.01424.

Tsunematsu, T. (2023). What are the neural mechanisms and physiological functions of dreams? *Neuroscience Research, 189*, 54–59. https://doi.org/10.1016/j.neures.2022.12.017.

Vallat, R., Nicolas, A., & Ruby, P. (2020). Brain functional connectivity upon awakening from sleep predicts interindividual differences in dream recall frequency. *Sleep, 43*(12), 1–11. https://doi.org/10.1093/sleep/zsaa116.

Vallat, R., Türker, B., Nicolas, A., & Ruby, P. (2022). High dream recall frequency is associated with increased creativity and default mode network connectivity. *Nature and Science of Sleep, 14*, 265–275. https://doi.org/10.2147/NSS.S342137.

van de Ven, G. M., Trouche, S., McNamara, C. G., Allen, K., & Dupret, D. (2016). Hippocampal offline reactivation consolidates recently formed cell assembly patterns during sharp wave-ripples. *Neuron, 92*(5), 968–974. https://doi.org/10.1016/j.neuron.2016.10.020.

Whinery, J. E. (1997). Psychophysiologic correlates of unconsciousness and near-death experiences. *Journal of Near-Death Studies, 15*(4), 231–258.

Winer, J. R., Mander, B. A., Kumar, S., Reed, M., Baker, S. L., Jagust, W. J., & Walker, M. P. (2020). Sleep disturbance forecasts β-amyloid accumulation across subsequent years. *Current Biology, 30*(21), 4291–4298. https://doi.org/10.1016/j.cub.2020.08.017.

Wohl, V. (2020). The sleep of reason: Sleep and the philosophical soul in ancient Greece. *Classical Antiquity, 39*(1), 126–151. https://doi.org/10.1525/ca.2020.39.1.126.

5 Extraterrestrial, Running Over Pedestrians*

Alien Abductions and the Science of Suggestibility

Barney and Betty Hill decided on a whim to take a trip to Niagara Falls in September of 1961. By all accounts, the trip itself was lovely, but what happened on the drive back home changed their lives forever.

Driving south on Route 3 in the White Mountains late at night, the Hills spotted lights in the sky. At first glance, nothing was amiss about the lights. After watching for a moment, Barney and Betty both came to the independent realization that the lights were moving in an erratic manner, unlike anything they had seen before. Barney suggested that they must have been from a satellite that somehow had gotten off its course. The couple watched the lights a little longer, neither of them very convinced that the lights were from a satellite.

The Hills became increasingly alarmed as the lights seemed to get closer to them. At this point, they could see that the lights were from a flying craft – a craft that appeared to be following them. As the story goes, the craft hovered just a few hundred feet away from them. Barney stopped the car in the middle of the road and Betty handed him binoculars. Barney stepped out of the car and began walking across the road, into a field. In the field, he pressed the binoculars to his eyes and looked at the craft. He saw a long row of large windows, and on the other side of the windows, he saw human-like beings, at least six of them. They appeared to be operating a control board. A ladder emerged from the craft, which was also lowering itself toward the ground. By now, Barney was terrified and he bolted back to the car.

* The chapter title references a lyric from the song "My name is" by Eminem (1999).

He threw himself into the driver's seat and sped away. Betty looked back for the craft, but it had vanished.

The Hills made their way back home in a daze. They were confused and disoriented about the events of the night and, barely speaking, went to bed. The next day, Barney discovered that the strap of the binoculars was inexplicably broken and that the tops of his shoes were scuffed. The couple felt on edge. Betty's sister once had claimed to have seen a UFO, which led Betty to become a tentative believer. Betty began to think that maybe that's what had happened to her and Barney – that extraterrestrials had made contact with them and somehow modified their memories. She made a call to the US Air Force and eventually spoke with someone who saved her report (Betty's report had stated that she saw the UFO, but she left out Barney's recollection of seeing human-like figures on board). She went to the library and borrowed a book on UFO sightings. Later, she wrote to the author of that book, Major Donald Kehoe. Major Kehoe forwarded Betty Hill's letter on, and eventually the letter reached Walter Webb, a scientific adviser to the National Investigations Committee on Aerial Phenomena. Webb later interviewed Barney and Betty independently and declared their abduction story "iron-clad" (Fuller, 1966, p. 34).

The persisting anxiety related to that night led the Hills to eventually seek psychiatric treatment. They found Dr. Benjamin Simon, who was a Boston psychiatrist interested in uncovering the underlying source of the anxiety, insomnia, and ulcers that had been plaguing the Hills. Under several hypnosis sessions, Betty recounted details that her conscious mind didn't seem to have access to before. She came to believe that she had repressed these memories, and Dr. Simon was able to use hypnosis to bring them to the surface.

Under hypnosis, Betty recalled that she and her husband were brought onto the extraterrestrial spacecraft. The couple was separated once on board the ship. Betty underwent a painful medical examination, including a "pregnancy test" that consisted of a long needle being inserted into her navel. She then had a rich conversation with one of the interstellar visitors, who was apparently the "leader." The leader showed her a map of intergalactic trading routes. Betty felt silly because she couldn't find Earth on the map. She also felt silly because she had trouble answering questions like, "What is a vegetable?" and "What is yellow?" Betty was in awe of these conversations and expressed remorse that no one at home would believe her. The leader offered Betty one of their books to take home, as proof of the experience. Later, though, this book was confiscated by the other visitors. Betty's impression was that they didn't *want* her to share her story. Finally, they brought Barney to her. He had been instructed by the visitors to keep his eyes tightly closed. He didn't see anything on board the ship.

The Hills' experience became the first widely publicized close encounter of the fourth kind. The experience has been met with support – and skepticism. Since then, thousands of people have claimed to have been abducted (Holden & French, 2002). Is it at all possible that so many people have been abducted, in secret, from the rest of the world? Are they making it all up?

Or is there another explanation?

WHAT IS A MEMORY?

Thousands of people have claimed to have been abducted and taken aboard extraterrestrial spacecraft. There are three potential explanations for these claims:

(1) They are lying
(2) There are some psychological or neurological factors at play to cause people to believe they have been abducted
(3) Or, they really have been abducted

It's tempting to think that abduction claims are simply bald-faced lies. It is certainly a parsimonious explanation. But, while it may be parsimonious, psychologists believe that the vast majority of abduction claims are not hoaxes. Abductees rarely seek publicity about their experience, or they prefer anonymity when they do speak out. This suggests that any fame and fortune that might befall them from a moment in the spotlight is not a motivator for claiming to be abducted (although, certainly, some claims are indeed hoaxes) (French et al., 2008; Holden & French, 2002)

If abductees aren't lying about their experiences, this means they truly believe they have been abducted. Therefore, either their memories are distorted, or they have in fact been abducted. Let's explore the former theory first, before we explore the possibility of abduction. But first, we must delve into the science of memories.

A memory is the neural representation of a sensory experience. Sensory experiences change our brains in ways that allow the experiences to live on in our brains. The experiences are stored in strengthened synaptic connections in neural networks. Activation of individual nodes of that network is often enough to activate the rest of the network, thus triggering recall of that experience – of that memory. As experiences become encoded into long-term memories, they create stronger connections between neurons, so that communication between these groups of neurons becomes faster and more efficient. Donald Hebb first proposed this idea decades ago in his now-famous locution, "Cells that fire together, wire together" (Hebb, 1949). The gist of Hebb's Law (also described in Chapter 4) is that if one cell is near enough to another cell to repeatedly or persistently excite it, then the two cells will increase their mutual connections and synchronize their activity.

This molecular basis of learning was further supported by a marvelously serendipitous finding in the 1970s by Terje Lømo and Timothy Bliss. By Lømo's own account, the two scientists were simply at the right place at the right time (Lømo, 2016). The scientists were just starting to understand the role of the brain in memory formation, and specifically, the role of a seahorse-shaped structure called the hippocampus, buried in the temporal lobe. Sharing a mutual interest for neural pathways and synaptic plasticity, Bliss and Lømo decided to collaborate and elaborate on Lømo's earlier findings that suggested that, with the right stimulation, the hippocampus changed itself.

The input to the hippocampus is a group of axons called the perforent path. Recall that neurons are comprised of dendrites and a soma (the input zone) that gives rise to an axon. The axon is the conduction zone – it's the long tube of the neuron that conducts the action potential. As the action potential makes its way down the axon, it finally arrives at the axon terminal, where this neuron will meet another neuron at a synaptic connection. Signals from the action potential trigger a release of neurotransmitters from the presynaptic cell onto the dendrites and cell body of the postsynaptic cell. Here in the hippocampus, the perforent path axons make up the presynaptic cells, and they terminate on cell bodies of a region called the dentate gyrus. The dentate gyrus cells project to area CA3, which in turn projects to CA1 (refer back to Figure 4.3 for a schematic of the hippocampus).

Bliss and Lømo were interested in the plastic properties of the hippocampus. To investigate these properties, they delivered a high-frequency electrical stimulation to the perforent path axons in anesthetized rabbits, which mimicked a large number of consecutive action potentials. Bliss and Lømo then measured responses in the postsynaptic dentate gyrus cells in response to perforent path stimulation. To their amazement, Bliss and Lømo discovered that the dentate gyrus cells *increased* their response, but only after a very specific train of high-frequency stimulation. Even more astounding, when the high-frequency stimulation was replaced with other patterns of stimulation, the dentate gyrus cells maintained their heightened response for several hours. Other lower-frequency patterns of stimulation were unable to induce the potentiated response. Bliss and Lømo named this phenomenon *long-term potentiation (LTP)* (Bliss & Lomo, 1973). This research supported Hebb's initial postulations, that neurons that can reliably induce responses in their partners become linked – somehow – with those partners. This neural behavior ultimately underlies learning.

In the years that followed, neuroscientists would investigate the pharmacological properties of the process of LTP – the process of memory formation. Glutamate was identified as the neurotransmitter that was released from perforent path terminals. This led to the discovery that blocking glutamate receptors can block the induction of LTP and thus prevent learning from taking place (Morris et al., 1986). LTP causes a rapid upregulation of a subtype of glutamate receptor, called the AMPA receptor, as well as an increase in release of glutamate from the presynaptic cell. These changes in glutamate signaling make the postsynaptic neuron capable of having a potentiated, or increased, response. Thus, the synapse is strengthened in response to stimulation (Nicoll, 2017). These were pivotal findings in understanding the neurobiological correlates to learning, and allowed scientists to begin to characterize the role of hippocampal glutamate in memory formation.

And yet, these answers led to more questions. How can cooperative neural activity produce a memory? Is it possible to have cooperative neural activity that represents an experience, if that experience never took place? What happened in Betty Hill's brain when she formed a memory of her abduction?

Much of the research into memory formation has been conducted on the hippocampus. For a long time, psychologists understood that the hippocampus was crucial for learning to occur but didn't know how – until the contributions of someone named Henry Molaison.

Molaison wasn't an elite neuroscientist. Nor was he a neurosurgeon or psychologist. He wasn't even a scientist. He worked on an assembly line for a time but was struck with such severe epilepsy that he wasn't able to maintain work. For decades, Molaison was known to the scientific world by his initials, H.M. Patient H.M. is possibly the most famous case study in neuroscience and psychology to date. When he was twenty-seven years old, Molaison underwent experimental surgery with the goal of removing the epileptic loci in the brain. This included a bilateral removal of the temporal lobe, including the hippocampus, parahippocampal areas, and amygdala. Upon recovering from surgery, it became evident that Molaison could no longer form new declarative memories (Scoville & Milner, 1957).

Let's pause here for a moment to describe different types of memory. *Working memory*, or immediate memory, refers to information that is taken in, is mentally available, and can be rehearsed. An example is when someone tells you their phone number – you might repeat it back to yourself before you enter it into your phone, but you haven't memorized it. By contrast, information that is no longer immediate gets stored as a *long-term memory*. *Declarative long-term memory* is memory for facts and events, like when you recount that time you were chased through the woods by an axe-wielding maniac. Or like when Betty Hill recounted her experiences on board that UFO. Non-declarative, or *procedural long-term memory* is the memory for things that you learn by doing, like learning a skill (Cohen & Squire, 1980). The classic example is learning to ride a bike, or like a young alien learning how to drive its first spaceship (probably). In any case, you can't learn how to ride a bike or drive a spaceship by reading a book about it – you have to practice it to learn it.

Ok. Now that we've done that, we can return to Henry Molaison and the persisting repercussions of his "frankly experimental" (Draaisma, 2013) surgery.

Upon waking from surgery, Molaison had profound anterograde amnesia – he could no longer form new declarative memories. Even though he couldn't form new declarative memories, he notably had intact attention and working memory. He could keep information in his mind *as long as he could rehearse it*. If he was distracted from rehearsing the memory, he lost the memory for the entire event. Perhaps even more notably, when Molaison was asked to learn a procedural task (drawing a five-pointed star when he could only see his drawing as reflected in a mirror) he learned the task as well as non-amnesiac controls. His skill learning improved over several trials over three days – although he had no declarative memory of ever having learned the skill (Corkin, 1968). Although Molaison also had mostly intact declarative memories for events that happened before his surgery, he had some partial retrograde amnesia – he lost most memories from about three years prior to surgery but retained memories from earlier in his life.

These three pieces of information provide crucial information to the field of learning and memory: much as there are multiple types of memory, there are multiple memory systems in the brain. Molaison had intact attention and working memory. This tells us that the hippocampus is not required for these types of memories. Molaison was able to learn a procedural task. This tells us that procedural tasks don't require the hippocampal regions. Finally, Molaison was able to retain remote memories from his childhood. That tells us that long-term, persistent memories don't live in the hippocampus. Importantly, though, Molaison could no longer form *new* declarative memories – which tells us that consolidation into long-term memory requires the hippocampus. Molaison famously described his life like waking in a dream. Every day is alone in itself" (Milner et al., 1968, p. 217).

MEMORIES ARE FALLIBLE

I've hopefully convinced you that memories exist as strengthened connections between groups of neurons, and these connections contain a neural representation of an experience. Activating these connections allows us to relive, or remember, that experience. We've also learned that in order for these representations to persist into long-term memory, one must have an intact hippocampus to consolidate short-term to long-term episodic memories.

Let us accept, for a moment, the idea that abductees have a genuine belief that they had been taken aboard an alien spacecraft, even though they hadn't. How could one come to have this explicit, declarative memory of something that never happened? To conceptualize this, we must first understand that memories are not always accurate representations of the experience that transpired during encoding. More troubling still, perhaps, is the idea that we might even have a memory for something we never experienced. Let's first explore how an existing memory can come to be altered, and then we'll discuss how a brand-new false memory can exist in the brain.

Memory distortion was eloquently demonstrated in 1974 by Elizabeth Loftus and her colleagues. Loftus showed participants videos of a simulated car crash. She then asked participants, "How fast were the cars going when they hit each other?" In some conditions, the word *hit* was replaced with words like *collided, bumped, contacted,* or *smashed.* Participants reported that the cars were going much faster when they heard the word *smashed* compared to any other condition. Moreover, when asked a week later, people that heard the word *smashed* were more likely to report that there was broken glass in the accident, even though there was none (Loftus & Palmer, 1974). Clearly, memories are malleable and can be influenced by things like leading questions and misinformation. This work has been replicated by a number of groups and reviewed extensively (Loftus, 1979, 2019). I highly suggest that the reader take about twenty minutes to watch Elizabeth Loftus's TED Talk, *How Reliable is Your Memory?*

A radical idea took hold of memory research in the 1990s – the idea that an existing memory, when reactivated, can become vulnerable to disruption. At the time, it was well established that the formation of new proteins – protein synthesis – is crucial for memory consolidation. Protein synthesis is triggered by cooperative synaptic activity, which would give rise to LTP. New proteins are created that allow these synaptic connections to endure. When drugs that inhibit protein synthesis are injected during the consolidation window, the memory fails to persist. Up until that time, people believed that once memories became consolidated, they were relatively immune to disruption. This later proved to be completely untrue. The radical idea was that, when an established memory becomes reactivated (like when you recount your tale of being chased through the woods by that axe-murderer, or when Betty recounted her experiences on the UFO), the memory becomes *re*consolidated. This process of reconsolidation also requires new protein synthesis. While a memory is being reconsolidated, it is also vulnerable to distortion through impairment of protein synthesis. So, when Betty was recounting her experiences, she was reactivating and reconsolidating her existing memories. If she was supplied with additional information during the reconsolidation window, she would be more likely to incorporate this new information into her memory. For example, if someone said to her, "You said that the aliens were tall, Betty," (which she hadn't) Betty might then reply, "Yes, they were very tall." And that becomes part of her narrative, and part of her memory.

The experiment to test the role of protein synthesis in memory reconsolidation was simple. Rats were taught to associate a tone with a mild footshock – simple Pavlovian fear conditioning. After training, presentation of the tone by itself resulted in fear-like behavior in the rats, evidence that they had learned the association. Importantly, when the rats were exposed to the tone alone, the tone acted like a retrieval cue, asking the animals to remember (reactivate) the tone–shock association. When the retrieval cue was presented, a protein synthesis inhibitor was injected into the amygdala, an area that is crucial for Pavlovian fear conditioning. Twenty-four hours later, the rats were exposed to the tone alone again, but this time, *they didn't exhibit fear-like behavior*. To be sure that it was indeed reconsolidation that made the memory vulnerable, the protein synthesis inhibitor was injected into the amygdala of rats who did not hear the retrieval cue and were therefore not "reminded" of the tone–shock pairing. When tested twenty-four hours later, these animals still exhibited fear-like behavior (Nader et al., 2000). The importance of this finding cannot be understated – when a memory is reactivated, protein synthesis is required. If protein synthesis is blocked during reactivation, the memory is disrupted. This groundbreaking finding shed some of the first light on the vulnerability of existing memories. Our memories are not an infallible representation of the experience, after all.

Of course, we cannot ask a rat what it is remembering and what it isn't. We can only measure a change in behavior. When an animal demonstrates a decrease in fear-like behavior in response to a retrieval cue, we don't know why that behavior change occurs. Is the memory deleted from the rat's long-term memory? Or does the rat still remember the event, but the memory has lost its emotional salience? Research in human populations is ongoing, but this has huge clinical ramifications. Some work shows that treatment with a common blood pressure medication called propranolol can impair the recall of memory when propranolol is given both during the consolidation and reconsolidation stages (Lonergan et al., 2013). In addition to blocking a subtype of norepinephrine receptor (which makes this a great treatment for acute anxiety), propranolol can also exert central protein synthesis inhibition, which explains its memory-impairing effects. People with traumatic memories can benefit from treatment like this. Indeed, propranolol used as an adjunctive therapy in patients with post-traumatic stress disorder has been shown to reduce negative symptoms in these patients, although more work needs to be done on this therapy (Giustino et al., 2016; Roullet et al., 2021; Young & Butcher, 2020).

FALSE MEMORIES

And now we can get into the thick of it – *how can someone form a memory of an event that never occurred?* Elizabeth Loftus and Jacqueline Pickrell designed an experiment to attempt to plant wholly false memories in healthy participants – and it worked. They were successful in planting false memories of being lost in a shopping mall as a child in 25 percent of their participants. Memories like these are called *rich false memories* because they can be rich in detail, however false they might be. The participants who came to believe that they had been lost in a shopping mall believed that they were lost for an extended period of time, were highly upset, and were eventually rescued and reunited with their parents by a kind elderly person (Loftus & Pickrell, 1995). None of this ever happened.

Other subsequent experiments had similar findings – after as few as two interviews where it was suggested that a fabricated event had happened, at least 20 percent of participants came to "remember" the false event (Hyman et al., 1995). False memories have been embedded into the memory landscape of participants for traumatic events (e.g., being attacked by a dog, Porter et al., 1999) and relatively benign events (e.g., being sick after eating egg salad, Bernstein et al., 2005). Researchers have even successfully implanted rich false memories of committing a crime – including assault, assault with a weapon, and theft (Shaw & Porter, 2015). It appears that the emotional quality of the memories does not differ much between real and false memories – fabricated memories can be just as traumatic and upsetting as true memories. People also report fabricated memories with exquisite detail and confidence. Research shows, though, that even when a person is *confident* in reporting a memory, that doesn't mean the memory is accurate (Laney & Loftus, 2008). This has obvious and major implications for the criminal justice system. Incarceration should be based on objective evidence, not fallible and unreliable eyewitness memories.

Researchers have even successfully planted false memories into the brains of mice. Yes, you read that right. We can use cutting-edge techniques to create a false association in the brains of rodents, and the rodent's behavior changes as if that event had happened. To do this, scientists have to be able to tag a neural network during the encoding phase of memory formation. The process is a little complicated, stick with me. Researchers tag neurons with the instructions to insert light-sensitive ion channels into the membranes of neurons that are involved in the formation of that memory (you might want to refer back to Box 4.1 for a quick review of optogenetics).

First, researchers allow a mouse to explore a new context (let's pretend it's a non-haunted house). Then, animals are fear conditioned in a distinctly different context (now, let's pretend they see a ghost in a different, haunted, house. In this study, though, the mice weren't actually taken to a haunted house. They were placed in plastic boxes in a lab and trained to associate a tone with a footshock using a Pavlovian conditioning paradigm). During this fear conditioning phase, any active neurons become tagged with a light-sensitive ion channel so that the memory can later be reactivated by light. Animals were then returned to the first context (the non-haunted house). Researchers flipped on a switch that delivered light via fiber-optic cable to the brains of the mice. This light turned on all the neurons that contain that light-sensitive ion channel, therefore turning on all the neurons that are part of the memory of being scared by the ghost in the haunted house.

When the fear memory was reactivated by light, the mice displayed high amounts of freezing – a fear-like behavior. They displayed this behavior in the *non-haunted* house, even though they were never in fact scared in that context. This demonstrated that optogenetic reactivation of a contextual fear memory can induce behavioral responses to that memory.

Next, researchers employed these techniques to *insert* a memory for something that never happened. As before, a new group of animals explored context A, the non-haunted house. This time, the neurons that contained the memory for context A were tagged with the light-sensitive ion channel. The next day, animals were fear conditioned in context B, the haunted house. During fear conditioning, the neurons containing the memory for context A were optogenetically reactivated. The idea was that by reactivating the memory of context A while the animal was being fear conditioned in context B, the animal would then associate the fear conditioning with context A. And that's exactly what happened. When placed back in context A, animals displayed a high amount of freezing, even in the absence of reactivating the engram. They did not display any freezing in an entirely new context (context C) showing that the fear memory did not generalize across contexts. Even more interesting, animals didn't demonstrate freezing in context B – the environment that they were actually fear conditioned in! The reason for this is not entirely clear. When cues are presented simultaneously, there might be competition for which one is "remembered." Here, it appears that the mice remembered the more salient context, even though it was a false memory (Liu et al., 2014; Ramirez et al., 2013).

SUGGESTIBILITY AND THE MYTH OF REPRESSED MEMORIES

Consider the suggestion, "Very soon you will be playing the computer game. When I clap my hands, meaningless symbols will appear in the middle of the screen. They will feel like characters of a foreign language that you do not know, and you will not attempt to attribute any meaning to them. This gibberish will be printed in one of four ink colors: red, blue, green or yellow. Although you will only be able to attend to the symbols' ink color, you will look straight at the scrambled signs and crisply see all of them. Your job is to quickly and accurately depress the key that corresponds to the ink color shown. You will find that you can play this game easily and effortlessly"(Raz et al., 2002).

This quotation was a suggestion that was made to individuals – some of whom were hypnotized – prior to engaging in an attentional task called the Stroop Task. In this task, the names of different colors appear on a screen. In some conditions, the name of the color appears in that same color (i.e., the word red appears in red), and participants are instructed to read the word that they see. In other conditions, the name of the color appears in a different color, but participants are instructed to name the color, not to read the word (i.e., the word "red" might appear in blue, and the participant would say "blue"). This task becomes more difficult when the word and color are incongruent, and reaction times tend to slow (this is referred to as Stroop interference). The Stroop Task is a well-known measurement of attention and is frequently used in cognitive psychology research. If you'd like to try the Stroop Task yourself, you can go to www.psytoolkit.org/experiment-library/stroop.html. If you want to try it under hypnosis, you'll have to figure that part out for yourself.

When some individuals are under hypnosis and hear a suggestion that letters are meaningless symbols, the letters actually *become* meaningless symbols to them. That's right – highly hypnotizable individuals can respond to the suggestion that they can't read the words that are right in front of them, and they are able to say the names of the colors without any Stroop interference (Raz et al., 2002).

But what happens in our brains to make us more suggestible when under hypnosis? Under hypnosis, people can narrow their focus and lose attention toward external stimuli. The dorsal anterior cingulate cortex (dACC; attention) and prefrontal cortex (PFC; executive function) are two key brain structures involved in the ability to tune out the senses. Individuals with high hypnotizability show altered activation and connectivity between the dACC and PFC compared to people who are less hypnotizable (Hoeft et al., 2012). Hypnosis is a top-down ability to intentionally ignore external stimuli, so it makes sense that these structures are differentially affected under hypnosis. Brain imaging studies suggest that when under hypnosis, individuals decouple conflict monitoring and attentional control – thus allowing themselves to be in a relaxed but focused state (Egner et al., 2005). Taken together, this information suggests that hypnosis can make people more vulnerable to suggestion.

Some psychotherapists have suggested (although it has never been backed up scientifically) that traumatic memories can be repressed (Terr, 1991). The rationale is that, if a person lived through a horrific experience, the memory of that experience might be too traumatic to relive, and so some people attempt to cope by burying those memories. Proponents of this idea often believe that the buried memory can be recovered with certain techniques, like hypnosis. This was the case for Betty and Barney Hill – they underwent hypnosis, and across several sessions, they (mostly Betty) "recovered" memories of their abduction. This raises questions, though, about the nature of hypnosis. Is hypnosis creating a mental state in which people are so suggestible that they create false memories? Or is hypnosis truly revealing memories that were buried so deep that the conscious mind cannot access them?

Often, abductees turn to hypnotherapy because they have had a strange experience, struggle to understand it, and seek answers. These strange experiences share a lot of characteristics. Many abductees report experiences that sound a lot like an episode of sleep paralysis. An abductee might find themselves waking up in the night, unable to move, with a feeling of a presence in their bedroom. Hypnopompic hallucinations often occur, including flashing lights, buzzing sounds, tingling sensations, feelings of levitation, etc. Upon later reflection, they might feel like they had lost time. In fact, about 60 percent of abductions occur during the night, when the victim is asleep (Spanos et al., 1993). Confused and bewildered individuals then seek the help of a hypnotist to understand the experience and what happened to them during that lost time. During the hypnotic session, some people can come to "recall" being abducted (Clancy et al., 2002).

Unfortunately, well-meaning therapists may inadvertently feed misinformation or ask leading questions that can distort memory – or worse, create a wholly fabricated memory (Loftus, 1993). And this is particularly true for hypnotherapy. As we saw a moment ago, hypnotized patients can be so prone to suggestion that they can override their own cognition. This, in itself, isn't a bad thing. Hypnosis has been used for a variety of good things, including cessation of drug and alcohol use, ignoring pain during childbirth, and the relief from anxiety. A mere suggestion can abolish cravings, pain, and fear (Potter, 2004).

But are memories for unlikely events, like alien abduction, subject to the same level of memory distortion as more probable, but still fabricated, memories? One study, conducted by researchers at Harvard University, evaluated memory distortion in people who claimed to have been abducted by aliens. Some of the study participants had memories of being abducted (the "recovered" group), some believed that they have been abducted but have no memory of it (the "repressed" group), and some participants deny ever having been abducted by aliens (the "control" group). All participants were brought into the lab and given a test of false recall and false recognition. As expected, participants reporting the recovered memories showed more memory distortion compared to the control group in laboratory tests of false recall and false recognition. There were no group differences in true recall, suggesting that people who report recovered memories of alien abduction are more susceptible to fabricating a memory based on mere suggestion. Importantly, people who have the belief that they have been abducted – whether repressed or recovered – scored higher than controls on scales of belief in unusual forms of causality (magical ideation and perceptual aberration). The belief that one has been abducted by aliens may be a *source-monitoring error*. For example, a person may have watched a movie about alien abductions as a child and later gone on to have an anomalous sleep-paralysis episode. They might conclude that they have been abducted by aliens because they have a memory of an abduction event, although they have confused the source of the memory (movie versus real life).

Of course, for a person to come to believe that they have been abducted, they first need to believe extraterrestrial ships can visit Earth, *and* that occupants of these ships have the ability to extract humans from their homes and take them aboard the ships. There are frequent claims that these beings have "wiped the memory" of the abduction from abductees' minds, necessitating techniques like hypnosis to "recover" them.

For one to come to believe they've been abducted, one has to believe that alien abductions are plausible in the first place. Data show that abductees have a higher belief in the paranormal than non-abductees. In one study, hypnotic susceptibility was found to be related to belief in the paranormal, although not necessarily with claims of experiencing paranormal activity (Atkinson, 1994). Other studies have reported similar findings, and added that people more susceptible to hypnosis tend to have a stronger belief that God is in direct control of their health (Green & Hina, 2022). An interesting personality trait that may be associated with the belief that one has been abducted is called *fantasy-proneness*. Some reports estimate that about 4 percent of our population is highly fantasy-prone. People who are fantasy-prone are highly hypnotizable, live vivid fantasy lives, and even have difficulty distinguishing fantasy from reality (Newman & Baumeister, 1996; Spanos et al., 1993). These are, of course, correlational relationships and cannot imply causation.

Newman and Baumeister (1996) suggest that there are a number of factors that might come together to cause a perfectly sane person to falsely believe that they have been abducted by aliens. Highly suggestible individuals might "recover" such memories under hypnosis, especially if they have experienced the anomalous sensations that come with an episode of sleep paralysis. On top of this, people who report abductions also have a high need to escape the self. This might, at least partly, explain why so many people would create spurious memories of alien abduction in particular. Psychologist Roy Baumeister has argued that masochistic fantasies are the result of a high desire to escape from self-awareness and identity. Masochistic experiences that allow one to escape self-esteem and control might help people escape themselves. He believes that a number of cognitive factors (false memories, suggestibility) and motivational factors (need to escape, high fantasy proneness) converge in an effort to explain anomalous perceptions, like an episode of sleep paralysis (Baumeister, 1988; Newman & Baumeister, 1996).

But, we might never know for sure.

THE ET HYPOTHESIS: WHAT IF THE TRUTH REALLY IS OUT THERE?

Thousands of people have claimed that they have been abducted by space aliens. We have already established that these are non-psychotic people who, for the most part, sincerely believe what they claim. We have generated several theories about why a person might come to believe this highly unlikely event. But ... what if all these people have really been abducted?

This brings us to our third and final explanation of abduction reports, the idea that such reports might actually be real. This is known widely as the extraterrestrial (or ET) hypothesis. Newman and Baumeister muse, "Yet, if these recent startling accounts are to be believed, they suggest a large and increasing scope of intervention by extraterrestrials into human affairs, which might soon amount to one of the most spectacular and important developments in human history" (Newman & Baumeister, 1996, p. 99).

Readers might remember the July 2023 US congressional hearing where not one, not two, but *three* military veterans testified that they had knowledge of unidentified anomalous phenomena, or UAPs. Retired Major David Grusch was part of the Department of Defense UAP Task Force, then he turned whistleblower. He testified to having knowledge of not only UAPs in the possession of the United States, but also of nonhuman "biologics" that have been recovered from crash sites. Grusch admitted that he had never seen any of this first-hand, but that the information had come from the more than forty interviews he conducted in his role on the task force. While he denied sharing specifics publicly, he offered to share more details behind closed doors. Finally, Grusch testified that he feared for his life after coming forward and that he has been the victim of "administrative terrorism."

Perhaps even more compelling than Grusch's testimony were the testimonies of former Navy fighter pilot Ryan Graves and retired Commander David Fravor. In 2014, Graves reported a UAP sighting off the coast of Virginia Beach. This UAP was a "dark gray or black cube inside of a clear sphere," and it was stationary in the air, despite hurricane-strength winds. A decade prior to Graves's sighting, Fravor made his own remarkable sighting – with video evidence. In November of 2004, Fravor, the commander of the F/A-18-F squadron on the USS Nimitz, and his colleague, Lt. Cmdr. Alex Dietrich, responded to alerts from the ship's radar of "multiple anomalous aerial vehicles." Some of these vehicles appeared to be descending 80,000 ft. in less than a second. Fravor and Dietrich diverted their planes to investigate. They spoke about the incident in an interview on *60 Minutes* (Whitaker, 2021).

"Dude, do you see that thing?" Fravor exclaimed. He described a "white Tic Tac looking object." The UAP had no markings, no wings, no exhaust plumes, and when Fravor brought his plane closer, the UAP seemed to mirror his movements. When he tried to cut it off, it rapidly accelerated. The UAP was detected seconds later, some sixty miles away. During his congressional testimony, Fravor explained, "The technology that we faced was far superior to anything that we had. I'm not a UFO fanatic. But what we saw with four sets of eyes – we have nothing close to it. It was incredible technology" (Romo & Chappell, 2023). In 2021, the Pentagon declassified the video of the strange flying Tic Tac objects. A video search for "flying Tic Tac object" should bring it right up. The video itself is a bit underwhelming. Sure, the Tic Tacs seem to be flying in ways that most humans haven't seen planes fly. But, the official radar data of the UAPs is not available, so we don't know how fast they were really flying. Visual perception is flawed and memories can be distorted. So who's to say what the Tic Tacs in the sky really were?

To date, though, the US government denies any knowledge or evidence of extraterrestrials ever visiting Earth.

But what if life is out there, and we just haven't found it yet? Astrophysicist Adam Frank believes this is very possible. Beyond our solar system, there are about *200 billion trillion stars* – and that's only in our observable universe. Every star is the center of another solar system. That means that there are billions of trillions of planets out there, and some of them just might have the right conditions for life. Actually – its more than "just might." The odds of Earth being the only planet – ever – to sustain life is roughly one in ten billion trillion. Adam Frank puts it like this: "So another way to look at this is that the universe has run ten billion trillion experiments in life, planets, and civilization. And they'd have to all fail in order for us to be the only one, the only civilization ever in the history of the universe" (Zuckerman, 2023).

And we're starting to develop technology that can detect signatures of potential life on all these other planets. In September of 2023, NASA announced that the James Webb telescope has found evidence of carbon dioxide and methane gas on an exoplanet about 120 light years from Earth. This means that this planet could be hydrogen-rich – and contain habitable conditions for life (NASA Webb

Telescope Team, 2023a). In June of 2023, the James Webb telescope detected a brand-new carbon compound on a young star 1,350 light years away (NASA Webb Telescope Team, 2023b). The telescope also displayed some preliminary signatures on life on that same planet. Webb picked up tentative evidence of a molecule called dimethyl sulfide (DMS). Here on Earth, DMS is only produced by life, mainly phytoplankton (NASA Webb Telescope Team, 2023a). In 2024, NASA launched a satellite into space to investigate the biosignatures of ocean phytoplankton on Earth (Ramsayer & McNamee, 2023). Hopefully this information will allow us to search for these same biosignatures – out there.

CONCLUSIONS: DOES THE EVIDENCE STACK UP?

Barney and Betty Hill, along with thousands of others, claim that they were haplessly brought aboard an alien spacecraft. There are some striking similarities between abduction events. First, many abductions are sleep-related. Victims might wake up in the middle of the night, confused about the strange lights and an unknown presence in their rooms. Second, people don't tend to remember the abductions until much later, often with the aid of hypnosis. Once the memories are recovered, they can recount the events. The events often, but not always, include a medical exam. When the exam is concluded there is a debrief with the abductor, sometimes including an explanation of what information they are seeking by visiting Earth. And finally, the abductee is returned to the general location that they were taken from. They report feelings of lost time, confusion, and disorientation.

Although some certainly are, most claims of abduction are not hoaxes. The victims genuinely believe that they have been taken, and some have real trauma associated with the experience. If we accept that they are not lying, then either they really have been abducted, or their brains are creating a false memory and belief of the abduction event.

There's a lot of scientific support for the latter explanation, but not really any for the former. Some of the strange experiences can be explained by the victim having an episode of sleep paralysis. Sometimes sleep paralysis can be very frightening, confusing, and disorienting. It is often accompanied by hallucinations and a sensed presence. Humans don't like ambiguity, and so we search for answers. For a person who is highly hypnotizable, highly fantasy-prone, and already has a belief in the paranormal, being taken aboard an alien craft isn't that much of a leap. And if that becomes plausible, then our memories distort themselves to help create an explanation for a terrifying and bewildering experience.

Is there life elsewhere, and is it possible that intelligent life has visited Earth? There are hundreds of accounts of UAPs. Most of them can be explained by weather balloons, satellites, and other perfectly ordinary things. But a number of them have not been explained, at least not publicly, and there is a record of these accounts maintained by the Department of Defense. Retired military members have stepped forward with claims to have knowledge of alien ships visiting Earth. As of yet, though, there is a dearth of evidence. It still seems extremely unlikely that hundreds, if not thousands, of people have been taken onboard ships in complete secrecy from the rest of the population. But, perhaps, space aliens have developed technology of which we can only dream.

REFERENCES

Atkinson, R. P. (1994). Relationships of hypnotic susceptibility to paranormal beliefs and claimed experiences: Implications for hypnotic absorption. *The American Journal of Clinical Hypnosis*, *37*(1), 34–40. https://doi.org/10.1080/00029157.1994.10403107.

Baumeister, R. F. (1988). Masochism as escape from self. *Journal of Sex Research*, *25*(1), 28–59. https://doi.org/10.1080/00224498809551444.

Bernstein, D. M., Laney, C., Morris, E. K., & Loftus, E. F. (2005). False memories about food can lead to food avoidance. *Social Cognition*, *23*(1), 11–34. https://doi.org/10.1521/soco.23.1.11.59195.

Bliss, T. V., & Lomo, T. (1973). Long-lasting potentiation of synaptic transmission in the dentate area of the anaesthetized rabbit following stimulation of the perforant path. *The Journal of Physiology, 232*(2), 331–356. https://doi.org/10.1113/jphysiol.1973.sp010273.

Clancy, S. A., McNally, R. J., Schacter, D. L., Lenzenweger, M. F., & Pitman, R. K. (2002). Memory distortion in people reporting abduction by aliens. *Journal of Abnormal Psychology, 111*(3), 455–461. https://doi.org/10.1037//0021-843x.111.3.455.

Cohen, N. J., & Squire, L. R. (1980). Preserved learning and retention of pattern-analyzing skill in amnesia: Dissociation of knowing how and knowing that. *Science, 210*(4466), 207–210. https://doi.org/10.1126/science.7414331.

Corkin, S. (1968). Acquisition of motor skill after bilateral medial temporal-lobe excision. *Neuropsychologia, 6*(3), 255–265. https://doi.org/10.1016/0028-3932(68)90024-9.

Draaisma, D. (2013). Neuroscience: Losing the past. *Nature, 497*(7449), 313–314. https://doi.org/10.1038/497313a.

Egner, T., Jamieson, G., & Gruzelier, J. (2005). Hypnosis decouples cognitive control from conflict monitoring processes of the frontal lobe. *NeuroImage, 27*(4), 969–978. https://doi.org/10.1016/j.neuroimage.2005.05.002.

French, C. C., Santomauro, J., Hamilton, V., Fox, R., & Thalbourne, M. A. (2008). Psychological aspects of the alien contact experience. *Cortex, 44*(10), 1387–1395. https://doi.org/10.1016/j.cortex.2007.11.011.

Fuller, J. (1966). *The Interrupted Journey Two Lost Hours Aboard A Flying Saucer.* New York: The Dial Press. http://archive.org/details/1966JohnFullerTheInterruptedJourneyTwoLostHoursAboardAFlyingSaucernotOCR.

Giustino, T. F., Fitzgerald, P. J., & Maren, S. (2016). Revisiting propranolol and PTSD: Memory erasure or extinction enhancement? *Neurobiology of Learning and Memory, 130,* 26–33. https://doi.org/10.1016/j.nlm.2016.01.009.

Green, J. P., & Hina, S. R. (2022). God locus of health control, paranormal beliefs, and hypnotizability. *The International Journal of Clinical and Experimental Hypnosis, 70*(2), 174–195. https://doi.org/10.1080/00207144.2022.2049445.

Hebb, D. O. (1949). *The Organization of Behavior: A Psychological Theory.* New York: Wiley.

Hoeft, F., Gabrieli, J. D. E., Whitfield-Gabrieli, S., Haas, B. W., Bammer, R., Menon, V., & Spiegel, D. (2012). Functional brain basis of hypnotizability. *Archives of General Psychiatry, 69*(10), 1064–1072. https://doi.org/10.1001/archgenpsychiatry.2011.2190.

Holden, K. J., & French, C. C. (2002). Alien abduction experiences: Some clues from neuropsychology and neuropsychiatry. *Cognitive Neuropsychiatry, 7*(3), 163–178. https://doi.org/10.1080/13546800244000058.

Hyman, I. E., Husband, T. H., & Billings, F. J. (1995). False memories of childhood experiences. *Applied Cognitive Psychology, 9*(3), 181–197. https://doi.org/10.1002/acp.2350090302.

Laney, C., & Loftus, E. F. (2008). Emotional content of true and false memories. *Memory, 16*(5), 500–516. https://doi.org/10.1080/09658210802065939.

Liu, X., Ramirez, S., & Tonegawa, S. (2014). Inception of a false memory by optogenetic manipulation of a hippocampal memory engram. *Philosophical Transactions of the Royal Society B: Biological Sciences, 369*, 20130142. https://doi.org/10.1098/rstb.2013.0142.

Loftus, E. F. (1979). The malleability of human memory: Information introduced after we view an incident can transform memory. *American Scientist, 67*(3), 312–320.

Loftus, E. F. (1993). The reality of repressed memories. *American Psychologist, 48*(5), 518–537. https://doi.org/10.1037/0003-066X.48.5.518.

Loftus, E. F. (2019). Eyewitness testimony. *Applied Cognitive Psychology, 33*(4), 498–503. https://doi.org/10.1002/acp.3542.

Loftus, E. F., & Palmer, J. C. (1974). Reconstruction of automobile destruction: An example of the interaction between language and memory. *Journal of Verbal Learning and Verbal Behavior, 13*(5), 585–589. https://doi.org/10.1016/S0022-5371(74)80011-3.

Loftus, E. F., & Pickrell, J. E. (1995). The formation of false memories. *Psychiatric Annals, 25*(12), 720–725. https://doi.org/10.3928/0048-5713-19951201-07.

Lømo, T. (2016). Scientific discoveries: What is required for lasting impact. *Annual Review of Physiology, 78*(1), 1–21. https://doi.org/10.1146/annurev-physiol-021115-105257.

Lonergan, M. H., Olivera-Figueroa, L. A., Pitman, R. K., & Brunet, A. (2013). Propranolol's effects on the consolidation and reconsolidation of long-term emotional memory in healthy participants: A meta-analysis. *Journal of Psychiatry & Neuroscience, 38*(4), 222–231. https://doi.org/10.1503/jpn.120111.

Milner, B., Corkin, S., & Teuber, H.-L. (1968). Further analysis of the hippocampal amnesic syndrome: 14-year follow-up study of H.M. *Neuropsychologia, 6*(3), 215–234. https://doi.org/10.1016/0028-3932(68)90021-3.

Morris, R. G. M., Anderson, E., Lynch, G. S., & Baudry, M. (1986). Selective impairment of learning and blockade of long-term potentiation by an N-methyl-D-aspartate receptor antagonist, AP5. *Nature, 319*(6056), 774–776. https://doi.org/10.1038/319774a0.

Nader, K., Schafe, G. E., & Le Doux, J. E. (2000). Fear memories require protein synthesis in the amygdala for reconsolidation after retrieval. *Nature, 406*(6797), 722–726. https://doi.org/10.1038/35021052.

NASA Webb Telescope Team. (2023a). Webb Discovers Methane, Carbon Dioxide in Atmosphere of K2-18 b – NASA. www.nasa.gov/universe/exoplanets/webb-discovers-methane-carbon-dioxide-in-atmosphere-of-k2-18-b/.

NASA Webb Telescope Team. (2023b, June 26). Webb Makes First Detection of Crucial Carbon Molecule – NASA. www.nasa.gov/universe/webb-makes-first-detection-of-crucial-carbon-molecule/.

Newman, L. S., & Baumeister, R. F. (1996). Toward an explanation of the UFO abduction phenomenon: Hypnotic elaboration, extraterrestrial sadomasochism, and spurious memories. *Psychological Inquiry*, 7(2), 99–126. https://doi.org/10.1207/s15327965pli0702_1.

Nicoll, R. A. (2017). A brief history of long-term potentiation. *Neuron, 93*(2), 281–290. https://doi.org/10.1016/j.neuron.2016.12.015.

Porter, S., Yuille, J. C., & Lehman, D. R. (1999). The nature of real, implanted, and fabricated memories for emotional childhood events: Implications for the recovered memory debate. *Law and Human Behavior*, 23(5), 517–537. https://doi.org/10.1023/a:1022344128649.

Potter, G. (2004). Intensive therapy: Utilizing hypnosis in the treatment of substance abuse disorders. *The American Journal of Clinical Hypnosis*, 47(1), 21–28. https://doi.org/10.1080/00029157.2004.10401472.

Ramirez, S., Liu, X., Lin, P.-A., Suh, J., Pignatelli, M., Redondo, R. L., Ryan, T. J., & Tonegawa, S. (2013). Creating a false memory in the hippocampus. *Science, 341*(6144), 387–391. https://doi.org/10.1126/science.1239073.

Ramsayer, K. B., & McNamee, E. (2023). NASA Wants to Identify Phytoplankton Species from Space. Here's Why. – NASA. www.nasa.gov/centers-and-facilities/goddard/nasa-wants-to-identify-phytoplankton-species-from-space-heres-why/.

Raz, A., Shapiro, T., Fan, J., & Posner, M. I. (2002). Hypnotic suggestion and the modulation of Stroop interference. *Archives of General Psychiatry*, 59(12), 1155–1161. https://doi.org/10.1001/archpsyc.59.12.1155.

Romo, V., & Chappell, B. (2023, July 27). U.S. recovered non-human "biologics" from UFO crash sites, former Intel official says. *NPR*. www.npr.org/2023/07/27/1190390376/ufo-hearing-non-human-biologics-uaps.

Roullet, P., Vaiva, G., Véry, E., Bourcier, A., Yrondi, A., Dupuch, L., Lamy, P., Thalamas, C., Jasse, L., El Hage, W., & Birmes, P. (2021). Traumatic memory reactivation with or without propranolol for PTSD and comorbid MD symptoms: A randomised clinical trial. *Neuropsychopharmacology*, 46(9), 1643–1649. https://doi.org/10.1038/s41386-021-00984-w.

Scoville, W. B., & Milner, B. (1957). Loss of recent memory after bilateral hippocampal lesions. *Journal of Neurology, Neurosurgery, and Psychiatry*, 20(1), 11–21.

Shaw, J., & Porter, S. (2015). Constructing rich false memories of committing crime. *Psychological Science*, 26(3), 291–301. https://doi.org/10.1177/0956797614562862.

Spanos, N. P., Cross, P. A., Dickson, K., & DuBreuil, S. C. (1993). Close encounters: An examination of UFO experiences. *Journal of Abnormal Psychology*, *102*(4), 624–632. https://doi.org/10.1037/0021-843X.102.4.624.

Terr, L. C. (1991). Childhood traumas: An outline and overview. *The American Journal of Psychiatry*, *148*(1), 10–20. https://doi.org/10.1176/ajp.148.1.10.

Whitaker, B. (2021, May 16). *60 Minutes* [Interview]. www.cbsnews.com/news/ufo-military-intelligence-60-minutes-2021-05-16/.

Young, C., & Butcher, R. (2020). Propranolol for Post-Traumatic Stress Disorder: A Review of Clinical Effectiveness. Canadian Agency for Drugs and Technologies in Health. www.ncbi.nlm.nih.gov/books/NBK562942/.

Zuckerman, W. (2023). *UFOs: The Truth Is Right Here* [Broadcast]. https://gimletmedia.com/shows/science-vs/gmhnabeo.

6 Tea Leaves and Tarot Cards

Psychic Readings and Illusions of Cognition

I found Anthony by googling the phrase, "psychic near me." He was highly rated on the Internet, so I made an appointment for a Tarot reading. I told him I wanted to know my future. He said he could help.

I pulled my car into Anthony's driveway and looked around. There was a yard sign that read "Psychic readings" in the lawn, near the road. The front door didn't appear to be well used, but there was a walkway leading to a side door. As I got out of my car, I saw the silhouette of a man who I presumed to be Anthony behind the side door. He opened the door and greeted me while nudging a yapping dog into a side room. He was tall and gaunt. I'd guess he was in his mid-40s. He had messy, sandy brown hair, thick glasses, an unshaved face, and wore a tatty brown cardigan. Anthony ushered me inside and told me to sit at the kitchen table. The house smelled like incense and old cigarette smoke. The kitchen table was littered with toast crumbs, a tea towel with a picture of a rooster on it, and two crystal balls.

"So, the thing is," he began, in a thick Southern accent, "I tell everything – the good and the bad. I have to. So, you know, that means death, that means illness and so forth. I mean, I have to. The only thing I won't tell is if I see someone's death. I don't like to."

I figured it must take a huge cognitive toll to tell a person when they are going to die.

Anthony told me a lot of things about my future. He said that he saw big challenges for me in the upcoming years. A man with a J in his name is worried about finances. He saw travel for me, which is exciting because I love travel. He specifically saw travel up north to see a father figure, which was spot on, as my parents live in Massachusetts. An attractive man from out of state will come into my life (also very exciting!). Anthony finally predicted that I would witness a car accident involving a female stranger. I pressed him a little on the accident and he told me that it might be an accident I see in real life – or it might be on the news.

I want to believe, I really do. But by the end of the session, I wasn't wowed by Anthony's intuitions about my future. Anthony, though, was pleased with the reading. He said he has an accuracy rate of about 80 percent. I asked him how he knew that. He said he *feels* it.

I almost named this chapter, "You have to believe it to see it." You'll see why. The powers of expectation and assumption guide our perception in ways that seem fully supernatural. But as we'll see, psychology and neuroscience can go a long way in explaining the predictions that we read in tea leaves and crystal balls.

WHAT'S IN THE TEA LEAVES?

People report all the time that they visited a psychic for a reading, and the psychic knew rich details about the person – details they would have no way of knowing. Psychics predict future events and talk about past relationships. They can tell you about a love you lost years ago and financial gains yet to come. They may even channel those who have passed away, relaying messages from the dead. How can a stranger possibly know this much? It can seem like being psychic is the only way they could. But as it turns out, there's a lot of psychology at play when it comes to seeing the future. Let's jump into it.

I'll start by describing things psychics do to *appear* psychic. The first, of course, is to conduct *hot readings*. These are especially insidious ways psychics attempt to swindle their audience – by googling them before doing a so-called reading. Comedian television host John Oliver publicly speculated that Tyler Henry, aka the Hollywood Medium, seemed to have done a hot reading for Matt Lauer on *The Today Show*. The episode aired on August 2, 2016. Henry claimed to have channeled Lauer's deceased father. Henry relayed some specific information about the tragic death of the father. Then, he said he was receiving information from the father about a sentimental fishing trip. Lauer was blown away, and became obviously emotional at the accuracy of this information. He and his dad had indeed shared a special bond over fishing, and this was being communicated to Henry from beyond the veil.

John Oliver, though, identified many times that Lauer had spoken publicly – including on *The Today Show* – about special fishing trips with his dad. So, did Tyler Henry really channel Lauer's late father? Oliver suggested that Henry "Googled 'Matt Lauer Dad' and hit the f***ing jackpot" (Perota et al., 2019).

Hot readings feel like cheating (because they are). Many psychics, instead, rely on *cold readings*. Cold readings involve using excellent people-reading skills. These psychics pay attention to body language and minute facial expressions, and adapt the prediction based on what they observe from their client. Let's explore the psychology behind cold readings.

To understand how psychics employ people-reading, let's travel back in time to Berlin, Germany at the start of the twentieth century, to the home of a horse named Hans. Hans was owned by Wilhem von Osten, who was an arithmetic teacher. Naturally, von Osten decided to teach arithmetic to his horse. von Osten taught Hans how to do addition, subtraction, multiplication, division, fractions, how to read a calendar, and even to tell time. von Osten could pose an arithmetic question to Hans, and Hans would tap his hoof on the ground the correct number of times to answer the question. It was amazing. People flocked from all around to see Hans do complex arithmetic. Hans almost always answered correctly.

Naturally, skepticism of Han's impressive abilities emerged. von Osten was accused of trickery and fraud. An investigation ensued, called the "Hans Commission." The commissioners included well-known veterinarians, education specialists, and psychologists. They posed rigorous tests to Hans, and Hans passed all of them with flying colors. In the fall of 1904, the London Herald published the headline: *Clever Hans again. Expert commission concludes that the horse actually reasons.* Some people even wondered whether Hans was using telepathy (Sigmund Freud among them).

Enter Oskar Pfungst, a psychologist at the Berlin Institute of Psychology. Pfungst believed that the Hans Commission used flawed methodology that invited Type I error – a false positive. Pfungst, then, investigated Hans using methods that should reveal whether Hans was as clever as he seemed, or if there was subterfuge afoot. Pfungst's experiments revealed two important pieces of information. First, Hans answered nearly every question correctly *unless* he was unable to see his questioner. Second, Hans missed questions if the questioner themselves did not know the answer.

Pfungst thus determined that von Osten had been unwittingly teaching Hans to read the body language of his questioners. Most of the time, people who ask questions of Hans unconsciously lean forward slightly and furrow their brow, relaxing when Hans tapped his hoof to correct answer. This body language was so subtle that no one even knew they were doing it. So, it seems that Hans was indeed a clever horse, but not in the way that von Osten believed. Hans was simply adept at reading the body language of his questioners.

In psychology, it is crucial that the experimenter does not inadvertently influence the results of the experiment by asking leading questions, giving unconscious cues, etc. Psychologists call this effect experimenter bias. Hans, for one, became quite good at reading the unconscious cues of his questioners. This is also why *double-blind* research studies are the gold standard in research methods. These are experiments where neither the experimenter nor the participant knows which treatment condition the participant received. Double-blind studies significantly reduce the possibility of the experimenter accidentally influencing the results.

Clever Hans showed us that animals can become quite good at reading the body language of humans. Of course, humans can read body language, too. A good psychic will become very well trained in reading and decoding human body language. There is a lot that can be learned about a person if you just pay attention to body language and facial expressions. In one study, social psychologists Nicholas Rule and Nalini Ambady asked naïve participants to look at the headshots of CEOs of Fortune 500 companies and rate their faces for different traits, including leadership ability, trustworthiness, warmth, power, and profits. Amazingly, there was a clear and significant relationship between ratings of power traits and company profit, showing that judgments of their faces accurately assessed objective success. Thus, some aspects of leadership and profits must be conveyed in facial expressions of the CEOs (Rule & Ambady, 2008).

Decoding our microexpressions is one way that psychics can "read" our thoughts and emotions. Microexpressions are small, involuntary facial expressions that last only a fraction of a second. Most people don't notice them or even know that they are giving them. According to work by Paul Ekman, people can become quite skilled at reading microexpressions (Ekman & Frieson, 1978).

If participants can accurately assess the leadership ability of a person and the profits of a company based on a simple black and white photo, and if a horse can convince the whole world it can do math, what can a person who is well-trained in people-reading gather from our unconscious behavior?

Psychics are excellent people readers and observers. When you go in for a psychic reading, the psychic is noticing everything about you and making assumptions based on what they see – your approximate age, sex, race, clothing style, mannerisms, etc. Based on what they observe, they will likely start with a broad observation, something that is probably true for most people in your demographic. For example, Anthony told me that I had a friend who was feeling emotionally distant from their partner. Did Anthony read that in the cards, or was it a good guess that was based on the likelihood that most people in their forties know a couple who is feeling distant? And here's the thing. When a believer hears something like that, they cast about, wondering who in their life this could be true of. When they think of it, they'll exclaim, "Yes, my friend so-and-so has been feeling distant from their partner!" People unknowingly disclose information with verbal language, body language, and facial expressions, and this provides the psychic with the material they need to make accurate "predictions."

There are a few psychological tricks going on here. The first is called the *Barnum effect*, named after none other than P. T. Barnum, of Barnum & Bailey Circus. Barnum's claim to fame was the exploitation of Black people who were, for all intents and purposes, his slaves. He paraded them around, claiming they were oddities like "half man, half ape," or the 161-year-old former nurse of George Washington. It was all a hoax, of course, and Barnum charged admission for people coming from all around to come gawk at his slaves (who hardly saw a fraction of this income). Barnum is commonly credited with the phrase, "There's a sucker born every minute," although it is difficult to verify the quote (Lindfors, 1984). Psychics who employ the Barnum effect make suckers out of their clients by using broad statements that can apply to many people, but frame them in such a way that the statements seem specific to only you.

In cold readings, a psychic might tease information out of you by studying your reactions to broad, Barnum-like statements.

"I sense you have lost a loved one." You nod. Who *hasn't* lost a loved one?

"Their cause of death" – pause for dramatic effect – "something in the chest area." Hardly specific. This could include any number of heart or lung issues. Heart disease is the leading cause of death in older adults, followed by cancer (FastStats, 2023). Lung cancer is one of the most common cancers in both men and women (Hansen, 1998).

The psychic might also appeal to your emotions. "This person wants to reach out to you, to let you know they are all right. I can sense that you two were close. Is there someone whose name is Mitchell? Or Michael?"

And this is where your own psychology comes into play. Some sitters might fall victim to *confirmation bias*. In confirmation bias, people tend to pay attention to, and even seek out, information that aligns with their beliefs while ignoring information that does not align with their beliefs. We do this all the time with the news media that we choose to consume. I can watch a newscast that generally aligns with my political leanings, and I would be likely to believe the information conveyed in the newscast. Conversely, if I watch a news program that opposes my political views, I would be more likely to dismiss the information as wrong or untrue. Confirmation bias isn't necessarily a bad thing, but it is crucial to be aware of, as everybody does it from time to time.

A person who is falling victim to confirmation bias might hear the name Mitchell and Michael, then exclaim with amazement, "My grandfather's name was Matthew!" They are paying attention to the fact that the psychic was pretty darn close to knowing the name of their grandfather. There must have been some static in the ether, and the psychic misinterpreted the name. The sitter is *not* paying attention to the fact that the psychic didn't know the correct name of your grandfather, or that Mitchell, Michael, and Matthew are all very common names in the United States.

Another Barnum-esque technique a psychic might use in cold readings is to use empty truisms – statements that are true about almost everybody. "You are sometimes shy in a new social setting." They might use contradictory statements, where at least one part of the sentence must be true. "You are generally a hard worker, but also enjoy your lazy days," or "You love talking to people but also value your alone time." Believers find the truth in these statements, ignore what doesn't apply to them, and behave in ways that allow the psychic to intuit more about them. The sitter is driving the narrative, not the psychic. At the end of a reading, a psychic might have made several statements. Some are very likely to be true ("sometimes, you feel introverted"), while others may not be (perhaps your grandfather's name was actually Andrew, but he had a best friend named Michael). Because of confirmation bias, we're less likely to pay attention to the inaccuracies, and we attend to the seemingly accurate statements, even if they are so broad that they would apply to almost anybody. Because the accurate bits are what we pay attention to, they are subsequently what we remember from the reading. When people retell the story of their psychic reading, their memory becomes distorted, where they retell the true bits, but omit the false ones.

These Barnum predictions, empty-truisms, and contradictory statements are used by astrologers, too. My horoscope for today, in fact, tells me I should spend time outdoors in quiet reflection. It says I have been working especially hard and need some time to refill the "well of my soul" (Daily Horoscope: Pisces, 2024). Most people, regardless of their birth-month, will feel like this applies to them. When most people read the horoscope, though, they are reading it with hope and expectation. Expectation that a particular prediction will be specifically for them. Maybe someone hopes that their crush approaches them. The horoscope might read, "Someone is thinking about you today." This is a vague and untestable statement, and probably true no matter your astrological sign. But the person hoping that their crush might think of them would likely read this with a deep, romantic heart. If you look for truth in a broad statement, you're likely to find it.

MISSING WHAT'S RIGHT IN FRONT OF YOU

There is so much happening around us that we simply don't see because we're not paying attention. The world is constantly changing, but we're only aware of a small piece of it.

In one classic psychology experiment, researchers showed participants a video of a basketball game. In this video, there were six players, three wearing white shirts and three wearing black shirts. The participant was to count the number of times the ball bounced between players on one team. About forty-five seconds into the video, a person in a gorilla suit walked across the game and off camera. About *half* of the participants didn't notice the gorilla (Simons & Chabris, 1999)! This is a wonderful demonstration of a type of psychological blindness called *inattentional blindness*. When we're not paying attention to something, we quite literally don't see it. So again, when a person is sitting down for a psychic reading, and they are expecting the psychic to, well, be psychic, they're using confirmation bias to pay attention to the accurate statements made by the psychic. When a sitter is focused on accurate statements, they might not even notice the many inaccurate statements.

Humans have a stubborn tendency to become uncomfortable when we encounter information that doesn't fit within our schemas. When we encounter such information, we do whatever mental gymnastics we need to do to ease that *cognitive dissonance*. A fantastic example of this occurred in one study that used magic tricks to examine *choice blindness* and cognitive dissonance. Researchers asked participants to look at photographs of two different female faces and choose the face they found more attractive. On some trials, participants were asked to explain their choice. Unbeknownst to them, the experimenter used sleight of hand to surreptitiously swap the photo they had chosen with the one they had not. For example, if a participant selected the photo on the right, they were shown the one on the left and asked to justify that (incorrect) choice. The amazing part is that hardly any of the participants detected that their chosen photograph had been swapped for the other. This was true regardless of age or sex of the participant, or similarity of the face pairs.

Even more surprisingly, the participants justified their choices when they were questioned. Participants said things like, "She looks like an aunt of mine," and "She's radiant. I would rather have approached her at a bar than the other one. I like her earrings" (Johansson et al., 2005). But they were saying these things about faces that they hadn't even chosen! They were duped, and then acted as if they had made that choice all along. Psychologists call this *confabulation* – when people essentially make up stories to explain their cognitive dissonance. It's another perfect example of our natural dislike for ambiguity and desire to make sense of the nonsensical.

Our brains are constantly taking in a complete barrage of sensory information, and if we were aware of all of it, all the time, we'd go mad. So, our brain filters the "important" information from the "unimportant" information, like when we don't see a gorilla walking across the screen because we're busy counting ball passes. Sometimes, though, our brain makes guesses about what it thinks should be there, and we're not always privy to these guesses. This is called *top-down processing*. We use our prior knowledge, experience, belief, biases, and

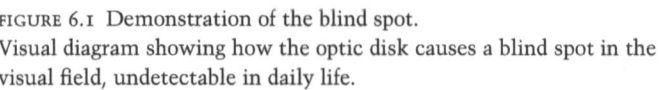

FIGURE 6.1 Demonstration of the blind spot.
Visual diagram showing how the optic disk causes a blind spot in the visual field, undetectable in daily life.

expectations to guide our perception of the world. This can cause us to see things not quite as they are.

Take, for instance, the bisected line in Figure 6.1. Clearly, the line is split into two. But try this: cover your right eye and fix the gaze of your left eye on the circle. Hold this book an inch or two in front of your face. Keeping your gaze on the circle, slowly move the book further from your face. When the book is about six inches from your face (give or take), the bisected line should appear as one. The line is clearly split, but you can't see it. This illusion of missing something that's obviously right in front of you (the bisection) is because we all have a *blind spot* in our eyes. The retina, at the back of the eyeballs, is rich with light-sensitive cells called *rods* and *cones*. Rods and cones are the basis of our vision. And of course, visual information needs to get from the eye to the brain. To accomplish this, rods and cones connect with *bipolar cells*, which in turn connect with *ganglion cells*. Thus, the dendrites and soma of the ganglion cells receive information from bipolar cells, and the long ganglionic axons converge and exit the retina. Recall that neurons propagate their action potentials along the axon. In this case, ganglion axons begin in the retina, and travel all the way to the thalamus, where they terminate. The thalamus (the lateral geniculate nucleus of the thalamus, to be precise) then directs visual information to the primary visual cortex in the occipital lobe. Back in the retina though, there are no rods or cones where the ganglion cells exit the eye. Therefore, there is a portion of each retina that can't detect light, rendering us blind. This is our blind spot. Any light that falls on that region of the retina is invisible to us. Now, we don't walk around with a deleted pixel in our visual fields. Part of the reason for this is that we have two eyes, so one eye can fill in the brain about what the other eye is missing. But when we close one eye, like you did a moment ago, the closed eye can't provide the brain with any visual information. When presented with missing information, the brain does its own confabulation and fills in the gaps with what it thinks should be there. Here, the brain doesn't know that the line is bisected. So it connects it for us.

Another reason we might miss things that are right in front of us is because of the ways our eyes move. Try looking at something off to your left, and, keeping your head still, slowly pan your gaze to the right. You'll find that your vision is sort of jerky. This jerky eye movement is called a *saccade*. Our eyes make saccadic movements to maximize the amount of light we can sense, although this causes us to miss a lot of visual stimuli. When our eyes pass quickly over an object, we only take in a small portion of the light from it, and our brain fills in the rest. In addition to that, light reflecting from objects in our visual fields makes its way to our retinas, but only a small portion of our retina is equipped to let us see that object in detail. Light shining on a region of the retina called the *fovea* is the only time we have decent visual acuity. Any light that shines outside the fovea will not be perceived clearly. You can prove this to yourself by holding a marker (or any small object with a single color, like a crayon or block) to the side of your head, so that it's just outside of your field of vision. Looking straight ahead, slowly move the marker toward the center of your vision. You'll be able to see the marker before you can make out any details, including the color of the marker. This is because the light reflecting from the marker is being projected outside the fovea while the marker is in your peripheral vision. You're unable to detect color or details of objects in the peripheral vision, but you can start making them out as the light from the marker makes its way closer to the fovea. Darting your eyes around, as you do with saccadic eye movements, ensures that more visual information will cross the fovea, but quantity is not quality. The vast majority of our vision is terrible, but we're not aware of that because the brain puts it all together in a seamless picture.

SEEING WHAT'S NOT REALLY THERE

Now you see how there are massive omissions in our perceptions of the world around us, and that we often confabulate to fill in this missing information. Confabulation is based on what we expect to experience. And when you're expecting to see something supernatural and you perceive something ambiguous that you can't make sense of, your brain will probably make up something supernatural.

It can be tough to use controlled experimental techniques to study ghosts, apparitions, and aliens to see if they're science or supernatural. One sneaky way to study the supernatural is to investigate *seemingly* supernatural things – magic tricks. Researchers at Oxford University created their very own magic trick called the Phantom Vanish Trick to measure whether participants "saw" the vanishing illusion. In this trick, a magician pantomimed the actions of presenting an object (holding it for the audience to see, etc.) and then making the object disappear. The trick was that *there was no object* – the magician never held anything in their hand. The magician created the illusion that there was a "phantom" object that was being vanished. In the experiment, each participant watched five silent videos of magic tricks, with the Phantom Vanish Trick as the fifth video. The participants were then asked a series of questions, with the critical question being, "*Please write a description of what was shown in the video. Do your best to describe specific actions and events in the order that they occurred.*"

A whopping 32 percent of descriptions included "seeing" the phantom object. Most of the 32 percent did not report a specific object, but 11 percent did name a specific object from the video. Most of the objects named were congruent with objects that they had seen in previous videos in this experiment (cup, silk scarf, etc.). Some participants described very specific objects and actions. One person even said, "The magician removed a silver coin from the cup and placed it in his hand before making it disappear" (Tompkins et al.,

2016). How can this many people describe in detail something that they "saw," when what they thought they saw never even happened?

The researchers behind this study suggest that the participants' top-down expectations outweighed the bottom-up sensory experience. In other words, the expectation to see an object was stronger than the actual visual information, at least for that 32 percent. Suggestion and expectation go a surprisingly long way in guiding what is perceived. Other studies have demonstrated similar findings. One study tracked the eye movements of participants while they watched a magic trick. In this trick, a magician threw a ball into the air two times, and, on the third throw, the ball disappeared. During each throw, the magician's gaze followed the ball. On the third throw, the magician used sleight of hand to feint throwing the ball which stayed in his hand, even though his facial cues suggested that the ball was thrown in the air. When surveyed, 68 percent of participants "saw" the illusion. The eye-tracking data revealed that, during the real ball tosses, the participants' eyes followed the ball (a type of eye movement called *smooth pursuit*, which is sort of the opposite of saccadic eye movement). On the fake throw, though, the participants had no ball to follow with their eyes, so they looked at the magician's face – *not* the would-be trajectory of the ball. The face of the magician appeared to watch the ball in the air, which gave the suggestion that the ball was in fact thrown. The participants who saw the illusion weren't even looking at the would-be trajectory, even though they thought they were (Kuhn & Land, 2006). This is yet another example of our brain influencing our perception of something that didn't really happen.

The Phantom Vanish Trick study utilized silent videos to avoid the confound of verbal suggestion from the magician. Other studies have used verbal suggestions, rather than visual, to induce expectation. One of my favorite studies was conducted by none other than Richard Wiseman, the same anomalistic psychologist who measured EMF fluctuations in Hampton Court Palace and the South Bridge vaults in Edinburgh. This time, he was interested in psychokinetic metal bending – bending a metal object like a key or spoon with nothing but the power of thought. Bizarre, right? In a typical metal-bending demonstration, the psychic holds the metal object lightly in their hand, making it clear that they are not applying force. To the audience's amazement, the metal bends. Even more bizarre, though, is that there is often an after effect. The psychic places the bent metal on a table and the metal continues to bend. How can this be possible?

Wiseman devised a clever study to test whether simply suggesting that metal is bending would be enough to cause a person to "see" it bend. In this study, participants watched a video of a fake psychic sitting at a table containing several objects. The camera pans in on the psychic's hands. The hands choose a key from the table. After a moment of lightly stroking the key, the key appears to bend. The psychic returns the key to the table, now with an obvious 25° bend in it (in reality, the bend was achieved by sleight of hand). In one condition, participants heard the psychic verbally, but briefly, suggest that the key was still bending after it was returned to the table (the suggestion condition). In the no-suggestion condition, this suggestion was omitted. Everything else about the video was identical between both conditions. Prior to watching the video, all participants filled out questionnaires asking about their belief in the paranormal, and afterward, about their observations of the video of the metal-bending.

Stop reading for just a moment and try to predict the results of this study. What percentage of participants in the suggestion versus no-suggestion condition do you think saw the after effect of the key bending?

Do you have your guess? If you think the participants saw the key bending when it wasn't, you were right. Almost *half* of participants in the suggestion condition were convinced they had seen the key bend when it was sitting on the table. This is compared to the 5 percent who saw the key bend in the no-suggestion condition. It seems that even a small verbal suggestion is enough to make a person believe the suggestion. Unexpectedly, this was *un*related to prior belief in the paranormal. People were equally likely to "see" the spoon bending, regardless of their prior beliefs. "When the key was put on the table the performer ... claimed it was still bending. This was difficult to see but it did appear to bend a little," reported one participant. Or, my favorite, "The key, which had already bent, continued bending without being touched by the performer" (Wiseman & Greening, 2005).

Wiseman has a history of duping his participants for the sake of science. Just how far can suggestion skew a person's perceptions?

In a more recent study, Wiseman used an actor to set up a fake séance. Participants at the séances were told that, for "ethical" purposes, this medium would not attempt to contact the dead but would instead attempt to guide the participants in psychically moving objects in the room. The medium asked the participants to join hands and to focus their energy on a maraca that lay on the table. The maraca rolled across the table and fell to the floor. Next, the medium asked the group to focus their attention on the ball. The ball rose several inches into the air and then fell. Of course, both of these objects had been rigged beforehand and the movement was nothing more than trickery. The medium then asked the group to attempt to psychically move a handbell that was on the table. The handbell remained stationary and the medium made no comment. Finally, the group was asked to levitate the whole table. The table did not levitate, but the medium suggested that it had by using phrases like, "That's good, the table's lifting up now...." To measure experiences, each participant responded to a questionnaire two weeks following the séance.

I'm sure you can see where this is going. Approximately 31 percent of participants incorrectly reported that the table had levitated. Approximately 10 percent incorrectly reported that the handbell had moved. This time, though, there was a positive relationship between prior belief in the paranormal, such that believers were more likely to report incorrect telekinetic movement (Wiseman et al., 2003).

As you have no doubt surmised, our brains can be tricked in ways that affect our perception and this calls into question everything that is in our realities. Sitting at a séance where the table appears to be levitating violates the laws of physics. This evokes massive cognitive dissonance – either your perception is false, or the laws of physics have been violated. Which is it? Researchers have clear evidence that the former is a possibility. To provide support for the latter, we need extraordinary evidence.

EXTRAORDINARY EVIDENCE

Back in the 1800s, hospitals were one of the most dangerous places to be in for a sick person. Doctors shunned handwashing and other forms of hygiene, saying it was unnecessary, even though hospitals were laden with infectious people. Germ theory hadn't yet been established, and the current thinking was that sickness was caused by a dysregulation of the "four humors" of the body (blood, phlegm, yellow bile, black bile), of which the traditional treatment was bloodletting. So, when Dr. Ignaz Semmelweis, a Hungarian physician, suggested that hospital staff wash hands between patients, the idea was met with ridicule and contempt. Semmelweis was ostracized from medical circles. Many physicians felt that their high position in society rendered them pure, and the suggestion that they wash their hands was frankly insulting. Nonetheless, Semmelweis instituted a handwashing policy at his own clinic, and patient mortality plummeted. But even in the face of data that should have been indisputable, Semmelweis's ideas were rejected by the medical community. Over the next two decades, Semmelweis's hygiene policies resulted in the almost eradication of certain infectious diseases in the clinics he worked in, yet his colleagues refused to adopt handwashing techniques. Semmelweis died in 1861, never to see the ultimate acceptance of his radical ideas (Ataman et al., 2013). Over time, more and more medical professionals spoke out about handwashing and hygiene, Florence Nightingale among them, and several ideas were formed to explain the spread of disease. But it wasn't until 1857 when Louis Pasteur presented his work on germ theory to the Academie des Sciences that the idea finally started to take hold (Ataman et al., 2013).

Nowadays, we take for granted that handwashing is one of the best ways to prevent the spread of diseases. But back in Semmelweis's day, when scientific data butted heads with belief, the majority of intelligent, educated, and reputable people chose to defy data and stick with their beliefs.

It seems a bit cliché to use the adage, "Extraordinary claims require extraordinary evidence," but here we are.

Social psychologist Daryl Bem would probably be among the first to agree with this statement. So, when Bem published a paper in 2011 with massively extraordinary claims, it was unsurprising that the scientific community naturally asked him to provide extraordinary evidence. But before I get into Bem's research, I want to discuss an important aspect of publishing scientific papers. In scientific research, we want to have a procedure to check over findings before they're published, to make sure a panel of experts agrees that the methods, analysis, and interpretation of the results are sound. This is called the *peer-review process*, and it is a crucial step in publishing high quality research. When a researcher has conducted a set of experiments and writes up the results, they submit it to a journal in their area of study. The editor of the journal organizes the peer-review. Experts review the manuscript and determine whether it meets the scientific rigor needed for publication. Bem submitted his work to the *Journal of Personality and Social Psychology*, a very well-regarded publication in psychology, published by the American Psychological Association. Bem's controversial paper was published in the 100th volume of the *Journal of Personality and Social Psychology* in 2011 (Bem, 2011).

Bem was a believer in psi, the passage of energy or information between individuals or individuals and their environment. Psi is, of yet, unexplained. In a series of nine studies, Bem claims to have demonstrated extraordinary evidence for the existence of psi. In one study, participants were shown a series of erotic and nonerotic pictures. Before they were shown the pictures, however, they were told to indicate the position (right or left) of the erotic picture. If psi was demonstrated, participants should be able to do this more than by chance. And indeed, psi was demonstrated. Erotic pictures were identified 53.1 percent of the time, across 100 sessions. Nonerotic pictures were only identified about 49.8 percent of the time.

Now, 53.1 percent is just over half. In the paper, Bem took care to explain that, though just over 50 percent, it was significantly higher identifying the erotic photographs by chance alone, and that this was supported by their statistical analyses of the data.

In another study in the same paper, Bem attempted to retroactively prime his participants. *Priming* is a common method in psychological science where subjects are influenced to respond a certain way. For example, when you drove past a billboard for McDonald's this morning you didn't pay much attention to it. But by lunchtime, you are specifically craving a Big Mac, *not* a Whopper. Advertisements rely heavily on priming. So do psychologists. A traditional priming experiment in psychology might look like this: A participant is briefly shown a picture on a screen and is asked to judge whether the picture is pleasant or unpleasant. Just before the picture is shown, a word is flashed (e.g., *beautiful* or *ugly*). If the word is congruent with the picture (e.g., seeing the word *adorable* and then being shown a basket of puppies), response times are faster. In *retroactive* priming, though, in Bem's research, the participant makes a judgment of the picture *before* the word is flashed. Lo and behold, when the word was congruent with the picture, Bem and colleagues recorded faster response times (Bem, 2011).

I think this concept needs to sit and marinate in your brain for a moment. Bem's research suggests that participants were influenced by words flashed on the screen, but the influence occurred before the words were actually flashed.

Still marinating? My students need to marinate for quite a while on this, too. In the words of one of my former students, "No, Dr. Maffeo. Just . . . no."

Not surprisingly, Bem's findings caused quite a stir in the scientific community. The research design and statistical analyses were met with a great deal of scrutiny and criticism. One reason for this is that the types of tests used in Bem's study are very likely to cause Type 1 error. Additionally, the size of the relationships observed in Bem's results was negatively related to the number of participants, possibly indicating that the trials ended when the desired data were collected (Rouder & Morey, 2011; Wagenmakers et al., 2011). Instead, Bem should have determined how many participants and trials were needed to have a satisfactory effect size and run all of the trials to completion. Finally, there have been repeated failed attempts at replicating Bem's findings. In one replication attempt, methods for three of Bem's nine studies were conducted almost exactly as Bem had done them. All three studies failed to replicate, even though the studies they chose to replicate were the ones that showed the strongest relationships and the ones that Bem himself suggested are the most replicable (Ritchie et al., 2012). Bem continues to defend his original dataset.

WHAT'S REALLY IN THE TEA LEAVES?

Uri Geller, a self-proclaimed psychic, is most well-known for his telekinetic spoon-bending ability. Geller claimed he could take a complete, intact, unbent spoon, and, with only the power of his mind, bend the spoon almost in half. Geller appeared regularly on television shows, performing unbelievable psychic feats for the hosts. He could ask people to write down anything they were thinking about, and he would draw it. It was quite amazing. Many people claimed it must be a hoax, but no one could figure out how. To this day, Geller maintains his claims of psychic abilities.

Other magicians, on the other hand, never claim to possess any supernatural abilities. Their magic and illusions are simply the product of sleight of hand, misdirection, suggestion, and knowing how to manipulate the audience's expectations and attention. Magicians like James Randi and Darren Brown work hard to expose fraudulent claims of psychic ability. Fun and games, are, well, fun and games, but sometimes people get hoodwinked into making seriously bad choices. On the one hand, talking to a deceased loved one through a psychic or medium might bring peace or closure. If this is the case, is there any harm done? But on the other hand, a charlatan psychic might reap financial benefits from the grief of others. In the words of John Oliver, "Hold on here. Where is the downside in telling people their grandmother loved them? But I would argue that, at best, it is reckless for a stranger to take a stab at ventriloquizing the dead. Loss is complicated and mourning doesn't look the same for everyone. But at worst, when psychic abilities are presented as authentic, it emboldens a vast underworld of unscrupulous vultures more than happy to make money by offering an open line to the afterlife, as well as many other bullshit services" (Perota et al., 2019).

One of these unscrupulous vultures was a con artist by the name of Rose Marks. Marks and her family ran businesses offering fraudulent psychic services in both New York and Florida. As part of their hoax, Marks told her wealthy clients that their money needed to be "cleansed" to remove any negativity from it. Marks needed to have the money in her account so that she could perform the cleansing ritual. Supposedly, she would return the money to the client after it had been cleansed, but no money was ever returned. Other ridiculous schemes including telling clients that Marks had a psychic gift that was given to her by God, and the client must make a monetary sacrifice to benefit from Marks's gift. Marks also suggested to her clients that they had been cursed in a prior life, and the only way to break the curse was to pay a large sum of money. These poor victims were swindled for *millions* of dollars. In 2011, Marks and her family members were charged with fourteen federal crimes spanning twenty years. Two years later, they were convicted of all fourteen charges. Marks was sentenced to ten years in federal prison.

You can see why magicians like Randi feel the need to publicly debunk psychic services. Randi claims that supernatural abilities don't exist, and therefore none of these people are truly psychic. When Randi publicly debunked the famous Uri Geller, it caused quite a stir. Randi stated publicly that Geller is a fraud, and his so-called magic could be attributed to sleight of hand and other tricks. Randi demonstrated how each trick was done, without any magic at all. For example, spoon bending is an old sleight of hand trick that can be achieved through several methods. One way is to start with three spoons. The magician asks a participant to hold one spoon against their forehead and to tell them when it starts to feel warm. Meanwhile, while all the attention is on the person with a spoon on their forehead, the magician brings the other two spoons together, surreptitiously bending them both at the neck. They can be held together in one hand in a way that makes them appear unbent. Then, the magician turns the spoons, causing them to apparently bend in his hand. Meanwhile, they take the third spoon, bend it with the other hand, while the audience's attention is on the two spoons "bending" in the magician's hand. The magician then takes the supposedly unbent third spoon in both hands, and, with the power of concentration, turns the spoons, seemingly making it bend in their hand. And voila, the magic of spoon bending.

Geller countered all of Randi's accusations and maintained that he was given his psychic ability by extraterrestrials. Geller sued Randi multiple times for slandering and libel, but lost every case. Randi never paid a cent to Geller.

Randi and others have created multiple opportunities for a person to prove their psychic powers. Randi is the founder of the James Randi Educational Foundation, a foundation that encourages intellectual curiosity, critical thought, and healthy skepticism. Randi also sponsored a Million Dollar Challenge for any person who could show concrete evidence of being psychic. Although more than 1,000 people entered the contest, not a single person could prove their abilities. Before his retirement, Randi terminated the contest to use the funds for other intellectual pursuits (Time is running out for paranormal prize, 2008). Randi died on October 20, 2020, and left behind a legacy of debunking pseudoscience.

CONCLUSIONS

So, what's really in the tea leaves? Do some people have psychic abilities to feel the past as well as the future? Do mediums have a direct channel of communication with the dead? Or are psychics and mediums simply adept at reading subtle expressions, directing and misdirecting attention, some sleight of hand, and a lot of charisma?

Let's weigh the evidence. Psychics can conduct hot readings by researching their clients before the session. Psychics can also read their clients' faces and body language extraordinarily well. People, especially believers, give inadvertent clues about the veracity of the psychic's statements. The psychic can use these clues to guide their narrative from broad, Barnum statements to more specific "predictions." I think we can all agree that none of this is supernatural.

And then, there are the perceptions of the client. Because of our tendency to seek out information that supports our beliefs, we are more likely to pay attention to, and thus remember, the statements that seem to be true. If we encounter information that is in discordance with our mental schemas, we can confabulate to ease the discomfort of cognitive dissonance. Finally, suggestion alone carries a lot of power. With mere suggestion, people might see an object that was never there, see a spoon bend or table levitate, when, in reality, none of that is happening. When all of these things happen at once, paired with belief in psychic abilities, it makes a lot of sense why people might walk away from a psychic reading believing it was real. There's a lot of cool psychology here, but still, nothing supernatural.

Finally, we should consider the feelings of the psychic, as well. Like Clever Hans's owner who truly believed his horse could do math, many psychics truly believe they are using precognitive psychic abilities. This belief is probably projected to the client, further supporting the illusion.

At this point, I'll leave it up to you to draw conclusions from the research. Are the tea leaves just tea leaves, or might they reveal our destinies?

REFERENCES

Ataman, A. D., Vatanoğlu-Lutz, E. E., & Yıldırım, G. (2013). Medicine in stamps-Ignaz Semmelweis and puerperal fever. *Journal of the Turkish German Gynecological Association, 14*(1), 35–39. https://doi.org/10.5152/jtgga.2013.08.

Bem, D. J. (2011). Feeling the future: Experimental evidence for anomalous retroactive influences on cognition and affect. *Journal of Personality and Social Psychology, 100*(3), 407–425. https://doi.org/10.1037/a0021524.

Bem, D. J., Utts, J., & Johnson, W. O. (2011). Must psychologists change the way they analyze their data? *Journal of Personality and Social Psychology, 101*(4), 716–719. https://doi.org/10.1037/a0024777.

Daily Horoscope: Pisces. (2024). www.horoscope.com/us/horoscopes/general/horoscope-general-daily-tomorrow.aspx?sign=12&ladate=20240101.

Ekman, Paul, & Friesen, W. V. (1978). Facial Action Coding System. *Facial Action Coding System (FACS) [Database Record].* https://psycnet.apa.org/doiLanding?doi=10.1037%2Ft27734-000.

Centers for Disease Control and Prevention. (2023). www.cdc.gov/nchs/fastats/older-american-health.htm.

Hansen, J. (1998). Common cancers in the elderly. *Drugs & Aging, 13*(6), 467–478. https://doi.org/10.2165/00002512-199813060-00005.

Johansson, P., Hall, L., Sikström, S., & Olsson, A. (2005). Failure to detect mismatches between intention and outcome in a simple decision task. *Science, 310*(5745), 116–119. https://doi.org/10.1126/science.1111709.

Kuhn, G., & Land, M. F. (2006). There's more to magic than meets the eye. *Current Biology, 16*(22), R950–951. https://doi.org/10.1016/j.cub.2006.10.012.

Lindfors, B. (1984). P. T. Barnum and Africa. *Studies in Popular Culture, 7*, 18–27.

Perota, J., Werner, C., Hoskinson, J., Pennolino, P., & Leddy, B. (Directors). (2019, February 24). Last Week Tonight with John Oliver (151). HBO.

Ritchie, S. J., Wiseman, R., & French, C. C. (2012). Failing the future: Three unsuccessful attempts to replicate Bem's 'retroactive facilitation of recall' effect. *PLOS ONE, 7*(3), e33423. https://doi.org/10.1371/journal.pone.0033423.

Rouder, J. N., & Morey, R. D. (2011). A Bayes factor meta-analysis of Bem's ESP claim. *Psychonomic Bulletin & Review, 18*(4), 682–689. https://doi.org/10.3758/s13423-011-0088-7.

Rule, N. O., & Ambady, N. (2008). The face of success: Inferences from chief executive officers' appearance predict company profits. *Psychological Science, 19*(2), 109–111. https://doi.org/10.1111/j.1467-9280.2008.02054.x.

Simons, D. J., & Chabris, C. F. (1999). Gorillas in our midst: Sustained inattentional blindness for dynamic events. *Perception, 28*(9), 1059–1074. https://doi.org/10.1068/p281059.

Simons, D. J., & Chabris, C. F. (2008). Time is running out for paranormal prize. *Nature, 451*(235). www.nature.com/articles/451235e.

Tompkins, M. L., Woods, A. T., & Aimola Davies, A. M. (2016). The phantom vanish magic trick: Investigating the disappearance of a non-existent object in a dynamic scene. *Frontiers in Psychology, 7*, 950. https://doi.org/10.3389/fpsyg.2016.00950.

Wagenmakers, E.-J., Wetzels, R., Borsboom, D., & van der Maas, H. L. J. (2011). Why psychologists must change the way they analyze their data: The case of psi: Comment on Bem (2011). *Journal of Personality and Social Psychology, 100*(3), 426–432. https://doi.org/10.1037/a0022790.

Wiseman, R., & Greening, E. (2005). "It's still bending": Verbal suggestion and alleged psychokinetic ability. *British Journal of Psychology, 96*(1), 115–127. https://doi.org/10.1348/000712604X15428.

Wiseman, R., Greening, E., & Smith, M. (2003). Belief in the paranormal and suggestion in the seance room. *British Journal of Psychology, 94*(3), 285–297. https://doi.org/10.1348/000712603767876235.

7 The Call Is Coming From Inside the House

Rabies, Parasites, and the Truth behind Zombies

Before I graduated to reading Stephen King, I read quite a bit of *Scary Stories to Tell in the Dark*. My favorite story was the one about the babysitter. In the story, a young woman was hired to watch two children while their parents went out. The babysitter fed the children dinner, played with them, and put them to bed before she settled on the sofa to watch TV. Suddenly, the phone rang. On the other end of the line, a distorted voice said, "I'm on my way. I'll be there in 10 minutes." She was a little freaked out, but figured it was probably the dad, with poor service, saying they were on the way home.

The phone rang again. "Five minutes away now."

And again. "I'll be there any minute."

A little panicky, she called the parents of the children. There was no answer. She called the police, who traced the call. "Get out now," the operator said. "The call is coming from inside the house."

Just then, a door on the second floor opened and closed, and heavy footsteps started thudding down the stairs.

This story is a little different than the other scary stories because it is about a totally plausible event – something that is not at all supernatural. In the preceding chapters of this book, we've talked about natural explanations for supernatural occurrences. But there are other things to be afraid of, too. I want to shift gears a little and talk about something that is a real threat, and a danger to every single one of us. That's right. I want to talk about zombies.

Hear me out.

When you think about zombies, you're probably thinking about the reanimated corpses from the *Night of the Living Dead*, which is what most modern zombie lore is based on. Fun fact: *Night of the Living Dead* never used the word zombie. That term was coined later. There is a lot that can be learned about neuroscience and psychology from zombie lore, and I suggest that the interested reader pick up a copy of *Do Zombies Dream of Undead Sheep*, by Timothy Verstynen and Bradley Voytek. It does a fantastic deep dive into the zombie brain, making inferences about zombie neurobiology based on human neuroscience (Verstynen & Voytek, 2014).

Verstynen and Voytek did such a great job diving into the neurobiology of zombies in their book. Instead of trying to out-zombie them (which I never could), I'd like to spend this chapter exploring real-life zombies.

ZOMBI CORPS CADAVRE

In Haitian culture, there is an elusive religion, or more accurately, tradition, that was born out of the mixture of cultures of native Haitians, West African slaves brought to Haiti by Europeans, and even Catholicism (which was also brought by Europeans). Please don't confuse traditional Vodou with the made-up religion of voodoo (McGee, 2012). Vodou is a complex tradition centered upon spiritual healing and ancestry veneration. I'm afraid that if I tried to explain that complexity here, I would not even come close to doing it justice. For the purposes of this book, I'll focus on a sliver of Vodou tradition: zombie lore. According to folk belief, there are two types of zombies. The first is a spirit zombie. To create a spirit zombie, a sorcerer, or bokor, captures part of the soul of his victim. If released, the spirit zombie will wander Earth, but the spirit will forever be under the control of the bokor. The other type of zombie is probably closer to what you think of when you think of a zombie. This type of zombie, the *zombi corps cadavre*, is also the victim of a bokor. Instead of enslaving the spirit, the bokor enslaves the flesh. The bokor reanimates the corpse of his victim and uses it to do his bidding. There are many, many references to *zombi corps cadavre* in Vodou accounts, and, unsurprisingly, they are not substantiated. Because a person cannot raise the dead and control the reanimated corpses for their own malevolent purposes . . . right?

Clairvius Narcisse would beg to differ. On April 30, 1962, Narcisse was admitted to a hospital in west Haiti. On May 2, 1962, Narcisse died. Two physicians and his sister Angelina were present at his death. After her brother died, Angelina contacted the rest of the family. An elder sister arrived, identified Narcisse's body, and affixed her thumbprint to his death certificate. After twenty hours in cold storage, Narcisse was buried. A concrete slab was placed over his grave.

Eighteen years later, Clairvius Narcisse approached Angelina in a crowded marketplace and introduced himself by his childhood nickname. Naturally, Angelina was shocked and didn't immediately believe this person could possibly be her dead brother. But this person knew things that only the real Clairvius Narcisse would have known. The case was examined by a number of reputable people, and it was agreed – this man was indeed Clairvius Narcisse. But what happened to him?

Narcisse remembered his death. He remembered his sister weeping by his bedside and being lowered into his grave. He was fully conscious and aware, but unable to communicate. He also remembered when the bokor opened his grave and reanimated him with magic. The bokor had been hired by Narcisse's brother because of a family land dispute. Upon resurrection, the bokor beat and enslaved Narcisse, forcing Narcisse to work alongside other zombies. For two years he worked, until the bokor was killed and the zombies thus freed. Narcisse, afraid to go home and face his brother, wandered the country for the next sixteen years, only returning home when he heard of the death of his brother.

Before Narcisse, Vodou lore had been just that – lore. Zombies had been lore. Here was a person, in the (undead) flesh, claiming to have died and then been resurrected. Naturally, this garnered some attention. This was the first *documented* case of a Haitian zombie. An ethnobotanist named Wade Davis, at the time a Harvard graduate student, came onto the scene, fascinated by the so-called zombie powder used by the bokor. According to lore, the bokor blew the zombie powder into the face of his victim, or else sprinkled the doorway of the victim's home with the powder. Narcisse, in his interviews, had referenced a powder. Davis was certain that, if this powder existed, he could figure out what it was and solve the peculiar case of Clairvius Narcisse.

Naturally, Davis interviewed Narcisse. Narcisse said that when he died, his flesh felt like it was on fire. After death, he remained fully conscious while in cold storage and while he was being buried. The man claiming to be Narcisse even had a scar on his cheek. Apparently, when the nails were hammered into his coffin, one hit his face. And he again referenced the mysterious powder.

Davis speculated for months on what that zombie powder might be. He examined the flora and fauna native to the region and found some interesting candidate ingredients. One of these ingredients was the psychedelic poison from the skin of the *Bufo marinus* toad. Another came from the flowering plant, *Datura stramonium*, known for its toxic and psychedelic seeds. The problem with these hypotheses, though, is that neither toxin would slow a person's breathing so much that they appeared to be dead.

Finally, Davis gained access to bokor powder from different regions across Haiti. He analyzed the contents and found that the powders varied significantly from region to region ... but some ingredients were common to all the powders. Among these ingredients were human remains, various poison frog and toad species, and, importantly, *pufferfish*.

The pufferfish, and its cousin, the porcupine fish (along with many other marine species) contain a deadly poison called tetrodotoxin. When a person ingests tetrodotoxin, the toxin blocks ion channels on the peripheral nerves, preventing sodium from entering the neuron. When sodium enters a neuron, it generally results in that neuron firing an action potential, the basis of neural communication. When tetrodotoxin is present, say, if a person has come into contact with zombie poison, their neurons would not be able to send any signals to other neurons or muscles. The person couldn't move. Couldn't speak. Couldn't give a sign of life. Breathing and heart rate would be slowed – or stopped. That person could easily appear dead. Or, more likely, *become* dead.

FUGU, WOULD YOU?

Tetrodotoxin is one of the deadliest compounds on the planet, and yet, pufferfish that accumulate it are considered a delicacy in many southeast Asian countries. Tetrodotoxin accumulates in the liver, gonads, and scales of pufferfish and other members of the family Tetraodontiformes. Tetrodotoxin is more than 10,000 times more toxic than cyanide – the amount that would fit on the head of a pin could kill a person. To learn how to prepare pufferfish suitable for consumption, a dish known as fugu, a chef must train for years and pass a rigid test. If you're willing to take the risk, fugu is a coveted delicacy in Asia.

There are between 50–100 cases of tetrodotoxin poisoning in Japan each year, and roughly ten of these are fatal (Hossain, 2024). Many of these cases are from fish prepared by uncertified chefs, or worse, fisherman who catch the fish and attempt to fillet it on their own. Let's say you accidentally took a bite of a pufferfish, ingesting some tetrodotoxin. Your first sign of tetrodotoxin poisoning is paresthesia, or a tingling in the lips. The tingling and burning will spread through your face and soon, you'll start sweating. You'll probably experience gastrointestinal pain with nausea and diarrhea. Your motor neurons become unable to send signals to the muscles and you become paralyzed. If the paralysis spreads to the respiratory muscles, you will stop breathing and death becomes imminent. There is no antidote.

Bokors don't create zombies by serving their victims poorly prepared pufferfish. Instead, the bokor dries and crushes the pufferfish liver into a powder. The powder is mixed with other ingredients, sometimes human remains, sometimes *Datura* or *Bufo*, and various other animals and plants. The psychedelic compounds might help explain why the "corpse" is so suggestible once it has been "resurrected." The bokor then takes this powder and poisons his victim, either by blowing the powder in their face or sprinkling it in the victim's doorway.

Having tetrodotoxin blown in your face will not have the same effects as ingesting it (nor will walking through it). One reason for the discrepancy in effects has to do with the speed at which tetrodotoxin is absorbed into your bloodstream. Another part of it is the varying dose. And this is where the tetrodotoxin story gets a little dicey. Bokors don't exactly have highly precise laboratory scales to weigh out the exact amount of pufferfish liver needed to incapacitate, but not kill, their victims. Ideally, the victim will be fully paralyzed, with respiration and heart rate becoming so slow they appear to have stopped. Even a small accidental overdose would result in a fatality, which would deprive the bokor of a victim, if we believe that zombies are not actually reanimated corpses.

One of the coolest things about tetrodotoxin (besides how deadly it is) is that it is a defensive mechanism used by many species, not just pufferfish. The bizarre part is that the evolutionary arms race has given tetrodotoxin many paths to existence. In the pufferfish, for example, tetrodotoxin is highly concentrated in the liver and gonads (this varies a bit from species to species). Evidence suggests that pufferfish don't make their own tetrodotoxin. Instead, pufferfish accumulate it from tetrodotoxin produced by marine bacteria. We know this because pufferfish that are bred in captivity don't have tetrodotoxin. If they're fed tetrodotoxin, they are protected from its toxic effects *and* they take it up for accumulation in various organs (Noguchi et al., 2006)! But wait, it gets better. Not only do the captive fish start accumulating tetrodotoxin, they also physically grow bigger and have lower levels of stress hormones in their hypothalamus and pituitary gland (Amano et al., 2019). Feeding tetrodotoxin to a pufferfish is a lot like feeding a can of spinach to Popeye. The pufferfish now has a liver-full of tetrodotoxin and seems to say to its predators, "Come at me, bro."

But wait, it *keeps getting better*. Some newt species also have tetrodotoxin – in their skin. The roughskin newt lives along the west coast of the United States and secretes tetrodotoxin from its skin in response to stress. Imagine a snake trying to take a bite of a newt. Maybe the snake was able to grab a bit of the newt's tail, only to get a mouthful of tetrodotoxin. The snake dies, and the newt tail regenerates. Defense against predation, indeed. Recent research has shown that, unlike pufferfish, roughskin newts produce their own tetrodotoxin rather than taking it from their environment (Cardall et al., 2004; Hanifin et al.,

2002). And what about the snake? One of the main predators of the roughskin newt is the garter snake. Much like the newt evolved to produce a toxin to protect against predation, the garter snake has evolved tetrodotoxin-resistant sodium channels to protect itself from dangerous prey. The newt and the snake have both evolved survival mechanisms because of selective pressures of their environment – the need to eat, and the need to not be eaten. Coevolution like this is called *functional trait matching*. In regions of the country where newts produce high levels of tetrodotoxin, garter snakes have higher tetrodotoxin resistance. In parts of the country where the newts are less toxic, the snakes are less resistant (Reimche et al., 2020).

Tetrodotoxin is clearly an adaptive defense that newts have against predators. Amazingly, tetrodotoxin also protects newts from some infections. Tetrodotoxin varies widely among species of newts, and, as it turns out, tetrodotoxin negatively correlates with parasite infection. In other words, the animals with the lowest levels of tetrodotoxin in their skin had the highest parasite load. Not only are the high tetrodotoxin newts more toxic to snakes, the tetrodotoxin seems to help protect the newt against parasite infection. Evolution doesn't happen in a vacuum, and species depend on each other for survival.

RABIE, BABY

In Chapter 1, we talked about the use of horror fiction as mental preparation for real-life events. During the beginning months of the COVID-19 pandemic, for example, the movie *Contagion* was one of the most watched films, despite it being released almost ten years prior (Mack, 2020). In the movie, a deadly virus originates in Hong Kong. This highly contagious virus contained genetic material from pig- and bat-borne viruses and mutated to become zoonotic – it had the ability to pass from animal to human hosts. It spread rapidly through respiratory droplets, quickly turning into a global pandemic, killing millions of people worldwide. In March of 2020, the plot of *Contagion* was all too familiar. Some people, especially the morbidly curious like you and me, used fictional situations to mentally prepare for our real-life pandemic (Scrivner, 2021).

Lucky for us, coronaviruses aren't typically behavior-modifying. Let's take, for example, the plot of another pandemic thriller. In the 2002 movie, *28 Days Later*, a fictional "rage" virus travels from an infected chimpanzee to a human host. Immediately upon infection, the host becomes incredibly violent and either infects or kills anyone in their path. This is the classic zombie apocalypse premise, and it may be nearer than we think. The CDC urges citizens to have a plan for escape and survival, should a deadly pathogen spread throughout the world. The CDC went as far as creating a zombie apocalypse survival guide intended to help train leaders in the case of a crisis (Centers for Disease Control and Prevention, 2011; United States Strategic Command, 2011). The CDC probably intended to be a little tongue-in-cheek with the creation of these documents, but they also want us to bear in mind that there are deadly pathogens in the world, those pathogens do mutate, and we can't predict what's coming.

In the science versus supernatural conversation, a zombie apocalypse may *seem* supernatural. Unfortunately, a rage virus is very real. And it's called rabies.

The rabies virus is a virus in the genus Lyssavirus (after the Greek goddess of rage and madness, Lyssa). Rabies is believed to have been around for thousands of years, based on ancient writings about animals suddenly becoming aggressive, salivating, and biting (Tarantola, 2017). The behavioral effects were terrifyingly shown in Stephen King's *Cujo*, where a very cute St. Bernard dog was bitten by an infected bat and became aggressive, killing his human family and terrorizing a woman and small boy. Many iterations of zombie lore have been based on the strange behavioral effects of rabies. The sequence is identical – a victim is bitten and contracts the pathogen. After a short incubation period, the person begins to exhibit symptoms. The infected person becomes angry and aggressive and tries to bite other potential victims. The pathogen is thus spread from host to host through the saliva. Rabies is almost always fatal.

So how does rabies turn a cute dog into a killing machine who is hell-bent on biting as many other animals as possible? Glad you asked.

As we've already mentioned, rabies is transmitted from the saliva of an infected host. If a bite occurs, the virus-laden saliva will spread through the wound and the virus now has a pathway into the bloodstream. In the bloodstream, the virus will be carried to the nearest neuromuscular junction. This is the synapse between a motor neuron leaving the central nervous system and the muscle fiber that the motor neuron sends signals to. Motor neurons communicate with muscle fibers using the neurotransmitter *acetylcholine*. The muscle fiber contains a specific receptor for acetylcholine called the *nicotinic acetylcholine receptor*, or nAChr (this receptor is named for the first substance found to bind to it – nicotine). When acetylcholine is released from the motor neuron and binds to the receptor on the muscle, the receptor changes shape and opens the ion channel, allowing sodium ions to flow into the muscle. This triggers contraction of the muscle.

When the rabies virus arrives at the neuromuscular junction, it is taken up into the muscle fibers via nAChrs. Now the virus begins its first phase of replication – amplifying itself and preparing to invade the central nervous system. The water becomes murky here, though, because it's not entirely clear how the virus ultimately achieves neuroinvasion. The virus probably leaves the muscle fiber in a process called *exocytosis*, which is pretty much the cell spitting the virus out. Once in the cytoplasm, the virus enters the peripheral motor neuron through some sort of endocytosis, but this mechanism is not well understood. Rabies is sneaky, and it's in cahoots with one or more proteins that help it sneak its way into the neuron. The virus is now in the terminal of the neuron, but it has a problem. The environment in the terminal isn't a suitable place for replication, so the virus needs to find its way to the soma, which will take it to the central nervous system. So, the virus hitches a ride on endosomes that travel up the long axon toward the cell body of the neuron. This transport moves about 8–20 mm per day. Depending on the location of the bite (say, foot vs. shoulder), entrance in the central nervous system might be a few days or a few weeks (Lippi & Cervellin, 2021; Schnell et al., 2010). Remember that motor neurons connect the spinal cord to your muscles. If you're a tall person and a rabid dog has bitten your toe,

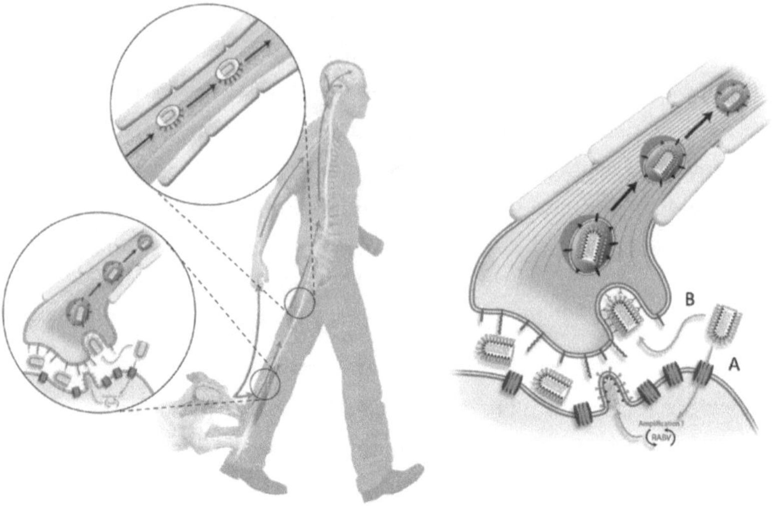

FIGURE 7.1 Process of rabies transmission from an infected animal bite to the leg. The virus enters the muscle at the site of the bite, and, by an unknown mechanism, enters the motor neuron terminal at the neuromuscular junction. The virus is then transported up the motor neuron axon toward and eventually enters the central nervous system. *Source*: Davis, B. M., Rall, G. F., & Schnell, M. J. (2015). Everything You Always Wanted to Know About Rabies Virus (But Were Afraid to Ask). Annual review of virology, 2(1), 451–471. https://doi-org.wake.idm.oclc.org/10.1146/annurev-virology-100114-055157

the virus must travel the distance from your toe to spinal cord, which could be a few feet. This process is depicted in Figure 7.1.

So here we have the rabies virus, secretly hitchhiking toward the soma of the peripheral motor neuron. Now in the spinal cord, the virus can invade a neuron in the central nervous system. And another. And another. But the virus is careful not to leave too much of a trace – it doesn't cause any major damage to neurons. Markers of neuronal damage would trigger an immune response in the host, potentially halting the virus in action before it has sufficiently spread (Schnell et al., 2010). So, the virus tiptoes past the immune system, quietly making more and more copies of itself with the goal of replicating so much that it spreads to another host. The zombification has begun.

The onset of clinical symptoms occurs when the virus invades the central nervous system, roughly 2–10 days after the bite. Rabies manifests itself in different ways. A rabies infection can either be "furious" (80 percent of cases; these are classical rabies symptoms, like aggression) or "paralytic" (the host becomes immobile). It is not clear why some hosts become furious and some become paralytic. Researchers observe that one strain of the virus can result in either manifestation of the disease. In a case study, two humans were bitten by the same rabid dog. One person developed furious rabies and the other developed paralytic rabies. Both died (Davis et al., 2015; Lippi & Cervellin, 2021).

In the central nervous system rabies continues to infect as many neurons as it can. Again, it's not clear how rabies interacts with neurons. Rabies probably acts like many snake venoms, that is, it interacts with nAChrs in the brain (Hueffer et al., 2017). Somehow the virus takes over the host's behaviors, making them irritable, aggressive, hyperactive, and, interestingly, hydrophobic – fearful of water. The host will die within a week of the virus arriving at the central nervous system.

Why would hydrophobia be advantageous for a virus infecting the brain? As the virus spreads throughout the central nervous system, it can move to other systems in the body. Rabies accumulates in the salivary glands, and as it does, stimulates the glands to overproduce saliva (remember Cujo foaming at the mouth?). Most animals are prone to biting when they become aggressive. Since the rabies virus is concentrated in the saliva, biting is a highly effective method of transmission. But, if the host had water in its mouth, the viral concentration would be diluted, decreasing the likelihood of transmission. How can rabies ensure the host doesn't get water in their mouth? By making them fear water.

Human-to-human rabies transmission is rare. Rabies is almost never transmitted by a human bite, with one possible exception. There was a case of human rabies in Ethiopia in the early 1990s. The victims were a forty-one-year-old woman and a five-year-old boy. The mother claimed that the boy bit her on the fingertip, although she never sought medical treatment. This bite is the most likely method of transmission from child to mother (Fekadu et al., 1996). Of course, the two could have shared a toothbrush, thus exchanging saliva, although this is unlikely. Rabies cannot live outside a host for very long, and if infected saliva were ingested, the virus would likely die before it had an opportunity to infect skeletal muscles or motor neurons.

Other methods of human-to-human transmission, like blood-borne transmission, are incredibly uncommon. Interestingly, there have been rare and anecdotal accounts of human-to-human transmission through sex (Gongal et al., 2012). So, if you start a love affair with a zombie, please use protection!

If there was documented human-to-human rabies transmission via a bite, that would be clear evidence of zombies. At the time of this writing, this method of transmission is highly unlikely. But if the virus were to mutate? What then? The rabies virus has clearly adapted to its environment quite well. What if humans were to become the ideal host for viral replication, and the virus mutates in a way to

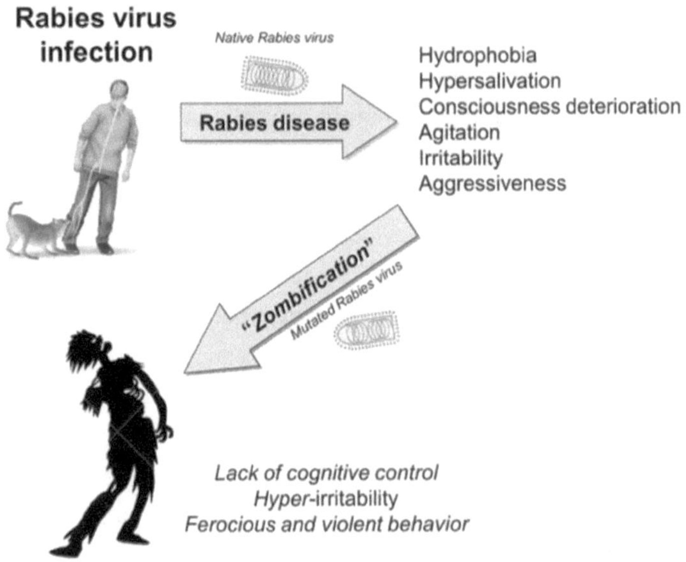

FIGURE 7.2 Rabies versus zombies.
Clinical similarities between rabies disease and zombification.
Source: Figure adapted from Lippi & Cervellin (2021), "Rabies: Still a challenge for the emergency physician?" Acta Biomed, 92(1), e2021045.

ensure more human infections occur? That could be a faster incubation time, higher aggression, and perhaps increased hunger to promote biting behavior. It could even look like longer survival time for the host – more time to bite people and spread the disease. The two conditions are rife with similarities, as illustrated in Figure 7.2.

THE CASE OF THE FEARLESS RAT

Zombie lore is rich with types of pathogens and modes of transmission that produce zombie symptoms. What all the lore has in common is the ability of the pathogen to control the behavior of its host in ways that maximize spread of the pathogen. Different pathogens achieve this by different means, and I think the argument for the rabies virus as a potential zombie pathogen is compelling. But, when it comes to zombie pathogens, there are more than just rabies. What if I told you that a tiny protozoan could infect the brain of the host, compelling that host to fearlessly approach its worst predator, to walk into almost certain death?

Let me introduce you to a little parasitic protozoan called *Toxoplasma gondii*. We'll call it 'Toxo' for short. Toxo is associated with the infection toxoplasmosis in its host, which infects about a third of the world's population. Toxoplasmosis affects about 11 percent of the population of the United States, which is low compared to other regions of the world (Centers for Disease Control and Prevention, 2019). Most human hosts to Toxo are asymptomatic and the infection doesn't do much harm. For some vulnerable populations, though, like immunocompromised individuals and developing fetuses, toxoplasmosis can be devastating. Humans can become infected with Toxo by eating infected food like undercooked meat or unpasteurized milk, but zoonotic transmission is the most common cause of human infection. Now is the time to give the side-eye to your cat, because it just might pass some Toxo on to you.

Cats play a huge role in the zoonotic transmission of toxo. Cats are the definitive hosts of Toxo, meaning that Toxo can *only* reproduce when infecting a cat, specifically in the gastrointestinal (GI) tract. The thing about GI tracts is that they are generally unidirectional. Whatever is in the GI tract tends to turn to fecal matter, and infected cats can poop out millions and millions of Toxo oocytes for weeks after an infection. The oocytes then progress to the next cycle of their life, where they become infectious. These infectious oocytes persist wherever the cat pooped – the litter box, the garden, the sandbox, etc. And the infectious oocytes can persist for a long time – weeks or months, even up to a year after being defecated. At some point, an animal will come into contact with the Toxo – eating some soil or a vegetable from the garden or drinking contaminated water. The issue for Toxo is that, while it can replicate itself asexually in intermediate hosts (like rats), it can only produce gametes and reproduce sexually, releasing oocytes, in the definitive host – the feline (Dubey, 2007). So Toxo needs to find a way to get from the rat to the cat.

Now inside the intestines of the rat, Toxo is transported across endothelial cells into the bloodstream, which causes an immune response in the rat. This should stop Toxo in its tracks, but Toxo has a plan. Toxo can infect immune cells like monocytes which then transport Toxo to the primary sites of infection – the skeletal muscles and the brain (Wohlfert et al., 2017). It makes sense for Toxo to accumulate in the skeletal muscle. If that rat becomes prey for a cat, it's most likely that the cat will preferentially eat the muscles over other tissue. But why the brain?

To eat the Toxo-laden muscles, the cat must first catch the rat. And Toxo *wants* to be eaten by the cat, so, it makes a few neural tweaks so that the rat is a little easier to catch. This adaptive behavioral manipulation on the part of the parasite is a powerful way to increase the chances that its intermediate host (the rat) gets eaten by the definitive host (the cat), with the goal of giving Toxo the best chances of sexual reproduction.

In the brain, Toxo interacts with proteins that ultimately increase excitatory neural signaling and decrease inhibitory neural signaling. Specifically, Toxo lowers the ability of a presynaptic neuron to take up excess glutamate (an excitatory neurotransmitter), thus causing an abundance of glutamate in the synaptic cleft. The abundance of glutamate will continually produce excitation in the postsynaptic cell. Similarly, Toxo decreases the ability of the presynaptic cell to produce GABA (an inhibitory neurotransmitter; Wohlfert et al., 2017). This causes increased activation in brain areas that are infected with Toxo.

So, what does all this mean? Well, in short, Toxo causes rats to demonstrate lower levels of fear and anxiety, making it less likely to run and hide when a cat comes along. But Toxo doesn't stop there. It increases activity in sexual areas of the rat brain, causing the rat to not only stop avoiding, but to actually *seek out* the cat (Berdoy et al., 2000; House et al., 2011; Vyas et al., 2007). Toxo does this through its spread through the limbic areas of the brain. The limbic areas are important for survival behaviors like defensiveness and sexual reproduction, as well as for various aspects of learning, memory, and emotion. Healthy rodents have an innate defensive response to the odor of cat urine. This is true even for rodents who have been raised in captivity and never experienced a cat or smelled cat urine. This is a highly conserved evolutionary response, since the cat is a natural predator of the rat.

Healthy male rats exposed to a sexually receptive female rat generally show increased brain activity in areas important for sexual behavior, like the medial amygdala. They also decrease activity in brain areas important for defensive behaviors, like the ventromedial hypothalamus. When male rats are infected with Toxo and then exposed to cat urine, they act as if they had been exposed to a sexually receptive female rat. That is, the medial amygdala and other "reproductive" structures in the limbic system increase activity in the same way for both cat urine and a female rat (House et al., 2011). Presumably, this leads to a fatal attraction of the rat to the cat. Here's the really messed up part, though. The rodent's lack of aversion to dangerous stimuli is *feline-specific*. Toxo infection does not decrease fear-learning, anxiety-like behavior, olfaction, or other forms of learning in rats (Vyas et al., 2007).

Toxo can therefore trigger a costly behavioral change – it causes the intermediate host to sacrifice itself to the definitive host, so that Toxo can replicate. As noted, this has been well-studied in rodents, but there is evidence of behavioral modification in other intermediate hosts, as well. Hyena cubs infected with Toxo approach lions more often and have higher lion-related mortality (Gering et al., 2021). Another study evaluated behavioral changes in gray wolves living in Yellowstone National Park. Wolves whose territories overlap with a definitive host (cougars, in this case) had a higher incidence of Toxo infection. Moreover, infected wolves were more likely to engage in risky behaviors like dispersing from their pack or becoming leaders of their pack (increasing their position on a dominance hierarchy). Toxo can also affect the behavior of primate species (Meyer et al., 2022). In one study, researchers infected chimpanzees with Toxo and measured the chimps' behavior toward urine of various species. The infected chimps investigated human, tiger, and leopard urine more than uninfected chimps, and spent more time approaching the leopard urine. Why would the chimps be more drawn to the leopard urine than the tiger urine? Well, chimps and tigers occupy separate geographic locations, therefore, a chimp is unlikely to encounter a tiger in the wild. Toxo can manipulate the brain of the chimp so strategically that it causes the chimp to prefer the scent of a predator that it has a higher likelihood of encountering (Poirotte et al., 2016).

Toxoplasma gondii clearly alters the behavior of many species of intermediate hosts. We know that up to a third of the word's human population can be infected with toxo. The next question is: What does Toxo do to humans?

The good news is that the majority of people who are infected with Toxo will be asymptomatic. For vulnerable populations like immunocompromised individuals and developing fetuses, toxoplasmosis infections can have devastating and permanent effects. At-risk people should take care when handling raw meat, gardening, and cleaning litter boxes.

It remains unclear what Toxo does in the brain of a healthy adult human. There is some research that suggests that Toxo is related to different personality profiles, like lower novelty seeking and lower impulsiveness. Toxo may cause an infected individual to have slower reaction times, and people with Toxo infections were more likely to be the cause of a car accident (Flegr et al., 2002, 2003; Havlícek et al., 2001). I know you're probably wondering whether you've been infected with Toxo, and if it has in any way shaped your relationship with your feline friend at home. And the answer is – maybe. One study gave various urine samples (feline among them) to humans with or without a Toxo infection and asked them to rate the pleasantness of the odor. Infected men rated cat urine as more attractive than did noninfected men. Interestingly, infected women rated cat urine as *less* pleasant than noninfected women, again, with little difference in ratings non-feline urine (Flegr et al., 2011).

IT'S A SCIENCE THING

So. Are zombies science, or supernatural?

At the time of this writing, outbreaks like the ones seen in *Night of the Living Dead, 28 Days Later, I am Legend,* and others have not occurred, although the CDC encourages us to be prepared for a devastating pandemic. Preparing for a pandemic (zombie or otherwise) is a prudent behavior that can help ensure survival. The COVID-19 pandemic is one that likely comes to mind for many readers. The early days of the pandemic were horribly uncertain. We didn't know how easily the virus spread or how dangerous it was. We stayed indoors and wiped down our groceries and mail. Victims of this coronavirus didn't exhibit behavioral changes like the ones described in this chapter, but the devastation was nevertheless profound. Preparing ourselves for uncertain situations like this can protect us in the long run.

There are pathogens in this world that modify the behavior of the host to ensure its own transmission and survival. We've discussed the rabies virus and the *Toxoplasma gondii* parasitic protozoan, but there are many behavior-modifying pathogens out there. These include other viruses, bacteria, even fungi. Currently, humans are not drastically affected by any of these pathogens, but what if the pathogens were to mutate? If the pathogen triggered self-destructive or aggressive behavior in its human hosts? Are we ready to face a very real zombie pandemic?

Throughout this book, I've argued that things that seem to be supernatural may be products of our own suggestable and mutable mind. This time, though, I will argue that zombies are very real unimagined potential threats.

Get those rabies shots.

REFERENCES

Amano, M., Amiya, N., Takaoka, M., Sato, H., Takatani, T., Arakawa, O., & Sakakura, Y. (2019). Tetrodotoxin functions as a stress relieving substance in juvenile tiger puffer Takifugu rubripes. *Toxicon, 171*, 54–61. https://doi.org/10.1016/j.toxicon.2019.09.024.

Berdoy, M., Webster, J. P., & Macdonald, D. W. (2000). Fatal attraction in rats infected with Toxoplasma gondii. *Proceedings of the Royal Society B: Biological Sciences, 267*(1452), 1591–1594. https://doi.org/10.1098/rspb.2000.1182.

Cardall, B. L., Brodie, E. D. Jr., Brodie, E. D. III, & Hanifin, C. T. (2004). Secretion and regeneration of tetrodotoxin in the rough-skin newt (Taricha granulosa). *Toxicon, 44*(8), 933–938. https://doi.org/10.1016/j.toxicon.2004.09.006.

Centers for Disease Control and Prevention. (2011). Preparedness 101: Zombie Pandemic. Retrieved January 23, 2024 from https://stacks.cdc.gov/view/cdc/6023.

Centers for Disease Control and Prevention. (2019, February 28). Toxoplasmosis—Epidemiology & Risk Factors. www.cdc.gov/parasites/toxoplasmosis/epi.html.

Davis, B. M., Rall, G. F., & Schnell, M. J. (2015). Everything you always wanted to know about rabies virus (but were afraid to ask). *Annual Review of Virology, 2*(1), 451–471. https://doi.org/10.1146/annurev-virology-100114-055157.

Dubey, J. P. (2007). 1—The history and life cycle of Toxoplasma gondii. In L. M. Weiss & K. Kim (Eds.), *Toxoplasma Gondii* (pp. 1–17). London: Academic Press. https://doi.org/10.1016/B978-012369542-0/50003-9.

Fekadu, M., Endeshaw, T., Alemu, W., Bogale, Y., Teshager, T., & Olson, J. G. (1996). Possible human-to-human transmission of rabies in Ethiopia. *Ethiopian Medical Journal, 34*(2), 123–127.

Flegr, J., Havlícek, J., Kodym, P., Malý, M., & Smahel, Z. (2002). Increased risk of traffic accidents in subjects with latent toxoplasmosis: A retrospective case-control study. *BMC Infectious Diseases*, *2*, 11. https://doi.org/10.1186/1471-2334-2-11.

Flegr, J., Lenochová, P., Hodný, Z., & Vondrová, M. (2011). Fatal attraction phenomenon in humans – Cat odour attractiveness increased for Toxoplasma-infected men while decreased for infected women. *PLoS Neglected Tropical Diseases*, *5*(11), e1389. https://doi.org/10.1371/journal.pntd.0001389.

Flegr, J., Preiss, M., Klose, J., Havlícek, J., Vitáková, M., & Kodym, P. (2003). Decreased level of psychobiological factor novelty seeking and lower intelligence in men latently infected with the protozoan parasite Toxoplasma gondii Dopamine, a missing link between schizophrenia and toxoplasmosis? *Biological Psychology*, *63*(3), 253–268. https://doi.org/10.1016/s0301-0511(03)00075-9.

Gering, E., Laubach, Z. M., Weber, P. S. D., Soboll Hussey, G., Lehmann, K. D. S., Montgomery, T. M., Turner, J. W., Perng, W., Pioon, M. O., Holekamp, K. E., & Getty, T. (2021). Toxoplasma gondii infections are associated with costly boldness toward felids in a wild host. *Nature Communications*, *121*, 3842. https://doi.org/10.1038/s41467-021-24092-x.

Gongal, G., Mudhusudana, S. M., Sudarshan, M. K., Mahendra, B. J., Hemachudha, T., & Wilde, H. (2012). Commentary. What is the risk of rabies transmission from patients to health care staff? *Asian Biomedicine*, *6*(6), 937–939.

Hanifin, C. T., Brodie, E. D. Jr., & Brodie, E. D. III. (2002). Tetrodotoxin levels of the rough-skin newt, Taricha granulosa, increase in long-term captivity. *Toxicon*, *40*(8), 1149–1153. https://doi.org/10.1016/S0041-0101(02)00115-0.

Havlícek, J., Gasová, Z. G., Smith, A. P., Zvára, K., & Flegr, J. (2001). Decrease of psychomotor performance in subjects with latent "asymptomatic" toxoplasmosis. *Parasitology*, *122*(5), 515–520. https://doi.org/10.1017/s0031182001007624.

Hossain, Z. (2024). Pseudomonas. In G. W. Smithers (Ed.), *Encyclopedia of Food Safety* (2nd ed., pp. 236–251). London: Academic Press. https://doi.org/10.1016/B978-0-12-822521-9.00257-4.

House, P. K., Vyas, A., & Sapolsky, R. (2011). Predator cat odors activate sexual arousal pathways in brains of Toxoplasma gondii infected rats. *PloS One*, *6*(8), e23277. https://doi.org/10.1371/journal.pone.0023277.

Hueffer, K., Khatri, S., Rideout, S., Harris, M. B., Papke, R. L., Stokes, C., & Schulte, M. K. (2017). Rabies virus modifies host behaviour through a snake-toxin like region of its glycoprotein that inhibits neurotransmitter receptors in the CNS. *Scientific Reports*, *7*(1), 12818. https://doi.org/10.1038/s41598-017-12726-4.

Lippi, G., & Cervellin, G. (2021). Updates on Rabies virus disease: Is evolution toward "Zombie virus" a tangible threat? *Acta Bio Medica: Atenei Parmensis*, *92*(1), e2021045. https://doi.org/10.23750/abm.v92i1.9153.

Mack, D. (2020, March 3). Everyone Is Watching "Contagion," A 9-Year-Old Movie About A Flu Outbreak. *BuzzFeed*. www.buzzfeednews.com/article/davidmack/contagion-movie-coronavirus.

McGee, A. M. (2012). Haitian Vodou and voodoo: Imagined religion and popular culture. *Studies in Religion/Sciences Religieuses*, *41*(2), 231–256. https://doi.org/10.1177/0008429812441311.

Meyer, C. J., Cassidy, K. A., Stahler, E. E., Brandell, E. E., Anton, C. B., Stahler, D. R., & Smith, D. W. (2022). Parasitic infection increases risk-taking in a social, intermediate host carnivore. *Communications Biology*, *5*(1), 1180. https://doi.org/10.1038/s42003-022-04122-0.

Noguchi, T., Arakawa, O., & Takatani, T. (2006). Toxicity of pufferfish Takifugu rubripes cultured in netcages at sea or aquaria on land. *Comparative Biochemistry and Physiology Part D: Genomics & Proteomics*, *1*(1), 153–157. https://doi.org/10.1016/j.cbd.2005.11.003.

Poirotte, C., Kappeler, P. M., Ngoubangoye, B., Bourgeois, S., Moussodji, M., & Charpentier, M. J. E. (2016). Morbid attraction to leopard urine in Toxoplasma-infected chimpanzees. *Current Biology*, *26*(3), R98–R99. https://doi.org/10.1016/j.cub.2015.12.020.

Reimche, J. S., Brodie, E. D. Jr., Stokes, A. N., Ely, E. J., Moniz, H. A., Thill, V. L., Hallas, J. M., Pfrender, M. E., Brodie, E. D. III, & Feldman, C. R. (2020). The geographic mosaic in parallel: Matching patterns of newt tetrodotoxin levels and snake resistance in multiple predator-prey pairs. *The Journal of Animal Ecology*, *89*(7), 1645–1657. https://doi.org/10.1111/1365-2656.13212.

Schnell, M. J., McGettigan, J. P., Wirblich, C., & Papaneri, A. (2010). The cell biology of rabies virus: Using stealth to reach the brain. *Nature Reviews Microbiology*, *8*(1), 51–61. https://doi.org/10.1038/nrmicro2260.

Scrivner, C. (2021). An infectious curiosity: Morbid curiosity and media preferences during a pandemic. *Evolutionary Studies in Imaginative Culture*, *5*(1), 1–12. https://doi.org/10.26613/esic.5.1.206.

Tarantola, A. (2017). Four thousand years of concepts relating to rabies in animals and humans, its prevention and its cure. *Tropical Medicine and Infectious Disease*, *2*(2), 5. https://doi.org/10.3390/tropicalmed2020005.

United States Strategic Command. (2011, April 30). CDRUSSTRATCOM CONPLAN 8888-11: Counter-Zombie Dominance. https://i2.cdn.turner.com/cnn/2014/images/05/16/dod.zombie.apocalypse.plan.pdf.

Verstynen, T., & Voytek, B. (2014). *Do Zombies Dream of Undead Sheep? A Neuroscientific View of the Zombie Brain*. Princeton: Princeton University Press.

Vyas, A., Kim, S.-K., Giacomini, N., Boothroyd, J. C., & Sapolsky, R. M. (2007). Behavioral changes induced by Toxoplasma infection of rodents are highly specific to aversion of cat odors. *Proceedings of the National Academy of Sciences, 104*(15), 6442–6447. https://doi.org/10.1073/pnas.0608310104.

Wohlfert, E. A., Blader, I. J., & Wilson, E. H. (2017). Brains and brawn: Toxoplasma infections of the central nervous system and skeletal muscle. *Trends in Parasitology*, 33(7), 519–531. https://doi.org/10.1016/j.pt.2017.04.001.

8 Your Brain on Infinity

Psychedelics, Mystical Experiences, and Altered States of Consciousness

"Blessings on your journey," Morgan whispered to me as the effects of the ayahuasca began to set in. We were sitting in a large circle with about fifteen other participants in the small lakeside town of San Marcos, Guatemala. We were in a large dome ivory tent under the shade of an enormous jocote tree (a tree with which two participants later described making love to during the night) in the manicured yard of Jaya's family home. On that warm night in December, I sat with a group of strangers chanting and singing. We were together, but on our own journeys.

Psychedelic drugs, like ayahuasca, have the power to induce profound mystical experiences in their users. Some believe that these substances allow people to cross from the natural to supernatural – that they let us communicate with God. Others say that the drugs enable us to be one with the universe, find answers from a higher power, or invoke wisdom from the divine to help us uncover truths within ourselves. For thousands of years, people have called upon psychedelics to bridge the divide between humanity and the cosmos. Are these mystical effects supernatural, or are users tapping into feelings of universal truth from a plant-induced shift in brain chemistry?

Some also argue that psychedelic drugs are not "drugs" at all, at least not in the abused sense. Most drugs of abuse are often taken in higher quantities than intended, can lead to tolerance and dependence, and produce dysphoric withdrawal symptoms as they leave the body. Psychedelic drugs do none of these things.[1] Moreover,

[1] Psychedelics can cause acute tolerance. In cases of acute tolerance, a single dose of the drug reduces the effectiveness of subsequent doses of the drug, such that multiple

psychedelic drugs are not self-administered by animals in laboratory settings, suggesting they don't cause the same euphoric effects of classically abused drugs (Johnson et al., 2018, 2019).

To emphasize this difference, the psychedelic community coined the term *entheogen* to distinguish psychedelics from recreational or addictive drugs. The term suggests that psychedelics can bring about transcendence, spirituality, and insight. The word entheogen carries mysticism in its roots – it derives from the Greek *enthos*, meaning "full of God," and *genestai*, meaning "come into being." While psychedelic communities have embraced this term, it has not yet gained widespread use in scientific literature. For clarity and consistency, I will continue to use the term *psychedelic* throughout this book.

PLANT-BASED MEDICINE

In Central and South America, psychedelic plants are used as sacraments in spiritual ceremonies to facilitate the deliverance of guidance, enlightenment, and connectedness from the divine. In traditional ayahauasca ceremonies, an ayahuasquero prepares a tea from the vines of the *Banisteriopsis caapi* plant and the leaves of the *Psychotria viridis* shrub. The latter plant contains the chemical N,N-Dimethyltryptamine (DMT), a powerful hallucinogen. DMT should sound familiar to readers. There is a popular, but largely unsupported, theory that DMT is released in our brain moments before death and causes the so-called near-death experience. Exogenous DMT certainly brings about intense psychedelic experiences. However, DMT is rapidly metabolized by the enzyme monoamine oxidase, and it is thus active in the human body for only a very short time. Ayahuasca also contains the *Banisteriopsis* vine, which

doses taken in a short time frame will have little to no effect (de la Fuente Revenga et al., 2022). This diminishes the abuse potential of psychedelics, as it is essentially impossible to binge on them. The probable mechanism of this is a rapid downregulation of the $5HT_{2A}$ receptor after acute psychedelic treatment (Nichols & Nichols, 2008).

contains a monoamine oxidase inhibitor. Thus, when ayahuasca tea is drunk, the psychedelic experience can last for hours.

When I drank the ayahuasca ("Its best to drink it quickly," Jaya had said), I found the taste to be unpleasant and vaguely familiar. Unsure of what to expect, I took a seat on an empty mat near Morgan, pulled the blanket up to my chest, and waited for Mother Ayahuasca to make her appearance. Early research on psychedelics showed that the user's state of mind and expectations, as well as physical setting, are of paramount importance in predicting a positive experience (Hartogsohn, 2017; Stevenson, 1966). Jaya had clearly gone to great lengths to create a relaxing and inviting set and setting. The space was comfortable and everyone in the group was kind. "Trust, and let go," I whispered to myself, not for the last time that night.

Very suddenly, I felt a new and tingling sensation in my scalp and head, like pins and needles. This feeling quickly engulfed my whole body, including my stomach. Emesis is a common side effect of ayahuasca, and even though I knew this beforehand, it didn't make it any less awful. I could feel my mouth begin to water in the way it only does before vomiting. I sat straighter, closed my eyes, and breathed slowly. After a few minutes, the feeling passed. My body felt warmer. What came next happened in waves – a weird sensation of being lifted into an undulating space. The wave subsided, and I was back on my mat in the tent. The not-pleasant-but-also-not-unpleasant wave came back a few more times, but I couldn't quite get *into* the place I was trying to go. Eventually the wave subsided for good. Everything around me seemed to be pulsating, and geometric patterns danced on the ceiling. I felt a little sad that the stronger sensations had dissipated, but on the other hand, I was glad to be rid of the nausea and be back in my own mind.

At The Forest Path Sanctuary, Jaya recreates traditional ayahuasca ceremonies and blends in his own flavor of New Age-y spirituality. There were about fifteen of us at that ceremony, sitting on our mats inside the large tent. In the center of the tent sat an altar that was adorned with flowers, candles, feathers, and other symbols of worship. Throughout the night, Jaya and his assistants danced, sang, chanted, and played instruments, while each of us gave into our experience. We didn't talk to each other during the ceremony, but the next morning, we shared our experiences. The woman beside me during the ceremony, Morgan, shared that she was battling cancer. She went into the ceremony looking for answers, and she received peace and tranquility. The ceremony gave her conviction that her treatment path was the right path. Kat, who had sat to my right during the ceremony, aptly told me that plants don't discriminate. "The medicine might not give you what you want or expect, but it will always give you what you need" (Kat, personal communication, December 14, 2022).

GOD'S FLESH

Human use of psychedelics can be traced back several thousands of years. One of the earliest pieces of evidence of psychedelic use was discovered in cave paintings in the Sahara Desert, Algeria. These paintings, which are estimated to be 7,000–9,000 years old, depict humans being levitated in the presence of a shaman who has mushrooms spouting from his body (Figure 8.1 shows the famous "Tassili Mushroom Man," painted in a cave in Algeria) (Winkelman, 2019). Evidence of psychedelic use by humans can be found in archeological remains from ancient Indian, Spanish, Grecian, Tanzanian, and Australian civilizations. The Aztec, Mayan, Olmec, and Zapotec societies of Central and South America used psychedelic plants in spiritual rituals. In fact, the Mayan and Aztek word for the psilocybin mushrooms is *teonanàcatl*, which translates to "Gods flesh." A great many psychedelic alkaloids are found in nature, and most of these have been used in traditional ceremonies. Aztecs and neighboring tribes also used the peyote cactus and ololiuqui seeds in their practices (Hofmann, 1971). The skin of the *Bufo* toad contains psychedelic chemicals, and Mesomaericans have used *Bufo*, along with wild tobacco, Jimson weed, *Salvia divinorum*, and water lilies for their psychoactive properties (Carod-Artal, 2015). And of course, South American tribes have used

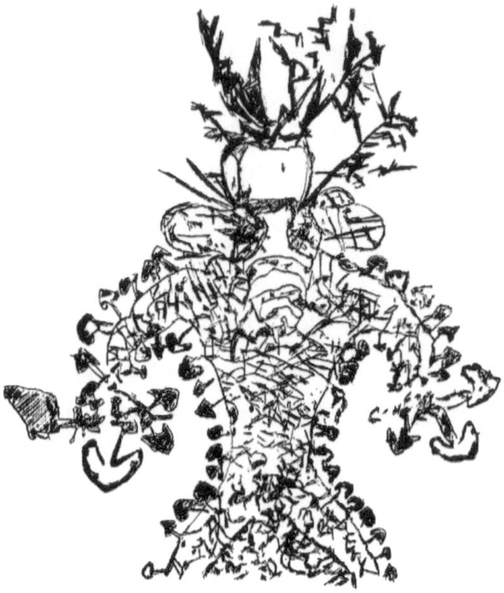

FIGURE 8.1 Tassili mushroom man.
Ancient rock art from the Tassili n'Ajjer plateau depicting a humanoid figure with mushrooms radiating from its body, often cited in psychedelic lore.

elixirs made from the psychedelic vines of the *Banisteriopsis caapi* plant and the leaves of the *Psychotria viridis* shrub for use in ayahuasca ceremonies (Carod-Artal, 2015; Rodd, 2008).

It's worth emphasizing that psychedelics have been used in spiritual practices for thousands of years. This means that people across the globe have independently discovered the mystical properties of psychedelics and come to the conclusion that these plants help them channel the cosmos.

Interesting, too, is that plants that produce psychedelic chemicals went relatively unnoticed by mainstream Westerners until the last 100 years. There are accounts of European colonists who sampled these plants, but these are few. For the most part, Spanish colonization attempted to squash indigenous tribes and their beliefs. It wasn't until the mid-1900s that word of a mysterious mushroom, teonanàcatl, reached the ears of R. Gordon Wasson. Wasson was the vice president of J. P. Morgan, and an amateur mycologist. He heard tales of a *curanadera*, or healer, named Maria Sabina who resided in Oaxaca, Mexico. Sabina was renowned for her abilities to cure ailments and connect with the divine through her use of ceremonies with psilocybin mushrooms, which she called her "holy children." In 1955, Wasson and photographer Allan Richardson traveled to Oaxaca and persuaded Sabina to let them partake in a mushroom ceremony. Of his experience, he wrote:

> We were left in darkness, and in darkness we remained until dawn. For a half hour we waited in silence. Allan felt cold and wrapped himself in a blanket. A few minutes later he leaned over to me and whispered, "Gordon, I am seeing things!" I told him not to worry, I was too. The visions had started. They reached a plateau of intensity deep in the night, and they continued at that level until about 4 o'clock . . . we were never more wide awake, and the visions came whether our eyes were open or closed. They emerged from the center of the field of vision, opening up as they came, now rushing, now slowly, at the pace that our will chose. They were in vivid color, always harmonious. They began with art motifs, angular such as might decorate carpets or textiles or wallpaper or the drawing boards of an architect. Then they evolved into palaces with courts arcaded, gardens – resplendent palaces all laid over with semiprecious stones. Then I saw a mythological beast drawing a regal chariot. Later it was as though the walls of our house had dissolved and my spirit had flown forth, and I was suspended in mid-air viewing landscapes of mountains, with camel caravans advancing slowly across the slopes, the mountains rising tier above tier to the very heavens . . . it seemed as though I was viewing a world of which I was not a part with which I could not hope to establish contact. There I was, poised in space, a disembodied eye, invisible, incorporeal, seeing but not seen. (Wasson, 1959, pp. 103 and 109)

The above account was published in the May 13th, 1957, edition of *Life* magazine, along with a series of photos taken during the ceremony. In large part due to the publication of this article, the United States saw an explosion of psychedelic awareness. Sadly, though, so did the town of Oaxaca (despite the attempts to hide Sabina's identity with a pseudonym). Americans flocked to the Sierra foothills in search of a glimpse of God, a transcendental experience, or just to get high. Sabina's tribe, the Mazatecs, turned on her, accusing her of selling their traditions for personal gain. Sabina was ostracized and died in solitude and poverty in 1985.

THE PROBLEM CHILD

The introduction of psychedelic plant medicine to Westerners happened not long after a separate and monumental psychedelic breakthrough – the serendipitous discovery of the remarkable properties of LSD by Albert Hofmann. "One often asks oneself," Hofmann mused in his address at the 1966 Worlds of Consciousness conference, "[w]hat roles planning and chance play in the realization of the most important events in our lives." As the story goes, Hofmann, working for the Swiss pharmaceutical company Sandoz, was researching derivatives of lysergic acid as a treatment for respiratory illness. He was suddenly struck by a (divine?) hunch and decided to resynthesize a compound he had first synthesized five years prior. This compound was called lysergic acid diethylamide-25 (LSD-25). Typically, compounds that show no pharmaceutical benefit are not resynthesized, but Hofmann decided to revisit this one. He "liked the structure," of that particular compound (Hofmann, 1996).

Now, Hofmann was a very careful scientist who took personal protection very seriously. He was meticulous about not coming into direct contact with the chemicals with which he worked. But on this day, with this chemical, his caution lapsed. A miniscule amount of LSD-25 must have been absorbed through his skin. What followed next was extraordinary. As Hofmann famously described it, he was suddenly overtaken by "a remarkable restlessness, with slight dizziness. At home I lay down and sank into a not unpleasant intoxicated-like condition, characterized by an extremely stimulated imagination. In a dreamlike state, with eyes closed (I found the light to be unpleasantly glaring), I perceived an uninterrupted stream of fantastic pictures, extraordinary shapes with intense, kaleidoscope play of colors" (Hofmann, 1980, p. 15). Three days later, Hofmann very carefully measured 250 μg of LSD, mixed it with a glass of water, and drank it. This day, April 19, 1943, has gone down in history as the infamous "Bicycle Day."

Bicycle Day has been written about extensively elsewhere (Hofmann, 1980), but I'll briefly summarize it here. After Hofmann drank the water with LSD, he was so afflicted that he required assistance on his journey back home from work (on a bicycle, a standard mode of transportation in wartime Basel). His initial perceptions and hallucinations were horrifying – he was certain that his neighbor was a malevolent witch trying to kill him, and that he, Hofmann, was surely poisoned. He believed that a demon had taken possession of his body, and he jumped and screamed trying to rid himself of the evil beast. Everything in his home assumed grotesque and horrifying shapes. He thought he had gone permanently mad. Perplexingly, the local doctor found nothing physically wrong with him. In time, though, the terror and anxiety faded, and a comfortable and peaceful state emerged. Hofmann enjoyed the kaleidoscope images and colors and felt satisfied, tranquil, and at peace. The following day, he woke feeling refreshed and noted that he remembered everything of his psychedelic experience. He knew he had unlocked something extraordinary and thus devoted his life to unraveling the mystery of LSD, and eventually, the mysteries of other psychedelics. In fact, rumor has it that after Wasson's fateful journey to Oaxaca, Mexico, it was to Albert Hofmann that Wasson sent lab-grown samples of Maria Sabina's holy mushrooms.

A PSYCHEDELIC REVOLUTION

The 1950s saw a psychedelic revolution. The first-ever research paper looking at perceptual and euphoric effects of LSD in humans was published in 1947 (Stoll, 1947, as referenced in Hofmann, 1980). Researchers were speaking out at events for organizations like the American College of Neuropharmacology and the Journal of the American Medical Association. Sandoz (the company that employed Hofmann when he synthesized LSD) manufactured LSD, and later, synthetic psilocybin, for use in research in psychotherapy. At Harvard University, a psychology professor named Timothy Leary became a key (maybe even *the* key) figure in the psychedelic revolution. Leary was enthralled with the potential for psychedelics to open the mind and expand the consciousness. Psychedelics became central in Leary's research life as well as personal life.

One seminal paper that came out of Leary's lab was published by his doctoral student, Walter Pahnke (Pahnke, 1963). The experiment was conducted on a self-selecting group of Boston University Divinity students attending Good Friday services and thus became known as the "Good Friday Experiment." All participants were given a pill containing either psilocybin or an active control. After the service ended and the psychedelic had worn off, all participants were asked about what they experienced. The questions included things like, "internal connectedness" and "fusion of self into the larger undifferentiated whole." Pahnke found that psilocybin-treated participants had profound and powerful experiences compared to controls, experiences that were overwhelmingly positive. One of the subjects wrote, "I saw the cosmos. It was all molten and plastic. Then I knew that I must be somewhere else. Where was myself? What am I? Where am I in the real (plastic) world? Then I was afraid no more" (Pahnke, 1963, p. 131). Thirty years after the Good Friday Experiment, all but one of these participants were tracked down and asked about that fateful Friday. Every participant said that psilocybin impacted their lives in a positive way and that they were appreciative of the opportunity to have participated in the study (Doblin, 1991).

Very unfortunately for the field of scientific inquiry into the potential of psychedelics, it was later learned that Leary and Pahnke were a bit lax when it came to reporting results. They failed to mention the incidents of anxiety that were experienced by some participants, and as you can imagine, this called everything into question. Psychedelics were already under massive political scrutiny. The unreported adverse events became fuel for the anti-hippie and anti-counterculture fire. It is rumored that President Nixon once called Leary the "most dangerous man alive" for his views on psychedelics, and counterculture more generally. Although psychedelics were legal at the time, Harvard University requested that Leary end the Psychedelic Drug Project, which Leary did not do. His employment was terminated under the auspice of unmet teaching responsibilities. Leary, however, was not silenced, and became an evangelist for psychedelic use, famously advising people to "Turn on, tune in, and drop out" (Stevenson, 1966).

But the war on drugs was on. In 1965, Sandoz halted production of LSD and psilocybin, and the prohibition of psychedelics began in the United States. Nixon signed the Controlled Substances Act in 1970, an Act that sorted drugs into categories called schedules. LSD and psilocybin, along with marijuana and heroin, were listed as Schedule I drugs – drugs that are highly addictive and have no medical benefit. This scheduling effectively eliminated all research into the potential benefits of psychedelics. In 1977, the last legal dose of psilocybin was given to a research participant for nearly two decades (Pollan, 2018).

Even while the US government was pushing back against the counterculture of people experimenting with psychedelics, scientists were still fascinated with these compounds and were certain that they could help unlock secrets of the unconscious and treat mental illness. Daniel X. Freedman, a pioneer in the studies of psychedelic chemicals, wrote that LSD could induce "'portentousness' – the capacity of the mind to see more than it can tell, to experience more than it can explicate, to believe in and be impressed with more than it can rationally justify, to experience boundlessness and 'boundaryless' events, from the banal to the profound" (Freedman, 1968, p. 331). Jerome Jaffe, head of the Special Office for Drug Abuse Prevention under Richard Nixon, is most well-known for his efforts to establish methadone clinics in the United States. Jaffe described psychedelics by saying, "the feature that distinguishes the psychedelic agents from other classes of drug is their capacity reliably to induce states of altered perception, thought, and feeling that are not experienced otherwise except in dreams or at times of religious exaltation" (Jaffe, 1990, p. 532) One can appreciate the uniqueness of these definitions. Well-respected scientists are suggesting that psychedelics can take the mind to places that it cannot normally go. Is it supernatural? I don't know, but I do know it's worth studying.

The late 1990s saw a small resurgence of psychedelic research in human subjects in Europe (Gouzoulis-Mayfrank et al., 1999; Vollenweider et al., 1998). In the United States, however, it was nearly impossible to gain approval to study psychedelics due to their Schedule I designation. Roland Griffiths, a neuroscientist at the Johns Hopkins School of Medicine, conducted the first legal study of psilocybin in humans since the enactment of the Controlled Substances Act more than thirty years prior. Griffiths effectively recreated the Good Friday Experiment, but with some important modifications. The modifications were primarily to increase the rigor of the research methods, and to include a two-month follow-up with all participants. The methodology of this project emphasized the importance of set and setting. The participants were all healthy adult volunteers who had gone through training with the researchers to gain trust and familiarity. The laboratory was set up to look like a comfortable living room. Each participant had two or three sessions. They were told that at least in one of those sessions, they would receive a moderate or high dose of psilocybin. In fact, the dose of psilocybin was 30 mg for all participants, the same dose chosen by Walter Pahnke in 1963. Participants were interviewed after the drug treatment and at a two-month follow-up. The results of this landmark study were irrefutable – psilocybin treatment under supportive conditions resulted in a variety of positive outcomes, most notably, feelings of mysticism and spiritual transcendence. Participants evaluated these experiences as deeply personal with great spiritual significance. These evaluations persisted at the two-month follow-up (Griffiths et al., 2006).

The question that remains is, what is the connection between psychedelics and the induction of spirituality, mysticism, and oneness? Mystical experiences induced by psychedelics are said to be similar to spontaneous mystical experiences that spiritual leaders and highly meditative people sometimes experience (Griffiths et al., 2019; Pollan, 2018). Are the neural underpinnings the same, too? Is it possible that psychedelics help us regular people relax our minds to accept the experiences and mysticism that we are probably *already* capable of generating, if only our minds were more disciplined? William James, the father of modern psychology, wrote about such spiritual experiences in his book, *The Varieties of Religious Experiences*. James believed that religious experiences were caused by an inflow of energy from the subconscious mind. Mysticism, James said, was the "root and cellar" of religious experiences and has four main criteria. Mystical, religious experiences must be ineffable, noetic, transient, and passive (James, 1902).

In his book, *How to Change Your Mind*, New York Times writer Michael Pollan likens transcendent psychedelic experiences with the properties of religious experiences as described by James. Pollan emphasizes the noetic aspect of mystical experiences, that is, the mysticism that occurs from insight into the self, unobstructed by external factors. High doses of psychedelic medicines can induce the deterioration of the self, this idea of *ego death*. If the "self" is a construct of the mind, and psychedelics can (temporarily) remove that construct, then I agree with Pollan, mystical experiences brought on by psychedelics are related to the noetic sense of the experience (Pollan, 2018). When one loses their entire sense of self, then one would lose the ability to distinguish between what is subjectively and objectively true. The very definition of consciousness changes. And the experience of existing in the universe, unencumbered by one's own self and one's own consciousness would thus allow a person to become aware of other things that may simultaneously coexist in the universe. I also believe that a person has to be ready to accept that temporary loss of self in order to reach this level of connectedness (again, the importance of mindset, or "set"). These were some of the ideas I explored with Jaya the morning after the ayahuasca ceremony as we discussed his role in guiding people's spiritual journeys.

Jaya founded The Forest Path Sanctuary to serve as a contemplative and meditative center for people to share in their spiritual journeys. The Forest Path offers spiritual guidance in many forms, including through the use of psychedelic journeys. The Forest Path "encourages a contemplative life," Jaya told me. "I discovered psychedelics when I was 14," Jaya began, describing how he came to be on this path of delivering spiritual guidance. Jaya had a spiritual upbringing in Queensland, Australia. When he discovered that psychedelics could deliver profound "irradiant" experiences, he took it upon himself to learn all he could. Shortly, he began to serve as a guide on other's journeys. Now, Jaya emphasizes the use of the ceremony to help the participant reach the shores of their own potential. "I try to give context to the teachings as we experience them, as we have experienced them. One can consume these medicines on their own and have a profound experience but be left in a scattered place of putting those pieces together for interpretation … on your own, you might not be able to navigate that, so the ceremony is a navigation system. There's places that we go, and places that we can go, and places that we can get to and things that we can move beyond and things that we can encounter that we didn't realize that were there, and it's very hard to get there if you're not in the boat of the ceremony navigating to these places." I asked Jaya what he believes happens in the connection between the medicine and the mind. Are the medicines delivering the Divine, or do we have the answers inside us all along, and the medicines help us access them? He coyly dodged my question. "The importance is in the questioning, and the medicines allow context. The ceremony is a guide to find the answers" (J. Roland, personal communication, December 13, 2023).

PSYCHEDELICS AND THE BRAIN

There is nothing *directly* supernatural about the mental state brought on by psychedelics. The chemical structure of psychedelics like psilocybin, LSD, and other hallucinogenic molecules is similar to the chemical structure of serotonin, a naturally occurring neurotransmitter in the brain and body. The discovery of this similarity was an important first step at understanding what psychedelics do in the brain – they mimic serotonin. Sort of.

Serotonin has been popularized as the "happiness" molecule (much like the amygdala has been popularized as the "fear" center), and popular science magazines have enumerated the ways you can hack your mood by boosting serotonin (no, a diet high in tryptophan will probably not improve your mental health). Most psychologists and neuroscientists disagree with the appropriation of serotonin as the "happiness" molecule; happiness is a complicated emotion that cannot be traced to a single molecule. It is true, though, that serotonin has been linked to mood, and medications that increase serotonin in the brain can be effective treatments for many mood disorders.

Our brains and bodies make serotonin from an amino acid, tryptophan, that we take in through our diet. Recall from Chapter 2 that a neuron stores neurotransmitters in vesicles in the axon terminal. Those neurotransmitters are released in response to an action potential. Neurotransmitters like serotonin bind to receptors on the surface of the postsynaptic neuron, resulting in a variety of changes in the neuron depending on the subtype of receptor that was activated. Activation of serotonin receptors can cause a huge diversity of postsynaptic effects, and this is largely because serotonin has at least fourteen different types of receptors! Each of these subtypes can cause a slightly different change in the postsynaptic neuron. By contrast, dopamine, another well-known neurotransmitter, has only five receptor subtypes, divided into two classes.

Because psychedelics have a chemical structure that is similar to serotonin, we have a clue about how psychedelics probably act in the brain. The fact that a chemical found in nature closely resembles chemicals that occur naturally in our bodies is far from unique. In fact, for many neurotransmitter systems, learning about the *exogenous* (originating outside the body) substances gives important clues to learning about the *endogenous* (originating inside the body) substances. One example of this is morphine. Morphine is an exogenous substance; it originates outside the body, from the opium poppy. By studying the chemical composition of morphine and which protein receptor morphine binds to, researchers were then able to discover an endogenous substance that resembles morphine. You've probably heard of endorphins – the word "endorphin" actually means "endogenous morphine!"

Knowing that the structure of psychedelics is like the structure of serotonin allowed researchers to hypothesize that psychedelics might bind to the same receptors as serotonin. Even so, it took decades of research to definitively tie the psychedelic effects of compounds like psilocybin and LSD to a specific receptor. Early research suggested that most psychedelics mimic serotonin at a few different serotonin receptors. Research projects called *receptor binding studies* allow us to see which specific receptors become occupied when the brain is treated with different compounds. Research from early receptor binding studies taught us that psychedelics primarily stimulate the $5HT_{2A}$ subtype of serotonin receptor (Glennon et al., 1984; McKenna et al., 1989). The stronger the drug binds at this receptor, the more potent the drug (Glennon et al., 1984). This brings us a bit closer to understanding what psychedelics do in the brain, but not how they bring about a mystical state.

Unfortunately, we can't exactly ask a lab rat if it is having a mystical experience. Nonetheless, there are some telltale signs a rat will give us that we believe indicate some kind of rat-psychedelic effect. As it turns out, treating a rat with psychedelics causes a unique head-twitch response. Researchers can block certain receptors and stimulate others and see what combination of receptor activation yields a head-twitch response. Stimulating the $5HT_{2A}$ serotonin receptor reliably causes a head-twitch response, but when that receptor is blocked, the head twitch goes away. This probably means that psychedelics exert their effects by stimulating the $5HT_{2A}$ receptor (Glennon et al., 1984). But is a rat head twitch a corollary to a psychedelic trip?

To answer that complicated question, we have to look toward human research. Similar experiments have been carried out in humans – blocking access to the $5HT_{2A}$ serotonin receptor blocks most of the effects of psychedelics, including euphoria and hallucinations (Siggaard Stenbæk et al., 2021; Vollenweider et al., 1998, 2007). Of course, the subjective (and beyond) effects of psychedelics are very complicated. Activating the $5HT_{2A}$ receptor must cause several other brain changes that we're only beginning to understand. Our understanding has been stalled thanks to the stringent scheduling of psychedelics, leading to a thirty-year gap in neuroscience research. However, with the progression in human neuroscience techniques like real-time brain imaging, we can begin to ask some intricate research questions.

One theory of how psychedelics exert their mind-altering effects is through alterations in information processing in areas of the brain that are important for sensory-motor integration. Our brains need to figure out what's going on around us, and for that, it relies on the senses. Recall that the thalamus takes information from the senses and sends it to the cortex. As you know, the cortex gives us a conscious experience based on a combination of bottom-up and top-down processing. Once the brain has figured out what's happening in our world, it needs to decide how to behave. For that, the cortex sends signals back down to the thalamus and striatum, a set of areas that are important for motivated behaviors. The thalamus and striatum put together a coordinated motor plan that is executed through interactions with muscles. These back-and-forth conversations between the thalamus and cortex are called *thalamocortical interactions*, and are widely believed to play an important role in consciousness (Edelman, 2003). If we expect that high doses of psychedelics will induce a drastically altered state of consciousness, then this circuit seems like a good place to start looking. If there are alterations in information processing between the cortex, thalamus, and striatum, the brain would lose its ability to filter information, thus losing its ability to screen what is not important for our conscious experience. As a result of that, *everything* becomes conscious, leading to a massive sensory overload and a breakdown of cognitive integrity. This in turn would likely cause hallucinations, psychosis, and a loss of a sense of self. Perhaps unsurprisingly, serotonin $5HT_{2A}$ receptors are highly expressed in this circuit (Quednow et al., 2012; Vollenweider et al., 1998; Vollenweider & Geyer, 2001).

Clearly, psychedelics have the ability to make strong changes in the brain during the user's experience. A technique called *resting state functional magnetic resonance imaging* (resting state fMRI) can measure global changes in activity by measuring small changes in blood flow in participants who are not engaging in an explicit task. Using this technique to measure psychedelic-induced changes in the brain is useful, because researchers can see changes unfold in the brain as the experience itself unfolds. One of the endpoint measurements of resting state fMRI is functional connectivity – how much a change in blood flow to one area of the brain correlates to a change in blood flow in others. Despite there being dozens of fMRI studies using classical psychedelics, the research is still in its infancy, and we have yet to paint a clear picture of how psychedelics change the brain (McCulloch et al., 2022).

fMRI studies evaluating global brain changes have largely focused their attention on a brain network called the Default Mode Network (DMN). Although not completely understood, this network of brain areas is related to our ability to focus attention inward for interoception, autobiographical memory retrieval, and self-referential processing (Broyd et al., 2009). This network includes structures that are involved in higher-level cognition like the precuneus, posterior cingulate cortex, medial prefrontal cortex, and inferior parietal cortex (Broyd et al., 2009). A number of studies support the idea that these structures are altered by psychedelics. First, structures in the DMN are rich with $5HT_{2A}$ receptors (Daws et al., 2022), making them plausible targets of psychedelics. Second, psychedelics increase connectivity between DMN structures, particularly the medial prefrontal cortex and the posterior cingulate cortex, and the connectivity changes correlate with subjective effects (Carhart-Harris et al., 2012, 2016). Other recording techniques show us that psychedelics change the conversations between core structures in the DMN and cerebral cortex in a way that changes the brain from an ordered to a more disordered state (Carhart-Harris et al., 2016; Nichols, 2016).

PSYCHEDELICS AND THE MIND

People report psychedelic experiences as some of the most positive and momentous experiences of their lives (Doblin, 1991; Pahnke, 1963). The ability of psychedelics to induce intense mystical experiences has been reported both anecdotally and experimentally (Griffiths et al., 2006). Psychedelics can cause people to turn inward, to flush out the external world. Not only is this life-changing in the mystical sense, but it can also be life-changing in the psychological sense. Many people believe that psychedelics may be an answer to treating psychiatric disorders – from treatment-resistant depression to fear of death in terminal cancer patients.

Much of this early work into psychedelic therapy came from the National Institute of Health–funded lines of work at the Spring Grove State Hospital in Maryland. A group at this psychiatric facility (later directed by Walter Pahnke, the former student of Timothy Leary) developed an extensive research program that evaluated the effects of psychedelic therapy on schizophrenia, depression, anxiety, and substance use disorders. Some of the earliest research was conducted on patients with terminal cancer and measured endpoints like improved mood and a decreased fear of death. These positive effects were seen in the majority of participants, and the effects persisted long after the cessation of psychedelic use (Grof et al., 1973; Pahnke et al., 1969). The Controlled Substances Act effectively shut down all research into psychedelic therapy, but some groups have been able to secure funding to further the research. One notable researcher is Roland Griffiths, who was described earlier in this chapter as the researcher who replicated the findings of Pahnke's Good Friday Experiment. At the time of this writing, Griffiths is the founding Director of the Center for Psychedelic and Consciousness Research at Hopkins and has been involved in psychedelic research for decades. Notably, Griffiths recently published a randomized, double-blind (the gold standard of experimental psychology) report corroborating the early work at the Spring Grove State Hospital – that treatment with a low dose of psilocybin drastically reduced depression and anxiety in patients with life-threatening cancer, and these effects persisted at least six months after treatment (Griffiths et al., 2016).

Work into the mental states of cancer patients is certainly the most well-documented therapeutic effect of psychedelics, but there is also evidence that psychedelics can be beneficial to other disorders, as well. For example, psychedelics have been shown to increase rates of abstinence in alcohol-use disorders (Bogenschutz et al., 2015) and in nicotine-use disorders (Johnson et al., 2017). They can also improve symptoms of treatment-resistant depression while increasing connectivity in the DMN, as compared to traditional antidepressants (Carhart-Harris et al., 2017; Daws et al., 2022).

HOW TO PERCEIVE THE WORLD

Although we tend to think our experiences are accurate portrayals of the world around us, this is far from the case. Our perception of the world is limited by the lens used by our brain to filter the world around us, and by our brain's ability to interpret this information. Psychedelics might widen this lens. During a psychedelic experience, our brains lose the ability to filter sensory experience from our conscious awareness, and as a result, we see and feel and hear everything, whether it's outside or within us. We are not equipped to handle everything at once, and in turn, we turn to nothing. Our cognition falters and then fails. Our very sense of self disintegrates. If one loses themselves, a concept called "ego death," they can be everywhere and everything, and at the same time, nowhere and nothing. This is the sense of connectedness that the psychedelic community describes. People lose themselves and become connected to everything on an interdimensional level. Time is nothing. People witness the start of the universe and the whole of evolution in mere moments.

When you're in a situation of ego death, you follow the only things you know to be true. For some, this is the sense of God. For some, it is many gods. The ghosts of our pasts. Love. Even the Big Bang. You find the one thing that you believe to be true and you hold on to it. When people have mystical experiences with psychedelics, they do not later dismiss their experiences as a weird dream. After their experience is over, most people feel certain that it was real and profound. And for many, this is life-altering. Psychedelics give people the ability to look inward and find connection to themselves, to the universe, and find a purpose. For many, this can look like accepting their imminent demise.

This experience can be confusing and scary. And this is where set and setting come in. Regardless of whether someone is a participant in a research study or drinking ayahuasca tea in the Guatemalan jungle, they must be able to trust and let go. People like Jaya can be a beacon with whom to place trust, who can help chart a path to a mystical, transcendental, even life-altering experience, whatever form that takes for you. Jaya's take is that it doesn't matter what you believe to be true, but anybody can use a guide to help them navigate the dimensions. "To give context to the teachings," as he said.

REFERENCES

Bogenschutz, M. P., Forcehimes, A. A., Pommy, J. A., Wilcox, C. E., Barbosa, P. C. R., & Strassman, R. J. (2015). Psilocybin-assisted treatment for alcohol dependence: A proof-of-concept study. *Journal of Psychopharmacology, 29*(3), 289–299. https://doi.org/10.1177/0269881114565144.

Broyd, S. J., Demanuele, C., Debener, S., Helps, S. K., James, C. J., & Sonuga-Barke, E. J. S. (2009). Default-mode brain dysfunction in mental disorders: A systematic review. *Neuroscience and Biobehavioral Reviews*, *33*(3), 279–296. https://doi.org/10.1016/j.neubiorev.2008.09.002.

Carhart-Harris, R. L., Erritzoe, D., Williams, T., Stone, J. M., Reed, L. J., Colasanti, A., Tyacke, R. J., Leech, R., Malizia, A. L., Murphy, K., Hobden, P., Evans, J., Feilding, A., Wise, R. G., & Nutt, D. J. (2012). Neural correlates of the psychedelic state as determined by fMRI studies with psilocybin. *Proceedings of the National Academy of Sciences*, *109*(6), 2138–2143. https://doi.org/10.1073/pnas.1119598109.

Carhart-Harris, R. L., Muthukumaraswamy, S., Roseman, L., Kaelen, M., Droog, W., Murphy, K., Tagliazucchi, E., Schenberg, E. E., Nest, T., Orban, C., Leech, R., Williams, L. T., Williams, T. M., Bolstridge, M., Sessa, B., McGonigle, J., Sereno, M. I., Nichols, D., Hellyer, P. J., Hobden, P., Evans, J., Singh, K. D., Wise, R. G., Curran, H. V., Feilding, A., & Nutt, D. J. (2016). Neural correlates of the LSD experience revealed by multimodal neuroimaging. *Proceedings of the National Academy of Sciences of the United States of America*, *113*(17), 4853–4858. https://doi.org/10.1073/pnas.1518377113.

Carhart-Harris, R. L., Roseman, L., Bolstridge, M., Demetriou, L., Pannekoek, J. N., Wall, M. B., Tanner, M., Kaelen, M., McGonigle, J., Murphy, K., Leech, R., Curran, H. V., & Nutt, D. J. (2017). Psilocybin for treatment-resistant depression: fMRI-measured brain mechanisms. *Scientific Reports*, *7*(1), 13187. https://doi.org/10.1038/s41598-017-13282-7.

Carod-Artal, F. J. (2015). Hallucinogenic drugs in pre-Columbian Mesoamerican cultures. *Neurología*, *30*(1), 42–49. https://doi.org/10.1016/j.nrleng.2011.07.010.

Daws, R. E., Timmermann, C., Giribaldi, B., Sexton, J. D., Wall, M. B., Erritzoe, D., Roseman, L., Nutt, D., & Carhart-Harris, R. (2022). Increased global integration in the brain after psilocybin therapy for depression. *Nature Medicine*, *28*(4), 844–851. https://doi.org/10.1038/s41591-022-01744-z.

de la Fuente Revenga, M., Jaster, A. M., McGinn, J., Silva, G., Saha, S., & González-Maeso, J. (2022). Tolerance and cross-tolerance among psychedelic and nonpsychedelic 5-HT2A receptor agonists in mice. *ACS Chemical Neuroscience*, *13*(16), 2436–2448. https://doi.org/10.1021/acschemneuro.2c00170.

Doblin, R. (1991). Pahnke's "Good Friday experiment": A long-term follow-up and methodological critique. *Journal of Transpersonal Psychology*, *23*(1), 1–28.

Edelman, G. M. (2003). Naturalizing consciousness: A theoretical framework. *Proceedings of the National Academy of Sciences*, *100*(9), 5520–5524. https://doi.org/10.1073/pnas.0931349100.

Freedman, D. X. (1968). On the use and abuse of LSD. *Archives of General Psychiatry*, *18*(3), 330–347. https://doi.org/10.1001/archpsyc.1968.01740030074008.

Glennon, R. A., Titeler, M., & McKenney, J. D. (1984). Evidence for 5-HT2 involvement in the mechanism of action of hallucinogenic agents. *Life Sciences*, *35*(25), 2505–2511. https://doi.org/10.1016/0024-3205(84)90436-3.

Gouzoulis-Mayfrank, E., Thelen, B., Habermeyer, E., Kunert, H. J., Kovar, K. A., Lindenblatt, H., Hermle, L., Spitzer, M., & Sass, H. (1999). Psychopathological, neuroendocrine and autonomic effects of 3,4-methylenedioxyethylamphetamine (MDE), psilocybin and d-methamphetamine in healthy volunteers: Results of an experimental double-blind placebo-controlled study. *Psychopharmacology*, *142*(1), 41–50. https://doi.org/10.1007/s002130050860.

Griffiths, R. R., Hurwitz, E. S., Davis, A. K., Johnson, M. W., & Jesse, R. (2019). Survey of subjective "God encounter experiences": Comparisons among naturally occurring experiences and those occasioned by the classic psychedelics psilocybin, LSD, ayahuasca, or DMT. *PloS One*, *14*(4), e0214377. https://doi.org/10.1371/journal.pone.0214377.

Griffiths, R. R., Johnson, M. W., Carducci, M. A., Umbricht, A., Richards, W. A., Richards, B. D., Cosimano, M. P., & Klinedinst, M. A. (2016). Psilocybin produces substantial and sustained decreases in depression and anxiety in patients with life-threatening cancer: A randomized double-blind trial. *Journal of Psychopharmacology*, *30*(12), 1181–1197. https://doi.org/10.1177/0269881116675513.

Griffiths, R. R., Richards, W. A., McCann, U., & Jesse, R. (2006). Psilocybin can occasion mystical-type experiences having substantial and sustained personal meaning and spiritual significance. *Psychopharmacology*, *187*(3), 268–283. https://doi.org/10.1007/s00213-006-0457-5.

Grof, S., Goodman, L. E., Richards, W. A., & Kurland, A. A. (1973). LSD-assisted psychotherapy in patients with terminal cancer. *International Pharmacopsychiatry*, *8*(3), 129–144. https://doi.org/10.1159/000467984.

Hartogsohn, I. (2017). Constructing drug effects: A history of set and setting. *Drug Science Policy and Law*, *3*(1), 1–17.

Hofmann, A. (1971). Teonanácatl and Ololiuqui, Two Ancient Magic Drugs of Mexico. United Nations Office on Drugs and Crime. www.unodc.org/unodc/en/data-and-analysis/bulletin/bulletin_1971-01-01_1_page003.html.

Hofmann, A. (1980). *LSD: My Problem Child*. Stuggart: McGraw-Hill.

Hofmann, A. (1996). LSD: Completely Personal. Newsletter of the Multidisciplinary Association for Psychedelic Studies. https://maps.org/news-letters/v06n3/06346hof.html.

Jaffe, J. (1990). Drug addiction and drug abuse. In G. Gilman, T. W. Rall, A. S. Nies, & P. Taylor (Eds.), *Goodman and Gilman's: The Pharmacological Basis of Therapeutics* (8th ed., pp. 522–573). New York: McGraw Hill.

James, W. (1902). *The Varieties of Religious Experience: A Study in Human Nature.* New York: Longmans, Green & Co.

Johnson, M. W., Garcia-Romeu, A., & Griffiths, R. R. (2017). Long-term follow-up of psilocybin-facilitated smoking cessation. *The American Journal of Drug and Alcohol Abuse*, *43*(1), 55–60. https://doi.org/10.3109/00952990.2016.1170135.

Johnson, M. W., Griffiths, R. R., Hendricks, P. S., & Henningfield, J. E. (2018). The abuse potential of medical psilocybin according to the 8 factors of the Controlled Substances Act. *Neuropharmacology, 142,* 143–166. https://doi.org/10.1016/j.neuropharm.2018.05.012.

Johnson, M. W., Hendricks, P. S., Barrett, F. S., & Griffiths, R. R. (2019). Classic psychedelics: An integrative review of epidemiology, therapeutics, mystical experience, and brain network function. *Pharmacology & Therapeutics, 197,* 83–102. https://doi.org/10.1016/j.pharmthera.2018.11.010.

McCulloch, D. E.-W., Knudsen, G. M., Barrett, F. S., Doss, M. K., Carhart-Harris, R. L., Rosas, F. E., Deco, G., Kringelbach, M. L., Preller, K. H., Ramaekers, J. G., Mason, N. L., Müller, F., & Fisher, P. M. (2022). Psychedelic resting-state neuroimaging: A review and perspective on balancing replication and novel analyses. *Neuroscience & Biobehavioral Reviews, 138,* 104689. https://doi.org/10.1016/j.neubiorev.2022.104689.

McKenna, D. J., Nazarali, A. J., Hoffman, A. J., Nichols, D. E., Mathis, C. A., & Saavedra, J. M. (1989). Common receptors for hallucinogens in rat brain: A comparative autoradiographic study using [125I]LSD and [125I]DOI, a new psychotomimetic radioligand. *Brain Research*, *476*(1), 45–56. https://doi.org/10.1016/0006-8993(89)91535-7.

Nichols, D. E. (2016). Psychedelics. *Pharmacological Reviews*, *68*(2), 264–355. https://doi.org/10.1124/pr.115.011478.

Nichols, D. E., & Nichols, C. D. (2008). Serotonin receptors. *Chemical Reviews*, *108*(5), 1614–1641.

Pahnke, W. (1963). Drugs and mysticism: An analysis of the relationship between psychedelic drugs and the mystical consciousness. Unpublished PhD thesis, Harvard University, Cambridge.

Pahnke, W. N., Kurland, A. A., Goodman, L. E., & Richards, W. A. (1969). LSD-assisted psychotherapy with terminal cancer patients. *Current Psychiatric Therapies*, *9*, 144–152.

Pollan, M. (2018). *How to Change Your Mind: What the New Science of Psychedelics Teaches Us About Consciousness, Dying, Addiction, Depression, and Transcendence.* New York: Penguin Press.

Quednow, B. B., Kometer, M., Geyer, M. A., & Vollenweider, F. X. (2012). Psilocybin-induced deficits in automatic and controlled inhibition are attenuated by ketanserin in healthy human volunteers. *Neuropsychopharmacology*, *37*(3), 630–640. https://doi.org/10.1038/npp.2011.228.

Rodd, R. (2008). Reassessing the cultural and psychopharmacological significance of Banisteriopsis caapi: Preparation, classification and use among the Piaroa of Southern Venezuela. *Journal of Psychoactive Drugs*, *40*(3), 301–307. https://doi.org/10.1080/02791072.2008.10400645.

Siggaard Stenbæk, D., Korsbak Madsen, M., Ozenne, B., Kristiansen, S., Burmester, D., Erritzoe, D., Moos Knudsen, G., & MacDonald Fisher, P. (2021). Brain serotonin 2A receptor binding predicts subjective temporal and mystical effects of psilocybin in healthy humans. *Journal of Psychopharmacology*, *35*(4), 459–468.

Stevenson, J. (1966). Celebration #1. The New Yorker. www.newyorker.com/magazine/1966/10/01/celebration-1?utm_source=chatgpt.com.

Stoll, W. A. (1947). Lysergsäure-diäthylamid, ein Phantastikum aus der Mutterkorngruppe [Lysergic acid diethylamide: A hallucinatory agent from the ergot group]. *Schweizer Archiv für Neurologie und Psychiatrie*, *60*, 279–323.

Vollenweider, F. X., Csomor, P. A., Knappe, B., Geyer, M. A., & Quednow, B. B. (2007). The effects of the preferential 5-HT2A agonist psilocybin on prepulse inhibition of startle in healthy human volunteers depend on interstimulus interval. *Neuropsychopharmacology*, *32*(9), 1876–1887. https://doi.org/10.1038/sj.npp.1301324.

Vollenweider, F. X., & Geyer, M. A. (2001). A systems model of altered consciousness: Integrating natural and drug-induced psychoses. *Brain Research Bulletin*, *56*(5), 495–507. https://doi.org/10.1016/s0361-9230(01)00646-3.

Vollenweider, F. X., Vollenweider-Scherpenhuyzen, M. F., Bäbler, A., Vogel, H., & Hell, D. (1998). Psilocybin induces schizophrenia-like psychosis in humans via a serotonin-2 agonist action. *Neuroreport*, *9*(17), 3897–3902. https://doi.org/10.1097/00001756-199812010-00024.

Wasson, R. G. (1959, May 13). Seeking the Magic Mushroom. Life magazine.

Winkelman, M. (2019). Introduction: Evidence for entheogen use in prehistory and world religions. *Journal of Psychedelic Studies*, *3*(2), 43–62. doi: 10.1556/2054.2019.024.

Conclusions

The Courage to Keep Asking Questions

If we're trying to come up with a theory to explain the sound of footsteps behind you, a feeling of a presence, lights that you can't explain, or the psychic who knows everything about you, we might be tempted to say that supernatural forces are at work. But we also know that each one of these instances can be easily explained with neuroscience and psychology. This is what I've attempted to do in this book.

A good theory is one that is parsimonious, well-organized, and falsifiable. Occam's Razor tells us that the simplest explanation is usually the right one. We have yet to produce definitive, empirical evidence that supernatural forces exist, but we have an abundance of empirical evidence that shows that our perceptions of reality and our memories of events aren't always accurate. They're shaped by what we expect, by what we believe, and our brain fills in the gaps with what it thinks should be there. An organized theory is one that explains as many observations as possible. I'd argue that supernatural occurrences are the result of complex neuroscientific and psychological factors, and this explanation can fit most, if not all, weird experiences. And finally, a theory needs to be falsifiable. We need to be able to find a way to disprove it. The suggestion that supernatural forces exist is non-falsifiable because it cannot be tested, at least not with our current technology. In contrast, the statement "activity in the temporal lobe can cause an illusory sensed presence," can, and has, been tested. The latter doesn't rule out the former, but it can at least provide more information.

For centuries, people believed that our four humors (blood, phlegm, yellow bile, black bile) need to be in balance with each other for optimal health. If they became unbalanced, disease would follow. These humors loosely translated to psychology, as Galen believed that sharpness and intelligence were caused by yellow bile, but that phlegm had no bearing on character, for example. In modern medicine, we know that there is no distinction between black and yellow bile, and phlegm means something very different today. We also know that diseases are not due to imbalances in our humors. Diseases are spread by germs.

Ignaz Semmelweis, a Hungarian obstetrician, was ridiculed by the medical community for requiring that medical workers in his clinic wash their hands regularly. At the time, most people believed that sickness was caused by an imbalance of the humors, and how dare he suggest that someone as dignified as a doctor has dirty hands that need washing! It was ludicrous that something invisible to the naked eye could cause so much devastation. Even when mortality dropped by almost 90 percent, Semmelweis was still ridiculed. He died not knowing the truth about germs. It wasn't until much later that we started to understand that pathogens can spread disease and that many of those pathogens can be easily killed by some soap and warm water. Just because we can't *yet* explain something doesn't mean that supernatural forces are at work.

Our friend, Clairvius Narcisse, the zombie, rose from the dead and was enslaved by a bokor for years. Without investigation, this absolutely seems supernatural. But after some deep digging, scientists came up with a plausible, non-supernatural theory to explain Narcisse's 'death.' Narcisse had very likely been poisoned with compounds that slowed his body so much that he appeared to be dead, and possibly with a psychedelic compound which would render him confused and highly suggestible. Instances like these seem supernatural to the unquestioning mind. But we can take a closer look and find a more parsimonious explanation.

Let me give another example. The "Double Slit" experiment was first conducted by Thomas Young in 1801. Young was researching the physical properties of light. At the time, it was not known whether light behaved like a wave or a particle. In the Double Slit experiment, a source of light is pointed at a large plate that has two parallel slits, and the light coming through the slits can be observed on a screen behind the plate. If the light behaved like particles, we'd expect to see two bright bands – one behind each slit. Young demonstrated that light behaves like a wave. Instead of two bands, the light formed an interference pattern: alternating bands of brightness and darkness. Many years later, quantum physicists used the double slit setup to shoot particles, like electrons, through the slits. It was expected that the particles would act like little bullets and go through one slit or the other. But they didn't. The particles showed up as light and dark bands just like the light waves did, indicating that they interfere with themselves and go through both slits as waves.

What makes this experiment truly mind-bending, though, is what happens when detectors are placed at the slits to observe which slit the particle goes through. The interference pattern disappears, and the particles behave like particles. When they are *not being observed*, particles behave like waves. This has been replicated with larger molecules – like buckyballs – showing that it holds true even beyond the microscopic world. This effect cannot fully be explained with our current understanding of quantum physics. I have no doubt that, with time, new technology and theory will emerge that helps us understand why measurement can change the behavior of matter. Until then, this experiment remains a provocative mystery. Is it science, or supernatural?

Anomalistic psychology implores critical thinking. It tells us that we need to keep asking questions, keep generating testable hypotheses, use empirical methods to test them, and remain parsimonious and objective when interpreting results. Critical thinking is both a set of skills and a mindset. Do we ask questions, stay curious, and keep our minds open to alternate explanations? Do we have the willingness to suspend judgment until we have all the possible information? Do we have the knowledge to understand when we have enough information, and the ability to assess the quality of that information? Do we have the courage and self-confidence to sit with the discomfort of cognitive dissonance?

Part of learning critical thinking skills is gaining knowledge of the content area to help us know what questions we should be asking. The goal of this book is to teach various areas of neuroscience and psychology that, at least in part, can explain "supernatural" experiences. We can take a non-falsifiable statement (the supernatural is real) and, using our knowledge of neuroscience and psychology, break it into observations that can then be the basis of a testable hypothesis. Maybe it's true that some people are more sensitive to EMF, ultrasound, and other environmental phenomena. Maybe some people experience episodes of sleep paralysis – terrifying, to be sure. They don't know what to make of the weird pressure on their chest, the strange sounds and lights, or the feeling of lost time. Or maybe someone has had their Tarot cards read, and the reader seems to know everything about them.

When we first encounter things like this, we believe what we've been told to believe. Trust your gut. The psychic knows all about you because they're psychic. If you sense a presence, then it's probably real. But as we learn more and gain critical thinking skills, we can stop and take account of the situation. Was the psychic *really* psychic, or have I been giving them unconscious cues? Was that really a ghost in my room, or did my bizarre dreams spill into wakefulness? Was there really an eerie face in the corner, or could my brain have made mistakes interpreting incomplete visual information during eye movements (saccades)?

Human minds don't like ambiguity. We like answers. We don't like things we can't explain and so we sometimes confabulate to find a way to explain ambiguity. We use mental shortcuts to save ourselves some of the effort of cognition. Be aware of these. Be wary of these. None of these are inherently bad things, but it is shortsighted to think that we are not victims of biases, heuristics, false memories, and faulty reasoning. Remember, *you have to believe it to see it.*

Our brains are powerful, messy, and sometimes misleading. They're also our best tools for making sense of this world.

And if you take nothing else from this book – please, don't mess with rabies.

Index

For EU product safety concerns, contact us at Calle de José Abascal, 56–1°,
28003 Madrid, Spain or eugpsr@cambridge.org.

www.ingramcontent.com/pod-product-compliance
Lightning Source LLC
LaVergne TN
LVHW041631060526
838200LV00040B/1539
* 9 7 8 1 0 0 9 3 2 2 3 7 9 *